T5-BCL-914

Violence and Truth

On the Work of René Girard

Violence and Truth

On the Work of
René Girard

Edited by
PAUL DUMOUCHEL

STANFORD UNIVERSITY PRESS
STANFORD, CALIFORNIA
1988

Stanford University Press
Stanford, California

Originally published in French 1985 by
Éditions Grasset & Fasquelle as
Violence et verité
Originating publishers of English edition:
The Athlone Press, London
First published in the U.S.A. by
Stanford University Press, 1988
Printed in Great Britain
ISBN 0-8047-1338-3
LC 87-61959

Contents

Introduction

> My claims are scandalously out of proportion with the general temper of the times and my literary background, which must be regarded by almost everybody as the worst possible recommendation for the type of research that interests me.[1]
>
> René Girard

Literary critic by profession, René Girard published, in the early 1960s, two books on the novel which revealed a somewhat peculiar point of view on the relationship between knowledge and literature.[2] The first, *Mensonge romantique et vérité romanesque*,[3] proposed a general theory of the novel and of its evolution, while the second, *Dostoïevski: du double a l'unité*,[4] was a short study dedicated to the development of Dostoevsky's literary production, from his earliest writings to *The Brothers Karamazov*. First we will turn to the second of these books.

In his *Dostoïevski* Girard suggested that literary criticism, in order to understand and analyse a text or an author, need not necessarily borrow from semiotics, psychoanalysis, philosophy or the sociology of knowledge the explanatory principles it uses for the interpretation of literature. Rather, argued Girard, it is sometimes possible to find within literary texts themselves a sufficient critical theory and the desired analytical tools. According to Girard, Dostoevsky provides an excellent example of this. His later works, beginning with *Notes from the Underground* and *The Eternal Husband*, generally picture the same types of human relations and conflicts as his earliest ones, but they throw upon them a very different light. Certain attitudes which the earlier works presented as characteristic examples of romantic generosity and abnegation, behaviour which was at first encouraged and given as an example to imitate, are in the works of Dostoevsky's maturity criticized and rejected: more precisely, they are shown to stem from envy and interpersonal conflicts.

This progress is not of mere debunking or cynicism but of

understanding and knowledge. The later Dostoevsky deconstructs into a network of human relationships the passions which the earlier works conceived as the spontaneous and simple expression of the romantic soul. Further, this deconstruction explains why an agent unwittingly caught within such a network of relations would spontaneously adopt upon his actions the viewpoint which the characters of the early novels embrace. Hence the superiority of the later works: they exhibit models not only of the situations found in the earlier ones but also of the explanations that there accompanied them.[5]

A crucial point is that Girard does not turn to the non-literary texts where the author discusses his work, critical essays, correspondence, etc. . . .[6] but to the later novels, which he sees as the implicit critique and reworking of the previous ones, or rather of certain situations and interpersonal relations that formed the web and texture of the earlier novels. The underlying idea is that literature itself is a form of knowledge and that the distance separating the earlier from the latter works indicates, sometimes, a growth and progression of understanding.

Clearly the later Dostoevsky thinks he grasps more accurately that which the characters of his early novels falsely believed they understood: the motives and meaning of their actions and desires. Through a skilful exploitation of situations reminiscent of those found in the early texts, the mature novels show for what they are – illusions and misunderstandings – the explanations originally proposed. Simultaneously, and through the same device, the later books adopt a critical distance towards attitudes and behaviour which the early novels unreservedly proposed as examples to imitate. The multiplicity of the situations and characters involved tends to indicate that the knowledge gained by Dostoevsky pertains to the networks of relations and desires common to the various characters and the repeated situations. His change of heart towards his characters' original 'explanations' tends to indicate that Dostoevsky shared their illusions. It follows that this knowledge is relevant not only to characters of fiction but also to each and every one of us inasmuch as we share these desires and partake in similar situations.

The various novels of Dostoevsky are successive steps in a cognitive experience. They inform us of the growth of his knowledge and self-understanding. To read them is to gain, perhaps, some of that knowledge and understanding.

What, then, is this knowledge? According to Girard, the illusion which a long tradition of novelists, including Dostoevsky, deconstructs is that of a spontaneous desire that links in a straight line the desiring subject to the desired object. It is of little importance here to know if this straight line is supposed to represent the subjectivity of desire, the transcendental ego's radically free choice of the object of his desire, or the objectivity of desire: the intrinsic qualities of the object which rationally justify its election. Both conceptualizations miss the essential, which great authors perceive, that desire is mimetic, imitative, or – to use Girard's early terminology – triangular. Our desires copy or mimic the desires of others. Desire is triangular because the object of our desire – knowledge, mate, position – is made desirable by the desires of others which also converge towards it. Desire is not a straight line. It is a triangle. Its vertices are occupied respectively by the other, the object, and ego. That is what the later Dostoevsky has discovered. He has learnt also that the dissonance which results from the collision of this fact with our cherished illusion of an autonomous desire breeds conflict and mystification.

Mensonge romantique et vérité romanesque, published two years before the essay on Dostoevsky, propounds a more general version of the same theses. Girard uncovers a tradition of novels that he calls 'romans romanesques', which reveal rather than reflect the influence and action of mimetic or triangular desire. It runs from Cervantes to Dostoevsky, through Flaubert, Stendhal and Proust.[7] The list given here should not be considered exhaustive or limited in time to the end of the nineteenth century. Later texts indicate that it extends to Kafka and Joyce.[8] But it should be considered exclusive of certain authors and texts: most of Balzac, Victor Hugo and Benjamin Constant, for example. In English literature it would exclude, among others, D.H. Lawrence and perhaps parts, but certainly not all, of George Eliot. This tradition divides, and the dividing line sometimes separates the works of one author, sometimes discerns certain novelists from other authors. Always it differentiates knowledge and understanding from misapprehensions and misunderstandings.

This is a strong claim, much stronger than viewing the evolution of one author as revealing the progress of his own knowledge. How can it be sustained?

Cervantes' hero, Don Quixote de la Mancha, engages upon a strange mimetic endeavour. He copies and imitates the knight-errants he has read so much about, especially Amadis of Gaul, whom he chooses as his model. Under the influence of this paragon he gathers the necessary equipment, changes his name and sets out on a quest of adventure and excellence. Quixote's mimesis is limitless; it is without bounds. He imitates not only how a knight-errant should dress or carry himself, but also what Amadis desires. The presence of this mediator, fictional as he may be, metamorphoses all things. It transforms a farm girl, Aldonza Lorenza, into a princess, Dulcinea del Tobosco, windmills into giants, and a barber's brass basin into Mambrino's golden helmet. Mimetic desire mystifies; it misrepresents the value and nature of the thing desired. It also deceives us about the quality and form of our desires.

Cervantes is not fooled by his hero's delusions. On the contrary, his irony unveils them and he takes care to show us how Quixote's lunacy slowly infects those who are near him; how – learned or illiterate, wise or unwise as they may be – they imitate him as he imitates Amadis of Gaul. The result of this is to weaken the distinction between fiction and reality and to show that if a fictional mediator like Amadis can be a real mediator, then a real mediator is always in a way fictional; his influence breeds fantasies and delusions. Cervantes' novel is an illustrative treatise on the contagious character of certain forms of madness. It is also a disquisition upon the role of literature in the epidemic.

The line that divides knowledge from misconceptions is drawn by Cervantes himself, and because novels are one of the protagonists of his novel the line is drawn through literature itself.[9] Girard uncovers, but does not invent, the tradition.

Don Quixote recognizes the influence of his mediator. He acknowledges that he is a disciple of Amadis of Gaul. He tells us, and Sancho, that his path leads him to imitate and to emulate his model, and he embarks on a series of ill-fated adventures. Yet Quixote never stumbles across Amadis himself; though the disciple and the model desire the same thing, the emulation never turns to rivalry, for they do not inhabit the same universe. Hence the slightly unreal and comical aspect of Quixote's quest.

Silas Marner and William Dane enjoy no such advantage. They belong to the same community, the church assembling at Lantern Yard. They both desire the same things: first to be shining instances of youthful piety, then to marry Sarah. They have been the best of friends for a long time when a mysterious fit of catalepsy, which occurs during a prayer meeting, singles out Silas in the eyes of the community as selected by God for a special purpose. William alone dissents from the general sympathy towards Silas, suggesting that the visitation may have been from the Devil instead. This disagreement does not impair their friendship. Silas has been engaged to Sarah for a few months and, we are told, 'it was a great delight to him that Sarah did not object to William's occasional presence in their Sunday interviews'.[10] Later, William successfully accuses Silas of a theft he himself committed. He has Silas expelled from the community and finally marries Sarah. The effect is anything but unreal and comical.

Is it a pure accident that Silas Marner will then become a miser, that his desire will be fixed upon the object that was designated to him by his happy rival? Is this behaviour new to Silas? Why is he so uncertain of the meaning of his apparent election? Is it because William dissents from common interpretation? Why does he take such delight in William's presence in his interviews with Sarah? Does he need his model to confirm the object of his desire? But who is William's model? William, who was also visited by God, who saw in a dream the words 'Calling and Election sure' written on a page of the Bible.[11] William, who also desires Sarah and who aspires to be, like his friend, a shining instance of youthful piety. William, it is true, is treacherous and deceitful, but only after he has suspected a lie and dissimulation in Silas' fit.

Silas Marner and William Dane are each other's model, but that is something which neither of them will recognize. They live in the same community and their mutual imitation leads them to conflict. The model indicates to his disciple the object he should desire and, in the same gesture, forbids him to proceed towards it. William tells Silas of his dream, but he rebukes him for his fit. Silas invites William to visit Sarah, but she is not for him. The conflict blinds the rivals to their reciprocal imitation, and it blinds us also.[12] As the rivalry unfolds, the antagonists strive to distance themselves from each other as much as possible. They struggle to become different from each other. Yet their efforts are in vain; their struggle renders them doubles of each other. William, in order to conquer Sarah, decides to obtain, by any means, the money whose absence was the only obstacle to Silas' wedding. In so doing he imitates the false and deceiving Silas he suspects. When Silas suddenly discovers the role William has played in the crime of which he is accused, he rejects the chance offered to defend himself. Silas will not accuse his accuser. Yet, by abandoning his fate to the drawing of lots, he solicits the same indubitable sign which the William he still believes in can claim. In the end, as Silas stands condemned, the two rivals become doubles of each other. Silas proclaims: 'There is no just God that Governs the earth righteously, but a God of lies that bears witness against the innocents.'[13] He makes his credo of the very belief upon which William has acted.[14]

Unlike Quixote and Amadis, William Dane and Silas Marner stumble across each other. They struggle and strive to be rid of each other. How could we suspect their imitation? Quixote protests far and wide the name of his model. William and Silas would both recoil at the idea that they counterfeit each other. Silas and William belong to a small, tightly knit, egalitarian religous sect. Quixote and Amadis belong to different universes; they will never meet. Yet it is that reduced distance between the model and the disciple which transforms the emulation into rivalry and finally destroys the distinction between model and disciples. In the end it makes the antagonists doubles of each other and establishes between them a complete, though negative, reciprocity.

This evolution of imitation from emulation to rivalry and enmity produces unanticipated situations and behaviour, behaviour which we do not commonly associate with imitation. It also confronts the authors with new problems of technique. Don Quixote is well aware of the mimetic nature of his desire. Consequently Cervantes can abandon to him the task of informing us of this. George Eliot has no such recourse. Silas and William cannot inform us of what they do not know. The author who transcribes for us the silent discourse of their hearts cannot speak directly. She can only stress the involuntary symmetry that arises from the rivalry, and indicate how the rivals converge towards the same objects.

There follows from this evolution a transformation of the concept of imitation itself. Don Quixote is conscious of his imitation, though he remains blind to most of its consequences.[15] His model is a model in every sense of the word, including representation. Cervantes' hero, we would say, is guided in his action by a representation, or a cluster of representations, of what it is to be a knight-errant. He has a certain idea and ideal in his mind and he acts upon it. The mimetic relation between Silas and William can hardly be described in those terms. Neither perceives the other as the prototype of his own behaviour. Their imitation entails no representation – no consciousness, however fleeting, of the other as a model to imitate.[16] [17] Girard's claim is that no such consciousness is needed. Imitation as exemplified in Silas and William's relationship should not be construed as an attitude of the characters towards their own thought contents, but as a disposition of the agents to act in similar ways and to converge towards the same objects. This imitation without representation, this disposition without intention, is what Girard refers to as mimetism or mimesis.

Mimesis as an inclination to reproduce the actions and gestures of others is prior to and more encompassing than imitation in the usual sense of the word. There is in *Silas Marner* a passage which illustrates this beautifully. Silas, upon entering his cottage, has found a young child. A short time later he discovers nearby, half buried in the snow, the dead body of the child's mother. Taking with him the little girl, he rushes to the Squire's house to fetch the Doctor. Once he is there and has informed everyone of the incident, Mrs Kimble suggests he should leave the child in her care. ' "No – No – I can't part with it, I can't let it go" said Silas, abruptly. "It's come to me – I've a right to keep it." ' George Eliot comments: 'The proposition to take the child from him had come to Silas quite unexpectedly, and his speech, uttered under a strong impulse, was almost like a revelation to himself: a minute before, he had no distinct intention about the child.'[18] There was a distinct intention behind Mrs Kimble's suggestion. Silas' desire sprang from the opposition and imitated hers. Yet he needed no image, idea, or model in order to map his behaviour upon her desire.

Furthermore, it is clear that even Mrs Kimble's *desire* is not needed here. We know from other passages that the Doctor and Mrs Kimble wanted a child. Her suggestion, none the less, could have been more innocent than at least her husband believed it to be and had the same effect upon Silas. He had no way of knowing her desire, and George Eliot in her comments refers only to 'the proposition to take the child from him' as motivating Silas' sudden ardour. Mrs Kimble's suggestion could simply reflect the fact that she thought it improper for an old and solitary man to take care of a young girl to whom he was not related. Silas' reaction can be compared to an unformulated hypothesis about Mrs Kimble's intention, but it need not have been right. On the contrary, Mrs Kimble's desire could very well proceed from Silas' sharp rebuttal of her inoffensive proposal.[19]

Desire is mimetic because what we commonly call desire originates in mimesis. Our representations are shaped and tinted by mimesis. Like a revelation a distinct intention suddenly settles in Silas' mind, and he will now act upon this, 'his' desire. He has a clear notion of it in his mind, and he thinks he knows what he wants. George Eliot describes how Silas' clear representation of what he wants originated and she knows what ill-fated consequences could follow from this origin.[20]

Mensonge romantique et vérité romanesque, through an analysis of the works of five great novelists, recounts the history of mimetic desire from the end of the sixteenth century to the end of the nineteenth. It is specifically a history of desire, and a history of the novel as the privileged form of expression of that culturally relative turn of our mimetic predicament.[21] Desire, resentment, 'envy, jealousy, and powerless hatred' are, according to Girard, typically modern sentiments, as Stendhal used to call them. They multiply and proliferate in a cultural environment where interpersonal conflicts lead less frequently to physical violence, and where the differences that once distinguished men from men or women and used to discern the various orders that constitute society tend to disappear. As the egalitarian ideal slowly pervades our universe, we refuse to allow others any kind of superiority. We are thus deprived of the possibility of that remote form of mediation which characterized Quixote's relation to Amadis. As our model closes in he becomes more and more an obstacle, a rival, the '*terzo incomodo*' that stands in our way. Like Silas, we do not understand that our imitation automatically arouses our rival and we vehemently refuse to accord our antagonist the least superiority. As a result, the evolution of mimetic desire accelerates the diffusion of egalitarian institutions and ideals which in return foster its multiplication.

A threefold history emerges from Girard's narrative: that of the simultaneous and interrelated development of the novel, of social and political institutions and ideals, and of mimetic interactions. What René Girard has discovered through literature is the mimetic dimension of human behaviour, its capacity to generate cultural forms. That is: the ability of mimesis to shape not only our actions but also our perception of our actions.

Violence and the Sacred,[22] published eleven years later, will systematically apply the mimetic insights gleaned from literature and elaborate them into a consistent body of hypotheses, a theory. The book opens, with due reference to Hubert and Mauss,[23] as an essay on the nature and function of sacrifice. Soon, beyond sacrifice, what unfolds is an inquiry into the nature and function of primitive religions in general, or if you prefer, the sacred. What emerges from this inquiry is a hypothesis about the origin of social order and a general theory of culture.

Anthropologists usually consider that such a general theory is in principle impossible. This is not a dogmatic opinion only; they have in fact many good reasons to justify their scepticism. The best case against general theories in anthropology was presented a few years ago by Professor Rodney Needham.[24] More than any other writer, Professor Needham has recognized the exact nature of the obstacle to generalizations in anthropology and has clearly stated the terms in which the problem stands.

Social institutions, rituals, incest prohibitions, systems of classification and of kinship, sacrifices, sacred kingships, myths – in short, most of the objects of anthropological research and knowledge – do not constitute, according to Needham, classes in the usual sense of the term. That is, words like sacrifice, rituals, or incest, which we use to group and to categorize cross-culturally various practices and institutions, do not in fact refer to sets of objects which all share certain common properties. Anthropological objects do not form (normal) monothetic classes defined by the invariable presence of certain common properties. It follows that what is known of one of these institutions is not necessarily true of another and that what Needham calls the principle of substitution cannot be applied.[25] There can hence, concludes Needham, be no general theory of such objects.[26]

It does not follow that anthropology is condemned to accumulate blindly unrelated data about every independent society or particular institution. The reason for this is that anthropological objects, if they do not constitute monothetic classes, do none the less cluster into polythetic classes. A polythetic class is a set of elements in which many defining features are distributed over all the members of the class but in such a way that (1) every member shares many defining features with most other member of the class and (2) no feature is common to every member.[27] In other words, a member of a polythetic class closely resembles most other members but does not resemble them all in the same way. Members of polythetic classes somehow look alike but they are not similar; they are related by what Wittgenstein used to call a 'family resemblance'.[28]

Most rituals strongly resemble most other rituals, but there is no reason to believe – and many reasons not to believe – that there is any characteristic feature common to all rituals. Rituals form a polythetic class. Therefore, concludes Needham, if general theories are unattainable, it does not follow that cautious comparisons between cultures and institutions are impossible or uninteresting; it simply means that such comparisons are made more difficult. Needham believes, in fact, that comparative studies can yield enlightenment about universal proclivities and perennial characteristics of the human mind.

Although I tend to agree with this assessment of the problem, I am not wholly convinced that the conclusion, at least the first part of it, is entirely vindicated. Professor Needham himself reminds us that the idea of polythetic classification is not proper to anthropology. In fact it has long been in use in biology, especially in zoology and taxonomy, where it established its hold under the influence of the theory of evolution by natural selection. The reason for this is simple. Once the members of a species were defined as 'having descended from a common ancestor' it became clear that no particular feature need be transmitted to all descendants or persist from generation to generation. Thereafter individuals tended to be grouped into species on the basis of overall resemblances, the greater number of features they share, rather than by arbitrarily eliciting one feature to decide membership in the group.[29]

The theory of evolution, as Professor Needham is well aware, is a general theory which deals with polythetic classes. It does even more, though this is not usually noticed. The theory of evolution by natural selection also explains why species tend to form polythetic rather than monothetic classes. The theory of evolution is a morphogenetic theory: it generates forms. It aims to explain how out of previous, more simple forms, later more complex ones can emerge. *Grosso modo*, its proposed answer is: out of random variations filtered by the environment. Given that species evolve, it is a necessary consequence of the theory that the members of a species aggregate into a polythetic class, not only because old features disappear but also because new ones appear. In other words, it is a strict prediction of the theory of evolution that the members of an individual species should constitute a polythetic class.[30] Because it is a morphogenetic theory, the theory of evolution not only bears upon polythetic classes but also explains why its objects should constitute such classes.

The lesson to be gathered from this short detour into evolution theory is that to postulate that general theories are impossible in anthropology because its objects form polythetic classes is to propound, in fact, that no morphogenetic theory is possible in anthropology, or at least that none is forthcoming.

According to Girard, mimesis is a universal proclivity of the human mind. We tend to copy each other in our actions and gestures, including the actions that are made to appropriate objects. We are drawn by the objects towards which others tend. This disposition leads us to conflict. This ability does not rest upon any representation in our mind of the other as a model to imitate. We counterfeit his motion spontaneously, so to speak. We need not know *that* we are imitating in order to know *how* to imitate; or, if you prefer, in order to imitate.[31] Imitation in the usual sense of the word is a special case of mimesis.

If mimesis needs no representations, it generates them, as we have already seen. Not just any representations follow from it but rather false representations, misunderstandings. Because the agents ignore the mechanism which guides their desires to the same object, they become protagonists in a conflict whose origin they do not understand. As their reciprocal imitation turns to enmity, the rivals progressively lose sight of the object that originally motivated their opposition. More and more they concentrate upon each other. Although they do not recognize the mimetic dimension of their behaviour, they do not fail to perceive the aggressive and harmful attitude of their antagonist. This justifies each one in a more resolute opposition which begets in turn even more animosity. Such a process of exasperation – if there is nothing or no one to stop it – must necessarily lead to physical violence, and from physical violence to death.

There are, it seems, only two things which may stop such a runaway process of violence: cultural institutions of some sort or dominance patterns. Among certain animal societies dominance patterns play this role. We usually perceive their psuedo-economic effects: they regulate the access of certain members of the community – i.e. young males – to certain valuables – i.e. females. They achieve this effect by regulating the outcome of conflicts that arise when many individuals converge towards the same object, and they prevent the intensification of such conflicts in two complementary ways. On the one hand they reduce the struggle to only one encounter. The dominance pattern maintains the outcome of that encounter. It establishes that outcome as a pattern of relationship between the two animals. On the other hand, it preserves the life of both antagonists. The animal who submits is spared. He will not challenge his new master again.[32]

Unfortunately dominance patterns are not available here. They rest upon a strong repugnance to intraspecific murder which humankind obviously lacks. To say that the conflict is mimetic is to say, in another way, that the outcome of the first encounter will not be maintained; that it will not become a pattern of behaviour between the two antagonists.[33] For evident reasons cultural institutions are also unavailable here. Mimesis is a universal disposition of the human mind, one which is clearly linked with our remarkable cognitive abilities, with our evolution from animalhood to humanity. The problems which follow from our mimetic disposition must have arisen before cultural institutions existed. They must be solved in the absence of dominance patterns.

We shall now see that there is no one to halt the mimetic process of violent intensification. The reason is simply that violence also is mimetic – first in its origin, as it proceeds from two greedy hands mimetically attracted to the same object. Then, it is mimetic inasmuch as it progressively transforms the antagonists into doubles of each other. Violence purifies the mimetic aspect of any conflict, especially physical violence: one blocks as the other hits, and vice versa, as one hits the other blocks. A violent exchange is always a dumb repetition of the same gestures. The longer the exchange lasts, the clearer this becomes. In the end, violence reduces both enemies to mirror-images of each other.

We usually fail to see this because we too often heed the words of the antagonists. Each one claims that an absolute difference separates him from his enemy, the great Satan, the empire of evil or the imperialist powers. We should know better and see through this, for the exchange of words but mimics the exchange of blows. On both sides the utterances are identical, enemies trade insults and threats, they make sure that the exchange is fair, that no one should receive less than he has given.

Thus our blindness points to the third way in which violence is mimetic. It is contagious. Violence, once it has erupted, has a strange ability to spread. It infects those who are near, even those who step into the conflict to put an end to it. They are usually brought, sooner or later, to perform the very actions which they set out to prevent. There is no one to stop the process of exasperation because violence never fails, especially when it is intense enough, to find allies and to turn even its enemies into its allies; often into its best allies, because they are so convinced of their good intentions.

In these circumstances, the problem which arises is not only that nothing, it seems, may stop the mimetic process, may alter the fact that the conflict will evolve to its violent outcome, but also that the struggle must progressively involve more and more people, until at last violence has infected the whole community. In the absence of dominance patterns, conflicts have no natural end. If violence is mimetic, all violence only arouses greater violence; every victory breeds new opponents and every conflict more warriors, more fighters, up to the point where all become part of the general discord and contention.

Once violence has reached a certain threshold, social and cultural institutions themselves are of no avail to limit its diffusion. Every attempt to defuse the conflict is seen as a further provocation and usual mechanisms of arbitration lose their transcendence. They are seen by all as a party in the quarrel rather than as a judge. Consequently their decisions are viewed as acts of hostility by some, and as vindications of further excesses by all. Just as violence reduces the individual opponents to mirror-images of each other, so it destroys the differences that normally distinguish justice from revenge, arbitrator from opponent, and finally friend from foe: '[A]nd by this means destroying all laws, both divine, and humane, reduce all Order, Government, and Society, to the first Chaos of Violence and Civill warre.'[34]

'Such being the case, that original state cannot subsist any longer, and the human race would perish if it did not alter its mode of existence.'[35] This is the problem. It is the problem of Hobbes and of Rousseau, and it is the problem of the origin of social order.

The solution, suggests Girard, rests on the expansion and evolution of the very process of mimetic violence that creates the problem. Mimesis of appropriation, our tendency to converge towards the same objects, divides and dissociates, pitches men one against the other. Yet once the violent process of undifferentiation has reached a certain point, once it has reduced all antagonists to mimetic doubles, it can suddenly reunite them in the shared hatred of a common enemy. If that hatred is unanimously distributed, the destruction of the common enemy will successfully put an end to the violence. There are two interrelated reasons why this is so. One, because all will simultaneously successfully vent their rage against the victim. Two, because this unanimity minus one ensures that no one will rise later to take the part of the victim, to avenge him and to punish its murderers. The mimetic character of the violence will ensure the unanimity of the process. As more and more converge against one, mimesis will realize the violent agreement of all and persuade everyone that the common hostility is justified. Yet the designation of the victim is arbitrary. In the dumb repetitive process of violence, mimesis suddenly amplifies a random fluctuation in the ever-changing distribution of alliances and counter-alliances; its very redundancy will stabilize this difference until finally the original chaos is structured by the raging convention of all against one.

This process is arbitrary; it is also obscure to the agents who perform it. They do not know their victim for what he is: a victim, the unlucky centre of an arbitrary process of convergence, the randomly designated focal point of a collective process of victimage. This misrecognition, of course, is not accidental; it is an essential part of the mechanism. It is necessary to its proper functioning. The convergence of all against one is the common conviction that this one, the victim, carries an ultimate responsibility in the ongoing violence. The peace that follows the victim's death confirms everyone in his previous belief. Peace follows only if that condition is fulfilled, if everyone thinks that this blood need not be avenged, that this dead person is not just another victim. This condition will be fulfilled if all sided against him.[36]

Given this, we may suspect that the now-reconciled opponents will see their victim in a strangely distorted way. He will appear to them as the source of all violence, as the cause of all evil, but also as the origin of all peace, as the fountainhead of order. They do not understand the process by which peace suddenly befalls them when violence reaches its paroxysm. They will associate the restoration of order with the victim's undoing because no other explanation offers itself. It follows that the victim will appear to have controlled the whole process of violent dissolution and restoration of order, including his own death. All-powerful to inflict evil and all-powerful to bestow good, the transfigured and absent victim is the sacred itself, an ambivalent power that is most holy and most impure. *Violence and the Sacred* propounds that the sacred emerges, with the social order, as a by-product, an unintended effect of a self-regulating mechanism of violence. The 'sacred' is the distorted and partial representation of that mechanism by the agents who unwittingly performed it.

The social order proceeds from the same origin. It is also, in its way, a partial representation of the crisis and of its resolution. Though it is obscure and confusing – or rather, because it is so unclear – the experience of the mimetic crisis and of its resolution demands, from those who lived it, urgent attention. This visitation from the sacred who run amok in the community must be understood if men are to protect themselves from its recurrence.

In an attempt to protect themselves from the return of the sacred, the agents could proscribe the gestures and actions – as prohibited by this higher being – that originated the crisis and characterized its development. They could also surround with rules the objects that first occasioned the conflict, erecting laws for their acquisition, ordinances regulating their exchange and purifications to protect those who make use of them. They would not consider these proscriptions and prohibitions as their own conventions but as instituted by the sacred itself. The agents do not understand the mechanical unfolding of the crisis and its sudden end. They try to read off their recollection of a sequence of events which they perceive as controlled by the victim/god, the obscure intentions of the divinity.

Conversely, attentive to the beneficial effects that accompanied the resolution of the crisis and in order to reinforce and maintain the recovered order, the agents could institute the re-enactment of the gestures that brought about the conclusion of the crisis, either periodically or whenever the social order was threatened. They would then prescribe, in those circumstances, the actions of violence and rivalry that hastened the end of the crisis and immolate a victim in an effort to recapture the original benefits they reaped from such behaviour. Such, according to Girard, is the origin of both sacrifice and ritual and the explanation of the fact that rituals so often prescribe the performance of those actions which are usually strictly prohibited.

Finally, myths would preserve the memory of that origin of society. They are distorted accounts of the mimetic mechanism and the process of victimage that concludes it.[37]

The social order emerges from the self-regulating mechanism of violence. It emerges as a means of protection against violence. To a certain extent this means of protection must be functional; it must successfully make up for the absence of dominance patterns. Ethnological data suggest that it does.[38] Prohibitions reduce occasions of mimetic conflict. Ritual prescriptions regulate the exercise of vengeance. Sacrifices, sometimes, provide an outlet for resentment and frustrations. This functionality is none the less limited. The misunderstanding characteristic of the resolution of the crisis prevents the agents from grasping the real nature of the danger that threatens them. It also condems them to gather from the crisis itself and its evolution the indications as to what is required of them.

There follows a strange ambivalence which was already visible in the contradiction between rituals and prohibitions that prescribe and proscribe the same actions. The result is that the very institutions which in normal times protect against violent contagion will in times of crisis precipitate its evolution. In the last resort, when everything else has failed, it is the mimetic mechanism of victimage itself that will protect the society against its own violence.

This process of victimage, then, is not an institution, for it functions only in the absence of all institutions, when all institutions dissolve under the pressure of internal violence. This mechanism would not happen only once or in only one community, but many times and in many places. Each time the exact form and content of the social order, the objects and gestures prohibited, the rules prescribed, the sequence of ritual, etc. . . . would depend on the contingent occasion that initiated the crisis and on the agents' recollection and partial understanding of the course of events. The crisis and its resolution constitute, according to Girard, the common origin of all institutions as an independently repeated self-regulating mechanism that is always formally identical but whose precise circumstances vary from case to case.

This hypothesis explains both resemblance and variety. It predicts that social and cultural institutions should share certain family resemblances; not that they should be identical, nor that any characteristic should be common to all sacrifices or rituals. In short, it predicts that anthropological objects should cluster into polythetic classes. This is not surprising, for the hypothesis is morphogenetic. The process of victimage is not an institution but the template from which all institutions proceed.

This template is a social mechanism, one which arises from the composition of the actions of many agents. It is also a blind mechanism. The reconciliation which follows the crisis is an unintended effect. That is why the mechanism is a self-regulating mechanism of violence. It rests solely on the unfolding of violence itself. In order to restore peace, it calls upon nothing but the murderous fury which moves the mimetic doubles. It requires from the agents no intention of reconciliation, no improbable discussion upon the advantages of peace. All the agents need do is to persist in their ferocious conflict in order, unwittingly, to restore or institute order. No one need design or will this order for it to exist; it is typically a spontaneous order.[39] Like the invisible hand which transforms private interests into the common interest, or private vices into public benefits,[40] the process of victimage diverts each individual's violence to the common peace and order.

The hypothesis of a self-regulating social mechanism resting on the mimetic character of violence can explain how a social order may have arisen out of what most threatens its existence, without anyone having to design or will this order. It also explains why societies, though they have always resulted from human actions, have almost everywhere conceived of themselves as instituted by the sacred: by powers beyond the reach of humanity. In this, it continues the great Durkheimian tradition of sociology.

Although the self-regulating mechanism postulated here is hypothetical, and although it is a model of social institutions rather than one institution in particular, it is, by hypothesis, a real event. The hypothesis refers to a set of real events, to a collection of actual victimages that really took place. A rigorously realist epistemology is inescapable here.[41]

Those events, none the less, cannot be directly documented. It is not because no documents exist, but the documents bear only an indirect and incomplete testimony. Given the structure of the mechanism, they hide the essential. They hide the fact that the victim is a victim. They disguise him as a god and consequently distort the process of victimage; they dress up the events in a fantastic way. This deception, of course, is not accidental; it is an essential part of the mechanism itself. Nor is it voluntary; it is a self-deception also. The mechanism defines what may be termed a successful persecution. But a successful persecution is by definition invisible, for all reports of it come from the persecutors themselves. Conversely, an unsuccessful persecution is not one that does not make any victims, but on the contrary a persecution that is visible and makes perhaps even more victims because it is visible, because someone always arises to avenge them.

In these circumstances, the existence of a religious tradition which – as both Nietzsche and Max Weber noticed – always takes the part of the victim is rather surprising.[42] The Judaeo-Christian tradition constitutes, from the viewpoint of Girard's theory, a religion which should not exist. A religion which preaches forgiveness not only towards the innocents but also towards the guilty, towards one's own enemies, reaches out to the heart of the mimetic mechanism that generates the sacred and destroys it, or at least endangers its proper functioning. Such a religion cannot proceed from that mechanism.

In the sense in which the term is used in the philosophy of science, Christianity falsifies Girard's theory of culture and religion. It provides the rigorous counter-example which shows that the theory cannot be applied to all religions. Yet this falsification, as Professor Girard is quick to point out, has some rather strange and unexpected consequences, both theological and epistemological. The two dimensions are, as we shall see, deeply interrelated.

If Christianity – according to the hypothesis of the mimetic crisis and its violent resolution – is a religion that should not exist, this is first and foremost for epistemological reasons. The gospels, through the Passion of Christ, provide in fact a complete rehearsal of the mechanism. But this time the narrative is such that it reveals, rather than hides, the nature of the process. Nothing is missing: not the collective and unmotivated aspect of the violence; nor the identity of God and the human victim; nor the fact that the crowd carried the day against the normal functioning of the institutions, liberating Barabbas and imposing the death of this man with whom Pilate had found no fault; nor the mimetic contagion and unanimity as the disciples are dispersed and as Peter, betrayed by his accent, denies that he knows this man. Further, Christ propounds precepts and rules of conduct which, if they were followed, would tend to prevent the recurrence of the crisis and its violent conclusion.

The problem is that this seems to entail a knowledge of the exact mechanism of the crisis and of its resolution and that this knowledge, by definition, is not available to anyone. If the whole of human culture arises out of the transfigured process of victimage, if all institutions proceed from it, and if a misunderstanding of the process is essential to its functioning, then knowledge of its exact mechanism is ruled out.

The theological conclusion is evident: this knowledge cannot be of human origin.[43] The epistemological conclusion is that Christianity constitutes historically the possibility condition of Girard's hypothesis. Both claims need to be detailed, and their intricate relations somewhat disentangled.

Girard's reading of the Bible entails, in fact, an important reinterpretation of the Christian texts: one that runs counter to St Paul's Epistle to the Hebrews, and to all renderings of Jesus' death as required by the Father in atonement for our sins. The God of Christianity is the God who refuses and rejects violence and whose revelation, according to Girard, unravels the violent origin of sacrificial institutions. He is not the ogre who orders the sacrifice of

His son. He does not take upon Himself the responsibility for human violence; He does not justify it. Girard proposes what he calls a 'non-sacrificial' interpretation of the gospels; he is well aware that this is a minority interpretation, both theologically and historically.[44]

This has repercussions upon the epistemological thesis. Given that Jesus' death took place – according to Girard, this was not for ever ordained but need not have happened – it is evident that His revelation was misunderstood and obscure. It is thus understandable that Christianity, historically, constituted itself around a sacrificial interpretation of the Passion. Yet it is also clear, argues Girard, that Christian precepts should slowly corrode sacrificial institutions[45] and progressively give rise to a radically different type of society.

Not a society that would be less violent, or where arbitrary processes of victimage would never take place, but a society that would eventually dismiss religion as the basis of the social order. A society that would progressively come to understand the purely human origin of the problem of violence and would attempt to solve it with the help of purely human institutions. Christianity, according to Girard, is the religion that gives rises to secular societies. This is not an entirely new idea. At least since Max Weber, sociologists and historians have advanced theses about the particular role of Christianity in the progressive 'disenchantment of the world'.[46] It has, none the less, interesting consequences.

According to Girard's hypothesis concerning the origin of religion and of the social order, this is precisely the type of effect which the Christian Revelation should have. It should desacralize the world and progressively divorce religion from the social, worldly, order. The result is that Christianity should then be written down on the side of corroborating rather than falsifying evidence. This conclusion is paradoxical; it is none the less sound. Whatever may be the origin of the gospels, if Girard's interpretation is right – if they do reveal the violent origin of the sacred, thereby destroying the social and cultural efficacy of the mimetic mechanism of victimage, and if the historical evidence is good – then Christianity has had the results which the theory predicts it should have had. It has given rise to secular forms of social organization.

The same cause made possible the sciences of culture and of social organizations. The reason for this is simple. As long as the origin and the legitimacy of the social order are sacred, divine, any questioning of the meaning of that order is a transgression and every attempt to propound purely human and social explanations for the order of society is a sacrilege. Sciences of society can develop only when the sacred has loosened its grip on society. In the last three hundred years, the extraordinary development of the social sciences in the occident has been clearly linked with the appearance of new forms of secular social and political organizations. Christianity, then, is the possibility condition of Professor Girard's hypothesis.

Problems remain, difficulties abound; let us mention but a few of the most obvious ones. If the general hypothesis about culture is exact, how can a society such as ours exist? Clearly we have abandoned most, if not all, the ancient means of protection against violence that structured traditional societies. Yet if we have inherited the destructive dimension of Christianity, its ability to corrode cultural forms, certainly we have not inherited the evangelical spirit of non-violence. How can a society like ours survive? What replaces the sacred as a self-regulating mechanism of violence in our secular societies? In *L'Enfer des choses*, Jean-Pierre Dupuy and I have tried to provide an answer to this question.[47]

The second very obvious difficulty is that Christianity, if it undoubtedly played a role in the particular cultural development of the occident, certainly was not the only cultural factor involved, nor is it obvious that it was the most important. In the present state of our knowledge, the peculiar version of the Weber thesis necessary for the vindication of Professor Girard's hypothesis remains uncertain. We know too little about the social and cultural factors that presided over the rise of capitalism and the modern world.[48]

The essays collected in this volume challenge these and other related problems. Gathered from a wide range of disciplines – from theology to anthropology, to aesthetics and economics – they demonstrate the fruitfulness of Professor Girard's research programme. They were first presented at an international symposium that took place in France, at the Centre Culturel International de Cerisy-la-Salle, in June 1983. The proceedings were published in French in 1985 by Les Éditions Bernard Grasset, and the present volume is a partial translation of those proceedings. Many of the essays have been extensively rewritten for this translation, and some which were written in English and translated for inclusion in the French volume have now recovered their original form.

Professor Girard is very well known in France, unfortunately not always for the best reasons. His claims, 'scandalously out of proportion with the general temper of the times', have often given rise to violent polemics. The present volume, which bears witness to the seriousness and the productiveness of his scientific enterprise should contribute to create, in the English-speaking world, a very different atmosphere.

Paul Dumouchel
University of Waterloo

Ouverture

PAUL DUMOUCHEL

Exactly two years ago, here at Cerisy-la-Salle, Jean-Pierre Dupuy and I accepted the direction of this symposium. We agreed, at that time, upon three objectives. The first was to inform the French public of all those who in other countries – especially in the United States, where René Girard has been teaching since 1947 – were influenced by him in their own work. The second was to follow and to carry on the interdisciplinary debates and avenues which Girard's work has opened up. Beginning from literary criticism and ending with a general theory of culture, through an explanation of the role of religion in primitive societies and a radical reinterpretation of Christianity, René Girard has completely modified the landscape in the social sciences. Ethnology, history of religion, philosophy, psychoanalysis, psychology and literary criticism are explicitly mobilized in this enterprise. Theology, economics and political sciences, history and sociology – in short, all the social sciences, and those that used to be called moral sciences – are influenced by it. Not that René Girard is a specialist in all these fields, but the stubborn attention he gives to the study of violence and of mimesis brings him to transgress the academic borders that isolate disciplines and to redefine their problems in terms of his own inquiries. There follows from this a situation which still prevails today: his relevance is recognized in each discipline, but his competence is rejected by all. It is important to find out how matters actually stand.

The third objective constitutes nearly, but not quite, a sub-category of the second. Rather, it is another version of it, orientated in a particular way by the interests – some would say the obsessions – of the two directors of this meeting. The fact is that another symposium, 'L'Auto-organisation de la physique au politique', which took place here in Cerisy and in which René Girard and others who are present today also took part, was to some extent the occasion out of which this one grew.[1] It was followed by another symposium, 'Disorder and Order', organized this time by Girard himself, which took place in September 1981 at Stanford University in California.[2] This initial movement gave rise to two research institutes, the 'Centre de Recherche Epistémologie et Autonomie', the CREA, of the Ecole Polytechnique, and the 'Laboratoire de dynamique de réseaux', the LDR, which together constitute the 'Groupe Science/Culture de la Montagne Sainte-Geneviève'.[3] At the CREA especially we carried on research on the relationship between the formal models of self-organization in the physical and biological sciences and recent development in the sciences of culture. In this research, the theory of mimesis and the hypothesis of the surrogate victim occupy a central place.[4] Thus, for many of us, this symposium is also an occasion to pursue this interest.

This said, it is clear that interdisciplinary meetings like this that assemble participants around only one man and his work can usually run aground in one of two ways. Each person arrives here from his own domain, the chosen land of his interest, with his own criticisms, questions, and criteria which he expresses in the language with which he is most familiar, that of his speciality. Carried from confusion to misunderstanding, the symposium risks dying of incoherence caused by a lack of minimal common language. Each misjudges the statements of all. Only noise is exchanged. Sonorous words meet in misunderstanding. The other danger seems entirely opposite, but it proceeds from the same causes. It consists in replacing this disorder by an excessively simple order, where all address only Girard. Displaced from his achievement to the man himself, the dismantled symposium hovers between sermonizing and rebellion.

I think we can escape these two pitfalls if we concentrate on what is most rigorous in Girard's work, and what founds its unity. Girard travels across the encyclopaedia and reorganizes problems in relation to his own preoccupations. If we want to succeed in talking together, we should focus on the string of precise reasons and the well-defined articulations that control this reorganization. Girard claims a scientific status for the theory of mimesis and for the hypothesis of the surrogate victim; I suggest we should take him seriously and consider the Girardian theory as an objective thought content, as what Popper calls an 'object of World 3': that is, as a theoretical ensemble relatively independent of its author and thus open to the inquiry and criticism of all. Girard is certainly a privileged interpreter of this theory, but he is none the less only one among others, often the one most surprised by the trails or deadlocks it contains.

Some will perhaps object that this attitude grants too much before even starting the inquiry. I believe, on the contrary, that this is the only way to grant and to refuse nothing, the only way of remaining faithful to the Cartesian precept: 'never judge anything without conceiving it clearly and distinctly'.[5] For it is the internal logic of a work, and the distance that separates what it achieves from what it pretends to, that allows criticism. The point is not to recognize *a priori* the scientificity of Girard's theory but to behave as if we do, to consider it as a scientific hypothesis to see if it survives the tests to which we submit it.

'To see if the hypothesis survives', 'to test it', 'object of World 3' – all these expressions betray the influence of one particular epistemology which is far from being universally recognized. This is certainly true, but I think that considering a theory as an objective thought content, independent of its author, is not proper to Popperian epistemology. I see only two forms of criticism of knowledge which proceed in a different way.

The first is a psychoanalysis of knowledge which reduces an intellectual work to the psychological dispositions of its author and a discourse to the unconscious which formulates it, beyond the subject who utters it. Thus the Freud of *Totem and Taboo* would treat us to the spectacle of his unconscious. The work would have no ethnological relevance and would only inform us about little Sigmund's Oedipus complex. Yet such a demonstration, even if it were possible, has the inconvenience of being inconclusive. Imagine, for example, that you succeeded in showing that René Girard was a particularly mimetic, envious and quarrelsome being. You will never know what you should conclude from this: that the mimetic theory only betrays in a universal language the aberrations of a particular psyche, or, on the contrary, that Girard's own character is a further corroboration of his theory. The question is unresolvable. At the end of the inquiry everyone is sent back to the opinion that was already his when it began.

The second way of not according theories the relative autonomy I ask here for Girard's work belongs to certain versions of sociology of knowledge. These reduce theories to their conditions of production, and statements to the interests of those who formulate them. The disadvantage of such an approach is that it must always have decided already the question of the truth or falsity of the theory it studies. Unless the sociologist distributes *a priori* the access to truth according to the social or historical position of the locutor – that is, unless he elaborates a pure theory of power that reduces the truth of statements to the authority of the locutor (including the truth of sociology of knowledge)[6] – he can only establish correlations between mistakes in the theory and the sociohistorical conditions of its production, or the interests of its author. This entails that before the beginning of his inquiry he can distinguish, within the theory he studies, truth from falsehood.

Thus it is not so much one particular epistemology that I propose here but a minimum procedure: one which allows us to address the question of the truth and scientificity of Girard's enterprise.

Some will object that it is unfair to Girard, and belittles his achievement, to take him seriously when he claims a scientific status for his enterprise. Have we not better and more important things to do than epistemological analyses? Is there not, beyond the theories and hypotheses, an achievement that appeals to us and questions us, a mixed discourse which is both anthropological and philosophical, but also moral and religious; even more so perhaps because Girard is sometimes tempted to deny it? Far be it from me to exclude these questions, but do they not preach in favour of the approach I suggest? Do they not indicate the distance written words often acquire in relationship to their author and to what he says of them?

I readily recognize that mimetism is not, and will not be absent from the attempt of collective appropriation, of kidnapping the work and expulsion of the author which I suggest. In counterpart, it offers Girard's work the chance of being recognized as what the author has always claimed it to be: a Truth that surpasses him.

A Gabonese Myth

RENÉ BUREAU

(Translated by Mark R. Anspach)

In *Le Bouc émissaire*, René Girard never misses an opportunity to speak ill of those he calls, rather peevishly, 'our' ethnologists. On page 38, he explains the reason for his irritation: 'Never do ethnologists identify the persecution schema in the societies they study.' They have in fact failed to read the author of *Violence and the Sacred*. The persecution schema has been hidden from them since the foundation of ethnology. Come now! There is no point in being thin-skinned. Let us make a liar of him instead. I read René Girard with enthusiasm and was inspired to reconsider a series of myths and a ritual corpus gathered in 1967 among the *Fang* of Gabon, adherents of a religious movement that is at once traditional and modern, the *Bwiti*. I would like to present here two serics of considerations concerning this review. First, the Girardian hypothesis has considerably illuminated for me the *Bwiti*'s myths of the origin of the world and of evil, both as to their primary meaning and as to the mechanisms of the concealment of this meaning; I was able to gather different versions of the oral traditions and to understand, I think, the reasons for the difference between the diverse states of the mythic story. Second, the ritual undertaking of the *Bwiti* initiates appeared to me in a new light: they behave like Girards of the bush, *mutatis mutandis* of course. It seemed to me that they, too, understand the surrogate victim mechanism.

Their religion, faithful to the original *Fang* cult centred on the ancestors, adopted and recast into a new and coherent whole an initiatory tradition from the midlands that of the *eboga* (hallucinogenic plant), at the same time as the most central biblical figures imported by the missionaries. Thus Christ, under the name of *Nzambi-a-Pongo*, assumed the principal place in their ceremonies. This adoption corresponds to a radical refusal of violence and sacrifice, which are represented by the witchcraft principle, *Evus*, also called *Nzambi-di-Békéké*, in so far as he is at once persecutor and persecuted.

We should say immediately that the *Bwiti Fang* appears as a fundamental statement of resistance to the white man's civilization, characterized by the conscious and accepted reign of *Evus*. But we need to get to the myth itself and to the rites. After that I will suggest 'Girardian' commentaries that will doubtless raise as many questions as they resolve.

I The *Bwiti Fang*

1. The Myths

You will have observed, I am sure, that tales of the origin of humanity weary us and fascinate us at the same time. It is impossible to read them in a lazy manner: they do not yield their meaning without a struggle. The same is true for primitives as for ourselves. Essential truths are not alluring at first blush. It is the long, drawn-out task of deciphering them which in the final reckoning, at the end of a lifetime, brings the mind pleasure. It is without doubt above all their transposition into community rites that makes them a source of delight. Members of the *Bwiti* with whom I spoke were never very eager to relate to me the basic texts by which they lived. You do not have to be a theologian to go the Mass.

I hope that you will be able to familiarize yourselves with the diverse vocables deriving from several vernacular tongues. Since it is impossible to reconstruct all the different versions for you, I will simplify where I can.

There is first of all *Mebeghe* (pronounced 'møbørø'). He has three offspring, *Nzame, Ninegone* and *None*: three beings who spring from the same placenta. From this placenta and the umbilical cord springs a fourth being: *Evus*. *Evus* himself has a double, *Ekurana*, who springs from the part of the umbilical cord that is cut and buried.

Through the intermediary of *Ekurana*, *Mebeghe* assigns to each of the four one direction (or one quadrant) of the universe. Crossing its borders is prohibited. *Nzame* is charged with the task of creation, particularly the creation of man. *Ninegone* violates the prohibition. She goes to find *Evus* and tells him of her jealousy *vis-à-vis* the prerogatives of her elder brother, *Nzame*. *Evus* says that he will show her how to make men after her own fashion. He reveals her femininity to her and enters her sex. Upon his return to the 'village', *Evus* behaves in a very exacting manner, devouring all the animals. *Nzame* retires. *Ninegone* initiates *None*, the third triplet, into sexuality. They procreate men, who will be mortal, unlike what *Mebeghe* had foreseen. *Evus* initiates *None* (whose name means 'anvil') into the technique of ironworking. From this moment on, the life of men is dominated by *Ninegone* and *Evus*.

I will add for now three mythic elements that are more or less integrated into the basic corpus, depending on the informants and the regions:

– We see *Nzame*, alone, carved up, losing his blood. According to one version, this 'sacrifice' is willed by *Mebeghe*.

– We see *Ekurana* dispatched by *Mebeghe* to punish *Evus* and to cast him into a hole.

– Reference is made to a myth borrowed from another ethnic group, in which a woman, *Benzogo*, has her throat cut in order to enter into communication with her deceased husband, thanks to the uses of the *eboga*, whose powers were revealed to her by supernatural beings. *Benzogo* is at the centre of the original *Bwiti*. She 'speaks' through the intermediary of *ngombi*, the harp, principal instrument of the cult.

2. *The rites*

The principal rites unfold in three phases, three successive ritual nights which represent thirty-six hours of cult activity. Here too I am obliged to be succinct. The three phases are as follows:

1. The origin, or birth. Origin of the world, of evil, of sex, of death, of man, of the *Fang* ethnic group, of each man, of the initiate, of Christ. It is the appearance of differences and divisions.

2. The world here below (*dissumba*), the struggle with *Evus*, death. The death of the initiate through the ingestion of *eboga*, the death of *Nzambi-a-Pongo* (Jesus), the death of each man, the eradication of *Evus*. The phase is symmetrical with the first: the woman's belly is in fact a tomb; the cord by which the cadavre is lowered into the grave is none other than the umblical cord.

3. The world beyond (*meyaya*), the death of death, the true birth, the return voyage to the bosom of God, the disappearance of differences. A preview of beatitude in which everyone turns back into a kind of 'cocoon', all united and dissolved together.

The first phase is that of the *prohibition* and of its transgression by woman. The second phase is that of the *rite*, organized by man. The third phase is the exit from time, with neither rite nor prohibition, as before the first phase.

The first phase corresponds to the rhythm of the musical rod (*obaka*) as it is struck by the hammer of the primordial forge: thunderbolt, bursting of the initial egg, first cry of a child, etc.

The second phase corresponds to the eight-stringed harp (*ngombi*): voice of the sacrificed victim.

The third phase: new clangour of the *obaka*: cry of agony (notably that of Christ), bursting of the cadavre, return to the mother's breast.

Another instrument, the musical bow (*bègn*), is played out of sight of the participants as a prelude to the original creation and transgression.

Among the personalities who direct the ceremonies, there are three principal roles:

– The *nganga*, the figure of *Nzame*, of *Benzogo*, of *Nzambi-a-Pongo* (Christ). He is assisted by two acolytes: the *yombo* who represents *Ninegone* and another *nganga* who represents *None*.

– The *kombo*, head of the community. He is stationed behind the altar, sometimes in a crypt. He speaks in an esoteric language in the middle of the night, then vanishes. An ambiguous figure, at once *Mebeghe* and *Evus*.

– The *ekambo*, an *Ekurana* figure, the double/enemy of *Evus*. He sits watching over the entrance to the temple, sacrificial sword in hand. In certain rites, he wields the torch which divides the world into quadrants.

In addition it is thought that, generally speaking, humans belong to one or another of the following three types:

– One who possesses a personal *evus*, the 'sorcerer' (*nem*). He eats the others and possesses the power here below. The *kombo* is necessarily a *nem*.

– One who knows the *evus*. He enjoys the same power of clairvoyance as the sorcerer, but he is not his accomplice. This is the *ngolengole*,'the intermediary'.

– One who does not even know of the existence of *Evus*, who is 'simple'. He is, however, enlightened and warned against the sorcerer by 'the intermediary'. The *nganga* is simple (*mimien*).

The first type is affiliated with *Ninegone*, the second with *None*, the third with *Nzame*.

To which type does *Nzambi-a-Pongo* (Christ) belong? We will find out later.

The ritual as a whole, structured like the initiation, presents itself as a combat against *Evus*, as a reconciliation between men and women, Blacks and Whites, the living and the dead. The first night begins in the 'hole of birth' at the temple's entry post and finishes at the 'head' of the temple, after the crossing of the central fire. The community's progress is known as the *Bwiti*'s 'road to the Cross' because everyone dies after the death of *Nzambi-a-Pongo*. On the morning of the third day power, sex and death no longer exist. Each person has again become the initial cocoon he once was. All are *mimien* (simple) like *Nzame*.

Here, in their dryness, are the cast, the camera angles and the essential sequences of the religion of the *Bwiti*. Let us try soaking the film in the Girardian developer in order to reveal the outlines of the realities it conceals.

II Attempt at Decoding

1. The initial crisis or the quadrants of the world

We thus start out with a gang of four. Or actually, three plus one, like the musketeers: *Nzame*, *Ninegone*, *None* and *Evus*. An order is established among them, based on primogeniture. Each is assigned to his own place. Mimetic rivalry manifests itself. The stakes: the divine prerogative of the production of men, attributed to *Nzame*. Mixing occurs: *Ninegone* crosses the forbidden border. *Evus* introduces bad reciprocity by provoking sexual division; he incorporates himself into *Ninegone*, who unites with *None*. The *Fang* designate the initial transgression by the word *nsem*, incest. A coalition is formed against the eldest, *Nzame*, who is put out of action.

The initial transgression was provoked by the jealousy of the youngest. The original spatial distribution was transformed into division and then into biological fusion. A plagiarism of divine production, procreation introduces death and its corollary, the separation between the living and the dead. The *Bwiti* is familiar with Cain and Abel; the first is called 'the-man-between-life-and-death'. As Claudel somewhere says, 'Cain verifies on his brother Abel the knowledge acquired by his parents.'

Finally, work, of which the forge is the symbol, plagiarizes the act of creation. It is said in the *Bwiti*: '*Evus* is the one who invented the word civilization.' He is often associated with the introduction of houses constructed of durable materials, with more than one storey. Consumption is no longer free. A disparity appears between those who produce more and those who produce less. It is in particular the gap between the 'civilized' and 'savages', between Whites and

Blacks. Numerous stories about the origin of the inequality of the races circulate among the *Fang* and testify to this interpretation of the role of *Evus*.

Thus the progeny of *Mebeghe* were divine; they become human. For the *Bwiti*, man can and should return to his divine state. The initiates sometimes say: 'In fact, we are gods.' Fallen gods or potential gods, which comes to the same thing. For the moment it is *dissumba*, the time of death, dominated by the couple *Evus–Ninegone*. The initiation anticipates the return to our true state. It is not only culture which is at issue (technical knowledge, power), but nature as well (sexuality, death).

2. The victim or the case of Nzame

The myth is discreet with regard to the fate of *Nzame*. Here, the analyses in *Le Bouc émissaire* proved particularly enlightening for me. The occultation of the collective murder is doubtless as important a phenomenon as the murder itself.

What appeared disconnected and bizarrely scattered in fragments of stories seems to have found its coherence. You recall that *Nzame* is sometimes presented as the victim of tortures, but that this scene is not integrated into the plot of the myth. It is said somewhere or other that it is on the orders of the 'Father' *Mebeghe* that *Nzame* is led to sacrifice himself. I am convinced that we are dealing here with a retrospective influence of the figure of Christ as presented by the catechisms. We will see this more clearly in a moment.

It is also said, in versions that are apparently older, that *Nzame* was punished 'because he had stolen the menses of his sister *Ninegone*'. The *Bwiti* does not keep this version. 'Men demand gods cleansed of all sin' (*Bouc émissaire*, p. 115). The mythology was moralized on contact with Christianity. A demon 'of reinforced guilt' – this must be *Evus* – appeared. We will see that he is also destined to be a scapegoat of the second degree. *Nzame* 'is specified as a good and divine power' facing 'a bad and demoniac power' (*B. E.*). We are shown in the *Bwiti* a disgusted and furious *Nzame* saying in so many words after *Ninegone* has brought *Evus* back to the village, 'Since that is how things are, you will have to manage on your own; I am retiring.' René Girard invokes here 'the theology of divine anger' as an explanation of violence.

As a matter of fact, the propensity to portray *Nzame* as innocent is a way of obscuring the original murder and the reasons invoked by the murderers. The traces of the victim's trial are erased.

But at the same time the acquittal of *Nzame*, who has become a figure of perfect innocence so as to conjure away the primitive lynching, permits a reversal. One dare not say that *Nzame* was killed by his twins but one does not, however, forget that he was cut into pieces. The hypothesis is launched that it is the Father who asked him to suffer, as the missionaries say. But in the last analysis – and this is, to my mind, the very great originality of the *Bwiti* – *Nzame* will be assimilated in the ritual to *Nzambi-a-Pongo* (Christ) and to *Benzogo*, the woman who was sacrificed and transformed into a harp, the voice of God. The whole cult revolves around the celebration of an innocent victim. It is the model of the Passion of Jesus that is reflected back on *Benzogo* and on *Nzame*. In the tradition, *Benzogo* was guilty of infringing the prohibition on entering into contact with the dead, of divinizing herself. The *Bwiti* affirms her innocence. *Nzame* was guilty of jealousy of his sister's fecundity and of stealing her menses. The *Bwiti* affirms his innocence. *Nzambi-a-Pongo* is the avatar of *Nzame*: he is the one who dies for no reason, the one with whom the *Bwiti* initiate identifies himself. When the initiate listens to *ngombi*, the sacred harp, the 'sacrament' of the divine presence among men, he hears the moans of the persecuted victim. 'Everything has gone through sacrifice [*okanzo*]', it is said in the *Bwiti*. *Mebeghe* is supposed to have sent *Ekurana*, his strong right arm, to tell men, 'There must be no more sacrifices.'

The chants take up the words attributed to Christ/*Nzame*, personified by the *nganga*, in the course of a symbolic celebration of the Passion, where one never knows whether it is a question of *Benzogo*, of *Nzame*, of Christ, of *Komba* (a Gabonese killed by the Whites) or of the initiate: 'I represent all men . . . All humanity doubted me . . . What did I do to men? . . . I take the road to the sky, the road of *Nzame* . . . I spoke to the men of this world and they did not understand.' Or again: 'God sent *Nzambi-a-Pongo* to us so that we eliminate sacrifices.' There is no question of sin, or of redemption. 'God entrusted the *eboga* to us so that we stop immolating men.' Advice is sung to the new initiate: 'Do not kill men . . . Do not act proud . . . Do not be resentful . . .' etc.

In the language of the *Bwiti*, the initiates 'turn their lives around'. 'We change our skin.' 'We perform the cult ceremonials to bring eternal life here below, so that everyone will be simple, so that all will speak the same tongue.' 'We await the day of the mingling, when all will be in the same place . . . That man become as a butterfly in its cocoon, that man may go everywhere, at every moment: that is what we call the happy life.'

Note for now this strange slide, already glimpsed, from culture to nature; this telescoping of history, this negation of the human condition in so far as it is distinct from that of God. And one never knows for sure if *Nzame* is a truly divine entity or if he is the number one creature; the *Bwiti* seems to have entered into the logic of the incorporation into Christ-God taken literally.

The 'operator' of this incredible transmutation is the *eboga*; its basis is the vision provoked by the sacred plant whose root is 'white like the bones of the sacrificed victim'. The *eboga* sprouted over the grave of *Nzambi-a-Pongo*. There would be no *Bwiti* without this primary experience – which each initiate undergoes once and for all – of fusion with the world of the dead, where 'one loses one's skin' (one's Black skin), where one finds oneself back in 'the abode of *Nzambi-a-Pongo*', in the company of all those who are no longer either men or women, elder or younger, chiefs or subordinates, Blacks or Whites, gods or men, but who are all divine. Realization of the Parousia, regression to the original matrix (isn't that so, Nicodemus?), abolition of the creation, eradication of violence by dilution of the antagonists. The disparity felt *vis-à-vis* the Europeans had to be really insupportable finally to provoke such an alienation.

The question of the relations between nature and culture is posed here, in connection with the Girardian theory. In their logic, the adherents of the *Bwiti* admit that even animals can be sorcerers or simple; one can even imagine their being initiated. Where does the crisis of undifferentiation begin? Resemblance is not in nature. How may we decide between what is innate and what is acquired? The mimesis of appropriation seems to be on the side of nature; culture comes in precisely with the victimage resolution that neutralizes it. Can one change one's culture without changing one's nature? The *Bwiti* answers no. As long as there are men . . . and women, *Nzame* will be executed. As long as there are houses with more than one storey, some will be higher than others. Is the problem any different? The *Bwiti* chooses to do away with *Evus*, the builder, *Nzame*'s challenger. We will come back to this point.

3. The doubles and the case of Evus

Who is the double of whom in this story of the primordial egg? Obviously, there are the three (or four) twinborn siblings of whom we have spoken. But more precisely?

Let us return for a moment to *Mebeghe*, the one who brought the siblings into existence. His name is practically never pronounced. When the missionaries sought a translation for the word 'God', they settled on *Nzame*. We are not even too sure whether it is *Mebeghe*, the father, or the eldest son, *Nzame*, who established the prohibition of the four quadrants; the accounts are vague on this point. *Mebeghe* is a plural form. Is it merely a generic term? It is said of *Mebeghe* that he has 'no father, nor mother, nor wife'. In fact, the first three offspring are called respectively *Nzame-Mebeghe, Ninegone-Mebeghe and None-Mebeghe*. Let us leave him out of the myth then, as is done for all practical purposes by the *Fang* themselves.

The *model-rival* is clearly *Nzame*. His double, 'the second after *Nzame*', as it is sometimes said, is *Evus*. 'At bottom, at bottom, *Evus* is not bad', an initiate told me. This reminds me of a sermon by an Ivorian prophet: 'The Devil is a spirit whom God loves.' In addition, the *Fang* assert that one would have to be stupid not to want to possess a personal *evus*.

The fact that *Nzame* and *Evus* may be two faces of the same being is attested by the figure of the *kombo*, the head of the community of initiates, the one who is secluded in his crypt during the rites and who speaks out with authority in the middle of the night of ritual. At once feared and venerated, he wields power in the world here below and is located at the top of the initiatory hierarchy; supreme chief, he is a God figure; but as the obvious manifestation of the inequality of status position in society, he is an accomplice of the demon. With the *kombo* the dualism appears, in a certain sense, as a duplicity. It is thought, moreover, that it is not possible to become *kombo* without sacrificing a human being. Léon Mba, the first president of Gabon, was a *kombo-bwiti*.

If the *nganga* (the innocent one) dominates the stage during the ceremonies, nobody forgets the presence of the *kombo* behind or under the altar.

The conjuncture becomes more complicated when one realizes that *Evus* has a true double, not an elder 'brother' like *Nzame* but an *alter ego* who sprang from the same umbilical cord, *Ekurana* (also called Saint Michael). It is *Ekurana* who sacrifices *Evus* by casting him into a hole dug by his spear. We thus have a double-rival and a double-enemy. The two antagonisms are not of the same nature. *Ekurana*, for his part, does not seek to become a god any more than he imitates *Evus*. He is the avenger who sees that justice is done.

Evus, the witchcraft force, the plagiarist of God, the wolf facing the lambs, the 'king of the earth', as he is sometimes called, the revealer of woman's desire, her possessor-possessed, the eater of wild meats, then of domesticated meats, then of human flesh, the initiator of the control of fire, the inventor of houses built of durable material, the chief, the one who knows and who profits from his knowledge, the White, the leaper of forbidden boundaries . . . is he not God behind another face? 'At bottom, at bottom, *Evus* is not bad.'

'The demoniac does justice on one hand to all the tendencies in conflict in human relations, to all the centrifugal forces within the community, and on the other hand to the cenripetal force that brings men together, to the mysterious cement binding this same community'(*Bouc émissaire*, p. 274). Is not *Evus* the true scapegoat, constantly employed to hide the mechanism of his own execution? 'The order that is lacking or that the scapegoat has compromised is established or re-established by the intervention of the one who at first disturbed it.' 'He wishes to be without rival, ahead of all the others, serving as their model but himself without model' (*B.E.*, p. 93). He represents 'the exacerbated form' of mimetic desire. 'The equilibrium is broken in the myths, sometimes in favour of the maleficent, sometimes in favour of the beneficent, sometimes in both directions at once, and the equivocal primitive divinity can split into both a perfectly good hero [*Nzame*] and a perfectly evil monster' (*B.E.*, p. 118). 'Paradox of the god who is useful by being harmful, who promotes order by instigating disorder.' 'An implicit scapegoat, like Cadmus who provokes disorders "only" to put an end to them . . . He does not reveal the secret of his own production.' 'False transcendence of violence.' These quotations apply perfectly, I believe, to the case of *Evus*.

Evus provokes the undifferentiation by transgressing the prohibition with the complicity of *Ninegone*. By so doing he introduces disparities: man/woman, living/dead, primitive gathering/technology, Whites/Blacks . . . Following his lead, the sorcerer, seer of the 'world of the night,' plays with the laws of nature: to be in several places at once, to transmigrate a man into an animal, to render sterile (for women), to wipe out the crops, to appropriate the substance of men in order to make them work as slaves at invisible tasks, and a thousand other powers whose source is the devouring of others, that is to say the mixture of what should be distinguished (individuals), and the practice of incest, another form of mixture of what should be distinguished (blood relatives). Given this, it is traditionally assumed that society cannot get along without sorcery, for it cannot get along without power. *Kombo*s are necessary as long as '*Bwiti* hasn't arrived'. And yet when the fragile social equilibrium is threatened society seeks out the sorcerer, subjects him to an ordeal and eliminates him. The recent increase in disparities has provoked a sort of inflation of suspicion and of witchcraft accusations. The origin myth has a tendency to veer towards Manichaeism. The Whites have contributed to rendering *Evus* radically evil.

The *Bwiti* is in contrast with this traditional logic. In a certain sense, it restores to *Evus* his (relative) innocence before getting rid of him. It respects his ambivalence. It desacralizes him in order to neutralize him. This operation is accomplished thanks to an indispensible godsend: the *ngolengole*.

Before coming directly to this 'intermediary', let us say a few words about the manner in which the *Bwiti* envisages the problem of evil. In *René Girard et le problème du mal*,[1] Christiane Frémont poses a question in relation to Leibniz: 'Are God and the Devil twins?' The *Bwiti* seems to reply in the affirmative. 'Believe in God or believe in the Devil, the universe will be no different for it: God as an absolute master ruling all things according to His caprice is indistinguishable from a spirit of mischief' (op. cit., p. 286). Yet these twins, *Nzame* and *Evus*, are not identical. In the last analysis,

> the Devil has no kingdom he can call his own . . . There is no duel between good and evil; rather, the second is included in the first. Universal good requires singular evil. Evil is not a principle, it is existential; it is the necessary correlate of the production of a whole. God would be evil if He hadn't created the world. He wishes for good and takes in evil: in doing so, He founds the order of things.

This God who 'takes in' evil receives a name in the *Bwiti*. He is called 'the third', 'the intermediary', the *ngolengole* who is figured by *Nzambi-a-Pongo*: that is, Jesus.

4. Neither model nor rival, the case of the ngolengole

Of the three deities who issued from the primordial mass, *None* apparently does little to attract attention. He takes no initiative. He is in point of fact the youngest. Yet *Ninegone* initiates him into sexuality, *Evus* into metalwork. Did he in fact participate in the murder of *Nzame*? Evidently, the question is not asked.

This discreet figure could well be central, or at least absolutely necessary. A *Fang* story concerning three brothers of whom the youngest is the only one to renounce the temptation of power and to refuse to violate the paternal interdict would tend to corroborate this way of looking at things.

It is said in the *Bwiti*: how could the sorcerer (*nem*) and the simple one (*mimien*) coexist without the presence of the *ngolengole*, the 'third'? In the ritual, then, this intermediary represents *None*. One might wonder if this last little one is truly a male; his name is that of the anvil struck by the masculine hammer. To be exact, the anvil does not receive the blows directly; it vibrates when the object to be forged (*Nzame*?) is pounded. Is not *None* what is called a *nyamogho*, generally an old man (or an ancestor) who transcends and assumes at the same time the masculine and feminine principles? Is he not the 'good including evil', behind or beyond the persecutor/persecuted duo which permits them to coexist? The *ngolengole*, a redoubled name, allows the group to survive. He knows *Evus*, he is an initiator, he 'sees' in the nocturnal world. But he is in no way the accomplice of *Evus* who, for his part, not only sees and knows but acts for his own advantage, thanks to his knowledge.

The *Bwiti* has not hesitated to make Christ (*Nzambi-a-Pongo*) into the *ngolengole par excellence*, the one 'who knows what lies in man's heart', but refuses the temptation of the desert. He is not a model, for he possesses nothing that one would like to appropriate ('not even a stone on which to rest his head') and, for this reason, he is not the rival of anyone. This being so, the 'simple' ones are, however, suspicious of his knowledge and the sorcerers resent his refusal to connive with them.

At the time of my field work in Gabon I read a novel by Louis Aragon, *La Mise à mort*,[2] and I fell upon a passage which I noted down. It concerns a character, Christian, who is said to examine himself in a mirror with three faces:

> Finally, for Christian, the system of Dr Jekyll and Mr Hyde seemed to be an interesting stage in the knowledge of man's abysses. The dichotomy between the philanthropist and the monster is based on a rather elementary idea of the cleavages that exist within a personality. It is simply a rupture between two poles . . . Stevenson made the monster win out over the philanthropist: Dr Jekyll fades away to the benefit of Mr Hyde . . . It is Stevenson who had the first insight into the duplicity of man [. . .] and thus is proclaimed the pre-eminence of evil over good. [. . .] Good and evil do not need to be incarnated in a symbolic manner: they coexist in the same man like a crossroads of the soul, and he who hates war quite honestly makes the gestures that unleash it. Do you follow me?

> Christian used to say that if two forces, one positive, the other negative, give birth through their coexistence to a current, that is because the poles have been separated, because someone, you understand, someone holds

> them apart. What Stevenson did not see is the third character, the arbiter between good and evil, who dozes off from time to time, letting evil carry the day against good, or vice versa. The Indifferent One, are you with me? The Indifferent One [. . .] The mirror with three faces had acted as a machine to divide Christian into his components. This reflecting machine had revealed to this well-dressed lad the mystery of the human trinity. The central image is formed by the equilibrium of Dr Jekyll and Mr Hyde; it expresses that strange mathematical phenomenon which contradicts our elementary knowledge according to which one plus one equals two, when in reality there is in the sum of one and one something which does not exist in either one: the plus, no doubt.

I have reproduced these long extracts in a Girardian spirit of respect for novelistic expression, for they summarize rather well – here at the level of the components of the personality – what the *Bwiti* intends, at a level we may call ontological, by this third figure whom it sometimes calls 'the independent one'.

In so far as He is 'innocent' or 'simple' (*mimien*), Christ is the avatar of *Nzame*, but in so far as He has aquired a first-hand knowledge of the *Evus* He is 'the arbiter between good and evil', the 'plus' in the sum of the antagonists (*Nzame*/*Evus*) – what Leibniz would call 'the best' in opposition to a good, for 'it produces a whole' by 'taking in evil' (cf. *supra*, Christiane Frémont).

The first ritual night sees the elimination, still more or less shrouded in obscurity, of *Nzame*; the second night sees the elimination of *Evus*; the third sees the death of *Nzambi-a-Pongo*, the *ngolengole*. The first celebrated the victory of *Evus*: it was a 'mortal' death, giving birth to the world here below (*dissumba*) with its divisions and antagonisms. The second established a 'false transcendence': the elimination of the second twin (*Evus*) does not abolish the antagonism itself. The third death is needed, the 'native' or 'natal' death, for violence to be eliminated; the mediator himself chooses his death; neither an innocent arbitrarily designated for the vengeance of the group, nor a creature of envy, *Nzambi-a-Pongo* is not 'sacrificed', even if his death presents itself as that of a banal surrogate victim, but he exposes the hidden violence against explicit or implicit victims and inaugurates the new era in which disparity itself will have been wiped out.

For the initiates, the unique source of knowledge is the *eboga*. The sacred plant plays the role of the operator in the action of 'turning life around' that characterizes the religious movement. To be exact – this point is much emphasized – it is not a matter, properly speaking, of knowledge, but of a vision. The *eboga* provides this without any merit on the part of the one who enjoys the vision unless it is that he must first purify himself, notably by confessing his 'witchcraft' crimes, and that the (difficult) ingestion of the bitter root provokes a grievous sensation of death. The *Bwiti* itself draws the comparison with Christianity: the latter is tied to the book; time is needed to gain knowledge and understanding of it.

Christians accept the passage of time, history, slow initiation through instruction. The *Bwiti* initiates, in accord with the cosmic burst symbolized by the clangour of the *obaka* (the resonant rod), 'see' the totality in a single experience. The shock is in fact necessary to provoke the rupture with *Evus*. This last, to whom the Whites appear to have sworn allegiance, supplies the banal knowledge of the world here below. This type of knowledge rules out the apprehension of what is essential; it implies a misrecognition (*méconnaissance*) of the intrinsically devouring character of the apparent successes of the kingdom of *Evus*. I often heard it said: 'The one who has more necessarily dispossessed the one who has less.' The recognition of this misrecognition is given only by the *eboga*. It is *Ekurana*, the double of *Evus*, who made the *eboga* grow over the grave of *Nzame/Nzambi-a-Pongo*. The *eboga* is the instrument that belongs specifically to the intermediary, to the third, to the best. It inserts itself between the rival doubles, it 'holds the poles apart', it opens a breech between life and death, it reveals to the initiate that life is a death and death a life. Let us be provocative: the *eboga* is the René Girard of the equator!

5. *Differences will always be with us*

One could doubtless say equally well that the *Bwiti* has understood everything and that it has understood nothing.

It seems to me that René Girard is lacking in precision as to the nature of these famous 'differences' and, as a result, of 'undifferentiation'. This vagueness impedes, to a certain extent, the clear understanding of a phenomenon like the *Bwiti Fang*. I have already alluded to this.

I would readily adopt as my own this criticism made by Lucien Scubla (in *René Girard et le problème du mal*, op. cit.):

> Doesn't the exclusive focus on the duality of the enemy brothers involve giving short shrift to the duality of the sexes and the duality of generations? Alongside the rivalry of enemy brothers which sets similar beings at odds with each other, shouldn't room be made for the

> antagonism between the sexes which pits different beings against each other and for the conflict between generations which pits unequal beings against each other? [. . .] We suspect that these types of opposition cannot be reduced to a single kind. (p. 148)[3]

And further on:

> Girard obviously cannot flatly deny the existence of differences before the primal lynching, since mimetic violence, which is supposed to erase all differences, presupposes precisely their existence. He can only attenuate their significance by refusing to see in them either autonomous sources of conflict or ramparts against the mimetic violence whose assaults they sustain. (p. 150)

The *Fang* myth, as we saw and emphasized, refers to very 'different' differences. There are those one could call cultural: power, wealth, technology, degrees of civilization. Then there are those which may concern man's biological nature: filiation, primogeniture, and above all sex and feminine superiority in procreation. One may recall that *Nzame* was supposed to have stolen his sister's menses. Finally, there are those one could call ontological: creator/creature, supernatural/natural, dead/living.

The *Bwiti* lumps these differences together and, in this logic, it stages a return to paradise lost, to the original matrix. In this way it telescopes history and can, quite naturally, disdain the disparity between Blacks and Whites, totally levelled out in the eschatological perspective. The resulting conception of the perfect man is that of a pure potentiality (the cocoon), undifferentiated through the absence of any specification; barely the foetal situation. This vision is opposite to that of the Incarnation. It is in this sense that the *Bwiti* has understood nothing (or understood too well?).

Yet it has understood that sacrificial ritual must be left behind and that this is the ultimate meaning of the death of Christ. Envisaging the possibility of an existence in the world here below from which all jealousy (*evus*) would be banned, from which all rivalry would be extirpated, from which all domination would be excluded (burying the *kombo* in his crypt) presupposes that one has grasped the inanity of the victimage mechanism.

How can we put into the same basket the disparities, inequalities, diverse degrees, rivalries, distances, dissimilarities, contrasts, incompatibilities, heterogeneities . . . which constitute, in all their indefinite nuances, human diversity, natural and cultural? Can a boundary be fixed between good and bad reciprocity? That, however, seems necessary if one does not wish to be engulfed in the regression characteristic of the *Bwiti* and to run the risk of wanting to abolish all creation (apocalypse . . .) at the same time as all culture. Until further notice, it is diversity which is good. But diversity is also the source of imitation . . . and of violence. Unification through the expulsion of the surrogate victim means resorting to a new violence. Just how far back in the chain of violences must we go, then, to find true peace? Renounce designating innocent victims, very well. But antagonism is there. It is redoubled, as in the case of the *ngolengole*, whom nobody can stand because he is lucid and non-violent. Root out antagonism and hold on to difference, but which difference?

Here I am seized with vertigo. If, enlightened by the revelation of the Revelation – reader, that is, of René Girard – I know that I, human, am a persecutor; and if I, believer, believe that it is possible to put behind us the detestable victimage mechanism by loving our persecutors rather than excluding indefinitely, in complicity with the others, those held responsible for our violence, this postulates on the one hand the perennial nature of persecution (of persecutors to love) and on the other hand makes it seem even more desirable to extirpate the reasons for persecution – jealousy, the driving force behind imitation – and finally to refuse diversity itself and to advocate undifferentiation (as in the *Bwiti*). In the turmoil into which the religion of the *eboga* (another name for the *Bwiti*) has thrown me, I find myself trapped back into a vicious circle. Moreover, the knowledge that I persecute and am persecuted makes my life more intolerable. The more I sense that René Girard is right, the more I find it irritating. In this way, I prove him all the more correct. All things considered, maybe I should have responded positively to the urgings of my *Bwiti* informants who told me I would know nothing without the vision gained through the *eboga*. Things would have been simpler. Although an initiate-initiator in the *Bwiti* confided to me one day: 'Those who see, like us, we are the ones who are the most doomed.'

Enough bantering. I will not be able to prove the master wrong. He explains to us, then, that the Scriptures disclose that we perpetuate and perpetrate an unavowed violence so as to neutralize the original violence. The knowledge that we have progressively acquired of this social mechanism, our growing aptitude for 'decoding' the persecuting attitude do not, of course, actually abolish the original violence. They only deprive us of the means of controlling it. The message of the Gospel doubtless does not mean that the mimesis of appropriation can itself disappear from the world here below, but that there exists a different route from that of the surrogate victim to cutting it off.

What good is there, in that case, in wanting to distinguish among motives for rivalry – that is to say among objects of appropriation – because in the last analysis what is at issue is the model-rival and not the apparently coveted object, since it is so true that this object can be utterly forgotten: the antagonism is more important that the reason for the antagonism. Then my irritation with René Girard's reticence at making distinctions among differences is doubtless without foundation. Any type of undifferentiation whatsoever will do to provoke the crisis.

Finally, to defuse the question, one can doubtless say – following both Genesis and the *Bwiti* – that all imitations are summed up in man's unique desire: to be like God. There is precisely one man – whom the religion of the *eboga* has placed at the centre of its ritual, just as Christianity has, each in its own way – one man who was not only like God, but who was God. The Word legitimizes all our desires, for it becomes possible to be like Him, in so far as He is in no way a rival.

I confess that the gnosis of the *Bwiti* has fascinated me, just as I am fascinated by the Girardian thesis. But the latter is not gnostic.

The Theology of the Wrath of God

RAYMUND SCHWAGER

The Problem of Allegory

According to Girard's theory, the sacred is the externalization and transference of a society's aggression on to a scapegoat. A consequence of this position is that religious accounts of divine acts of violence must be evaluated as human projections. Now many such accounts are found in the biblical writings. They are mainly connected with the major theme of divine wrath. How are these texts to be interpreted, especially as according to Girard it is precisely the Bible, first and alone, that has uncovered totally the underlying mechanism of violence?

I should like to tackle this question in an indirect way, in just that indirect way which Christian thought itself has taken. Language about the wrath of God was early on sensed to be a problem among Christians, but even earlier a similar problem had arisen in Greek thought in connection with mythology. For instance Isocrates (436–338 B.C.) gave the following verdict on the poets Homer and Hesiod: 'The poets have taught wicked things about the gods, such as they would not even allege about their personal enemies.'[1] The accounts of continual wars and sexual deviations were considered particularly scandalous. Nevertheless, to make the old stories acceptable to an ethically more critical consciousness, deeper hidden meanings were sought, and these began to be interpreted allegorically.[2] According to an author of the first Christian century, allegory is even an '*antipharmakon*' against impiety.[3] Myths were interpreted either in the physical sense as statements about the elements, parts and orders of the world; or psychologically and ethically as a presentation of spiritual powers and conflicts. In Plato we find an ambivalent attitude to allegorizing. On the one hand he rejects it, because he also wanted to expel the poets from his state. On the other, he himself used allegorically interpreted myths for central questions of his own philosophy.[4] By means of allegorical interpretation, he contested among other things the view that the gods could be envious. In the dialogue *Phaedrus* he says: 'Envy has been exiled from the divine choir.'[5] In the *Timaeus* he says of the demiurge: 'He was good, and what is good has no particle of envy in it.'[6]

After Plato it was Stoicism above all that further developed the view that the divine logos was dispassionate (*apatheia*) and without envy. This philosophical school also developed allegory into a fixed method by means of etymology. Finally Euhemerus (third century B.C.) introduced a new historical allegory. According to him, the gods were first only men. Tyrants appropriated superhuman powers to themselves and from them arose the evil deities. On the other hand, the great benefactors of the people earned undying fame for themselves and so became the benevolent deities.[7]

The allegorical method of the Stoics and central elements of their philosophy were adopted by Hellenistic Jews living outside Palestine among a Greek-speaking population and used to interpret their own scriptures. According to this method, the traditional language of the wrath of God refers on the one hand to the just punishment of the ungodly and on the other to the chastisement and education of the just (cf. 2 Macc. 6:12). It was particularly the Alexandrian Jew Philo who interpreted his people's scriptures entirely in the Greek allegorical sense. For him God is beyond all time, change and passion,[8] and so cannot in His being be enraged at all.[9] The stories about divine wrath were intended, as an educational deceit,[10] only for the unreasonable and the broad masses without insight into the truth, who need to be motivated to conversion by terrifying images.[11]

The world of Greek thought and Stoic allegory hardly penetrated Palestinian Judaism, because here there was an attempt to keep everything foreign at a distance. However, there is a certain resemblance to allegory in typology, which means the understanding of a present historical event in the light of a significant event in the past. Accordingly Deutero-Isaiah described the return of his people from the Babylonian captivity against the background of the tradition of the exodus from Egypt (Isa. 41:17–20; 42:10–44:23). For the typological method, unlike the Greek allegory, the problem of history was predominant. But the question of the wrath of God could not be directly approached in this way. This, however, was not a matter of urgency for the Palestinian Jews, as they had no problems with anthropomorphic language about God. The problem here was not divine wrath as such, but the question why the just often experience more of this wrath than the unjust (cf. Job).

In rabbinical theology we find – as an attempt to answer this question – the view that God's wrath against idolaters is eternal, but His anger against Israel lasts only a short time.[12] The question was, however, taken up more comprehensively by the same theology and harmonized with belief in the goodness of God. Starting from the prophetic discourse in which Yahweh laments over His unfaithful people, there arose the idea of the grief of God. God weeps continually for those Jews He was obliged to strike down in His anger,[13] and He is inconsolable for the Egyptians whom He caused to perish in the sea at Israel's exodus, as well as for those who were destroyed in the deluge.[14]

In the New Testament we find other ideas and a new kind of figurative speech: the parables. As distinct from allegory and typology an old tradition is not reinterpreted in them; rather, an event from daily life is narrated and made transparent to a deeper reality. So the sower scattering his seed, or the net cast into the sea, become likenesses of the Kingdom of God. As well as this figure of speech, the New Testament makes use of typology. Characters and events from the Old Testament are used as examples for Jesus and His destiny. At the same time this was a reinterpretation of the Old Testament. In this way a deeper insight into the working of God was gained, and so the traditional language of the wrath of God could be understood in a new way.

In the New Testament there arose the specific question: Why did God not destroy the enemies of His son in anger? Michel Corbin summarizes the decisive answer from the context of the whole New Testament as follows:

> If He [God] had sent legions of angels to defend His unjustly condemned Son, if He had allowed Him to come down from the cross to crush His enemies, as Psalm 2 foretold, He would have contradicted Himself, vindicating man's blind search for power.[15]

This gives the following consequences for an understanding of wrath in the New Testament:

> The wrath of God, in Paul as in Luke or John, is nothing other than this mechanism of blindness and violence unleashed around the false god, which strikes man down in the guise of an external fate, which seems all the more arbitrary, the more the mechanism of projections is unconscious. Wrath is called the wrath of God, it seems, because God alone, through His revelation in Jesus Christ, exposes its mechanism. Unmasking all the cover-ups of violence, He unstops ears and opens eyes.

> This is what justice is, all the more just for being a free pardon, so just that greater justice is unthinkable.[16]

This profound New Testament insight into divine wrath has to a great extent not been understood by Christians themselves, so the question has become a major problem. For instance, in the second century Marcion discovered the overwhelming greatness of the Pauline teaching on the justification of the sinner through the pure goodness of God. At the same time he was influenced by the Stoic concept of an entirely dispassionate and benevolent divinity.[17] From this Greek and New Testament view of God, the Old Testament statements about the passionate, wrathful Yahweh became completely untenable. So he was led to condemn these writings, attributing them to an inferior deity, and to reject everything Jewish. He may even have adopted the argument, well known to the Stoics, that 'When God is angry and jealous, aroused and moved, then He too declines and dies.'[18]

On the one hand Marcion found considerable support among Christians for his rejection of the Old Testament books, which mention the wrath of God; on the other the Church, led by the bishops, was neither able nor willing to follow him in condemning the Old Testament. The problems raised were temporarily solved, as the thinking of the Church itself had increasing recourse to Greek ideas and above all to the allegorical method. This is true of a considerable number of the second-century apologists and of Irenaeus. It was, however, the Alexandrians Clement and Origen above all who developed an exegesis which has much in common with Philo's. They used allegory comprehensively and supplemented it with biblical typology. Thus the stoic-Neo-Platonist concept of the immutability and impassibility of God was fully integrated into Christian thought and God's action towards mankind was interpreted as a great, wise, educational project. In the language about the wrath of God were seen merely statements about the just punishment of evil men.

Opposition to extreme forms of allegory arose later among Christians. Even so, this exegesis was never fundamentally questioned and was always resolutely defended by the great theologians. The essential arguments can most easily be found in Maximus the Confessor (580–662), who summarizes all patristic thought. He taught that the carnal sense should be rejected as being identical with Judaism.[19] Anyone who stops at the letter is, like the Jews, a killer of the divine Logos,[20] as the letters of the Scriptures are only the clothing of the divine Word.[21] A literal interpretation of the Old Testament scriptures attributes unjust judgements to God.[22] But even then, David (i.e. the spiritual sense) had killed the sons of Saul (i.e. the carnal sense).[23] To focus on the traditional historical events alone is to remain under the dominance of desire,[24] and to become entangled in contradictions.[25] In particular sacrifices should be understood in a spiritual sense, so as not to attribute passions to God.[26] Where Scripture speaks of such passions as wrath, this is only because God adapts Himself to our sensibilities.[27]

In a system of thought totally determined by spiritual-allegorical exegesis, all the biblical statements about divine wrath had lost their literal meaning and power to shock. They were consistently interpreted as statements about just punishment.[28] In his study *On the Wrath of God* M. Pohlenz could thus conclude:

> The 'philosophers' God' of Marcion, who was first felt to be an alien intruder, not only rapidly gained right of abode within the Christian churches, but also completely excluded the passionate Old Testament God disputed by Marcion. Even the Romans, initially only under the influence of the Christological disputes, accepted this God unconditionally. This victory is not questioned by the fact that Marcion's extreme conclusions were not shared, and that with Origen's exegesis a way was found to retain the authority of the Old Testament.[29]

This judgement is in certain aspects one-sided. Marcion was not merely influenced by the Stoics and although patristic theology took over the Greek concept of an immutable and dispassionate God, it simultaneously reinterpreted this concept in a Christian sense. For instance the idea of God's humility, which was far removed from Greek thought, was a central theme for Augustine, and Maximus the Confessor went so far as to understand true *apatheia* not merely negatively, as absence of passions, but also positively, as love of enemies.[30] Pohlenz is, however, correct in his view that the problem of divine wrath was primarily solved by the reception of Stoic allegory and the concept of a dispassionate God.

This process nevertheless left two problems unresolved. One concerned the allegorical method itself; the other the concept of divine punishment, which had replaced the language of divine wrath.

The Christian attempt to interpret the Old Testament allegorically was contested by many pagans. Celsus, for instance, mocked the biblical writings and made the following objections to the Christians:

> The allegories apparently written for their purposes [the books of the Old Testament] are far more shameful and absurd than the myths, because they attempt in a strange and utterly ridiculous fancy to relate things that have no connection whatsoever.[31]

Celsus considered, among other things, the Christian teaching about Satan to be particularly senseless and impious.[32] He was, however, at the same time a defender of Homeric epics and himself interpreted these allegorically, assuming in the process the existence of demons hostile to God.[33] He involved himself in contradictions, as J. Pépin has clearly brought out:

> This is the point where Celsus begins to fall victim to his own allegorizing, and to forget that he rejected the existence of Satan; for the interpretation he proposes for the Homeric gods . . . corresponds exactly with Christian demonology. It is hard to see what could be the nonsense perpetrated by the Christians in an eventual Homeric exegesis of their own, because it would be no different from that with which Celsus himself remains.[34]

Origen had already discovered and demonstrated the contradiction in Celsus. But the question arises whether he did not become involved in a similar contradiction, as he himself interpreted the Scriptures allegorically but criticized his opponent's allegorizing. His attacks were certainly more subtle than and consequently superior to those of Celsus. He could also rely on the fact that he did not arbitrarily apply his method to the biblical scriptures but that there is in the scriptures themselves a spiritual-typological interpretation of earlier statements. He also required that the allegorical interpretation should presuppose an acceptable literal sense, which was not the case with the Homeric epics.[35] Pépin, however, correctly judges:

> Even so he [Origen] is not entirely safe from paradoxes; the essence of his argument in favour of biblical allegory . . . consists of the statement: if pagan allegory is legitimate, then ours is also, *a fortiori*. Such argument though, assumes the recognition of some value in pagan allegory; if Origen attempts to ruin it completely, his own argument loses its force and becomes a paralogism, which the more summary criticism of Celsus avoided.[36]

Furthermore Origen, contrary to his own requirement, was unable to find any acceptable literal sense in many Old Testament accounts.[37]

Another pagan, Porphyry, also objected to Christian allegory and especially to Origen. He wrote:

> Certain men, desirous of finding an explanation for the wickedness of the Jewish Scriptures, but without breaking with them, have appealed to interpretations which are incompatible and in disagreement with what is written. They do not offer so much an apology for what is strange as a compliment and praise for their own fantasy.[38]

Porphyry further observes: 'The kind of absurdity comes from a man, whom I myself met when I was very young . . . from Origen.'[39] Porphyry had personally known Origen and contested his Christian allegory. He developed on his own account an allegorical interpretation of the pagan myths. Yet he no longer followed the Stoic method, but interpreted the epics in a Neo-Platonic sense against the background of a spiritual world. At the decisive moment, however, it can be said of him: 'Like Celsus and Origen, he remains an author who pronounces a ban on an exegetical process for as long as his adversaries use it, but does not hesitate to use it himself unreservedly.'[40] Pépin is able to show a similar ambivalence in the pagan emperor Julian and his Christian opponent, Gregory of Nazianzen.[41]

As a result the allegorical method was unable to solve the problem of rival interpretations. It also had a tendency, as we have seen more than once, to anti-Semitism.

The second unresolved problem lay, as the later history of the Christian West would show, in the interpretation of divine wrath as just punishment. For this view spontaneously linked itself with the idea that God could execute His judgement through men, particularly Christian princes and statesmen.[42] In this way even atrocities in the execution of 'just punishment' were justified, as it was a matter of carrying out God's judgement. For instance Bernard of Clairvaux wrote in a eulogy of the Knights Templar:

> The soldier of Christ is certain when he kills. He is even more certain when he dies. He honours himself when he dies. He kills with Christ, for he does not carry the sword without reason. He is a servant of God for the punishment of evil men and the praise of good men. When he kills an evil-doer, he is no murderer, but rather, I should say, a killer of evil and an avenger of Christ against those who do evil.[43]

So such phenomena as crusades, inquisitions and pogroms could come about and endure, with Christian inspiration and legitimation.

The futher question – who truly has the authority to judge truth and justice, and who might consequently proclaim himself the executor of the divine will – arose in the Western consciousness above all after the division of Christendom. The irreconcilable conflict and war between Catholic and Protestant cast doubts upon the violent claims of both sides. On this subject Walter Kasper writes:

> After the unity of faith – and with it the unitary basis of society until then – had collapsed as a result of the Reformation, the whole social order could not fail to be out of joint. The consequence was the religious wars of the sixteenth and seventeenth centuries, which brought society to the brink of destruction. This made it clear that religion had lost its integrating function. For the sake of the survival of society it was necessary to think out a new basis, other than religion, which could bind all together and be binding on all. For the sake of peace it was necessary to declare religion to be a private affair.'[44]

The transformation of the language of divine wrath into the language of just punishment had shown itself to be unsatisfactory. In the name of just punishment, Christianity had brought about a profound crisis in Western society.

But peace was hardly better served by the withdrawal from Christianity. It was replaced by a secular myth, which certainly had a great power for integration: the idea of the nation. But this new myth manifested itself concretely as a quantity of rival national myths, which were the occasion for new wars. Christians could even mix their traditional concept of participation in the just judgement of God with the idea of struggling in the just national cause. The contradictions this led to can be particularly clearly seen in the attitudes adopted by French and German Christians and Church leaders during the First World War. It was preached from German pulpits that evil was on the enemy's side. For instance: 'We see with horror how our neighbour nation, which a few years ago solemnly and officially separated itself from God – before whom we kneel in prayer – how this nation is subject to a terrible judgement.'[45] And yet more clearly: 'It is Germany's task, as God's instrument, to execute a world-historical divine judgement on our enemies, as they represent the spirit of darkness, the deadly enemy of the Kingdon of God.'[46] The other side made similar judgements, reversing only the roles of executor and guilty party. Germany's war aims were 'anti-Christian' and 'The lie is a constituent element at the innermost core of the German person.'[47]

The bloody history of the Christian West – and above all the fundamental contradictions in the judgement of what is in accordance with the justice of God – show that the idea of 'a just, divine judgement' is fraught with problems. It was precisely this high ideal of justice that served to veil personal prejudices and aggressions. Paul had already pointed out this mechanism of perversion in his Letter to the Romans (Rom. 7:7–25). This problem area, however, has up to now not been sufficiently considered by Christians either in the interpretation of Scripture or in the assessment of violent events.

The traditional allegorical method and the language of the just, divine punishment are inadequate to solve the problem of divine wrath. Simply to reject the Christian texts, as has been continually attempted since the seventeenth century, also leads no further. A comprehensive method is necessary, which assesses both pagan and Judaeo-Christian narratives by the same criteria. It must also be possible thereby to go beyond the ideal of justice and uncover and assess the collective mechanisms of aggression and concealment. This is precisely what Girard's theory attempts. So it offers progress where the greatest problems of Christian theology and occidental history have remained unresolved.

'I am Joseph': René Girard and the Prophetic Law

SANDOR GOODHART

> Il est juif et donc, dans son milieu et sa culture, il entend ce qu'il doit entendre, qu'il faut arrêter le sacrifice, qu'il faut un substitut . . .
>
> Michel Serres[1]

In 1973, Eric Gans wrote that René Girard's research in anthropology seemed to offer an 'Archimedian point' from which the human sciences could one day be rethought.[2] Gans may have underestimated the case. For what has occurred since Girard began writing in the early sixties is a veritable explosion of interest in his work in all major fields of Western inquiry. By the end of the seventies Girardian thinking had gained a foothold in literary studies, in classical studies, in anthropology, in psychoanalysis, and in religious studies.[3] But in the past two or three years, the 'mimetic hypothesis' has begun to be extended to fields less commonly associated with the human sciences, fields like economics and political science, and most recently the hard sciences of physics and biology.[4] If both the number and the kind of conferences that have been held recently (both in this country and abroad) can be taken as an index to this growing interest, then it may not be much longer before we discover in Girard's thought a model for talking responsibly about the conditions for both the humanities and the sciences – a basis, that is, for understanding in the most fundamental way the order of behaviour and of knowledge in human communities.[5]

My own contribution to this ongoing project – both in the present paper and in some forthcoming work – will be less to summarize Girard's ideas (there are already excellent accounts of his work) or to 'apply' them within my own field (which is literary criticism) than to highlight certain aspects of Girard's thinking that I think have been insufficiently emphasized – aspects that I call the 'prophetic'; in the second place, to undertake what I deem to be the next step of this research: to begin to uncover the roots of the Gospel revelation in that source of all prophetic thinking in our culture which is the Hebrew Torah. For that part of my presentation I will turn to certain texts at the conclusion of Genesis, texts concerning the story of Joseph and his brothers.

I

What René Girard's work offers us is neither more nor less than a theory of order and disorder in human communities. It emerged from the intellectual context of structuralism and post-structuralism in the late sixties and early seventies. Girard undertook to deal with the one problem evaded by the proponents both of textuality and of power – the problem of the sacred, a problem which, I suggest, comprehends each of these other two and goes beyond them.

In 1961, in *Mensonge romantique et vérité romanesque*, Girard proposed that desire is rooted neither in objects nor in subjects but in the deliberate appropriation by subjects of the objects of others.[6] The simplicity and elegance of this theory should not blind us to the enormity of its explanatory power. In a series of readings of five major European novelists (Cervantes, Stendhal, Flaubert, Dostoevsky, and Proust), Girard was able to show that the discovery of the imitative or mimetic nature of desire (in contrast to the romantic belief that desire is original or originary) structures the major fiction of these writers and makes available to us, if we would but read that fiction in the context of the writer's total output, an autocriticism of his own emergence from the underground prison of romantic belief.

In *La Violence et le sacré*, Girard generalized his theory of mediated desire to the level of cultural order at large.[7] What is the function of religion at the level of real human relations? If we have always had available to us imaginary theories of sacrifice – such as the kind Frazer and others in the nineteenth century proposed – or, more recently, with the advent of structural linguistics and structural anthropology; if we have tried to explain religion from within a network of social differences or symbolic exchanges – *à la* Marcel Mauss and Claude Lévi Strauss – then what Girard suggests in their place is a theory that would account for behaviour at the level of the real. Religion, Girard suggests, has the function of keeping violence out, of transcendentalizing it, of making it sacred. Thus the first equation towards this end of understanding the foundations for human community is the identity between violence and the sacred. The sacred is violence efficaciously removed from human communities, and violence is the sacred deviated from its divine position and creating havoc in the city.

But what is violence from a human perspective? Human beings argue, Girard asserts, not because they are different but because they are the same, because in their mutual differential accusations they have become enemy twins, human doubles, mirror-images of each other in their reciprocal enmity and violence. Thus violence is none other than difference itself, asserted in the extreme, no longer efficaciously guaranteeing its own propagation. It is difference gone wrong, as it were, the poison for which difference is the medicine. Such is the nature of the sacrificial crisis.

How do these identities offer us a theory of the origin of culture? In the midst of a sacrificial crisis which verges upon a war of all against all, an extraordinary thing can occur: the war of all against all can suddenly turn into the war of all against one. Since within the sacrificial crisis all approach a state of being identical to all, anyone approaches being identical to everyone and can, therefore, substitute for all those that each dreams of sacrificing. Thus the most arbitrary differences – hair colour, skin colour – can come to count absolutely. And in the wake of the successful expulsion of an enemy twin or double, peace is restored. Since the trouble was never anything other than human violence to begin with, the successful completion of the sacrificial project of each in the collective expulsion of an arbitrary scapegoat can restore difference to the human community. A complex network of ritual interactions can now be elaborated to prevent the recurrence of such a crisis, a prevention which can paradoxically take the form of its encouragement (in mock or commemorative form – and only up to a point) in order to reacquire its beneficial effects.

In *Des Choses cachées depuis la fondation du monde* and *Le Bouc émissaire*, Girard carries this development to its natural conclusion.[8] How has our knowledge of these sacrificial dynamics been made possible? Why is this very theory not just another sacrificial theory, protective of our own cultural ethnocentrism? The demystification of the sacrificial genesis of cultural order first makes its appearance in the Hebrew Bible and reaches its zenith, Girard argues, in the texts of the Christian Gospel, and in particular in the texts of the Passion. Texts like those of Cain and Abel or Jacob and Esau begin already to make available to us within the text this identicality of the sacred and human violence, but the full revelation comes only in the victimage of Christ. Christ, Girard argues, is the first innocent victim – a victim, that is, whose innocence renders visible for the first time the arbitrariness of the victims of primitive sacrificial behaviour and shows us where our violence is going.

For example, in the curses against the Pharisees, Christ tells the Pharisees:

> You say that, had you been there, you would not have stoned the prophets. Don't you see that in differentiating yourself from 'those who stoned the prophets', you do the same thing? You put yourself at a sacred remove from them which is neither more nor less than what they already were doing in 'stoning' their adversaries. Moreover, for telling you this truth of your own violence, you will differentiate yourself from or 'stone' me. What's more, those who come after you will repeat your very gestures. Believing they are different from you, they will in my name stone you, calling you Jews and themselves Christians.

The history of Christianity for Girard is permeated with such sacrificial misunderstandings, misunderstandings ironically of the demystification of sacrificial understanding itself.[9]

What does it mean, then, for me to call Girard's thinking prophetic? If we understand the notion of the prophetic as the recognition of the dramas in which human beings are engaged and the seeing in advance to the end of those dramas, then Girard's thought, which identifies itself with the gospel reading, is prophetic in the same way. Both elaborate for us the total picture of our implication in human violence, showing us where it has come from and where it is leading us, in order that we may give it up.

But where does such a notion of the prophetic itself come from? To ask this question is to necessitate an inquiry of a different sort.

The notion of the prophetic has particular meaning for us in the modern world, one which is associated for us with religiosity or a kind of false theologism as, for example, in the phrase '*nouveau prophétisme*'.[10] I would argue that if we have never recognized the true explanatory power of the prophetic, it is because we have lived within the confines of a Platonic essentialism which has barred that knowledge from us.[11] And yet I want to argue that the prophetic is more comprehensive than Platonism; that it is, if we understand the notion in its largest sense, the logic of ritual organization itself – a logic, moreover, that we share with every other culture on the planet and yet to which we remain indefatigably blind by virtue of our idolatry of Platonic reason. Therefore, it is a logic which raises as a stake our very ethnocentrism.

In what way? We live in a culture dominated by the thought of the logos, by discourse, by reason, by difference or decision-making – a thinking, in short, dominated by Plato. Within Platonic thinking there have been only two ways in which we have been able to conceive of the possibility of knowledge outside reason. On the one hand we have imagined it coming to us as the result of divine or providential intercession. Thus, for example, we have imagined poetic inspiration among the Greeks or the language of the Judaic prophets. On the other, we have imagined knowledge as possible for us through fantasies, illusion, dreams: in short, all those experiences of our lives that we feel to be the product of fiction or of desire. Thus Freud's discoveries, for example, far from unveiling for us a realm which is genuinely new, a knowledge which is other than conscious knowledge, only display for us a region which, from within Platonism, was, as it were, mapped out in advance. It is not coincidental that the two theories of dreams with which we are left after Freud is that they are either prophetic in the strictly literal sense of fortune-telling or the remnants of unconscious desire.

We have never, in short, been able to imagine the prophetic as a reading of the course of the dramas of human relations in front of us, a reading of what Michel Serres might call 'the excluded middle'.[12] And yet I want to suggest that there is such a conceptualization within our culture: one, moreover, that has been misunderstood precisely to the extent that we have felt it to be accessible to us within Platonism. I am thinking, of course, of Greek tragedy and the Judaeo-Christian Bible.

There is no time in the present context to specify how the prophetic makes its appearance within these two domains. Suffice it to say that I do not want to suggest that the Judaic Prophetic in the sixth century B.C. or Greek tragedy in the fifth century B.C. are simply extensions of Assyrio-Babylonian or other Mesopotamian rituals (for example, the mantic enthusiasm of the pre-Socratic philosophers), even a more profound version of those ritual traditions[13] Rather, what I would propose is that Greek tragedy and the prophetic tradition in Judaism appeared at a moment that Girard would identify as a sacrificial crisis of the possibility of religion itself, a moment when no sacrificial system seems to work, when all sacrifices lead only to more violence and all victimage leads only to more victimage and therefore to the need for more sacrifice. Without trying to pinpoint such a moment historically or culturally, I will say that Judaism and to a lesser extent Greek tragedy formulate a response to the following question: How can I live in a world in which there are no longer any gods of the sacrificial kind? How is it possible to be prophetic in the face of the collapse of the prophetic?

Apart from the answer Greek tragedy would offer us, the response Judaism poses to this question is one that has always been understood from within Judaism as an orthodox reading, although the path by which I will come to this reading may seem somewhat unorthodox; this response is, of course, the law of anti-idolatry.[14] At the heart of Judaism is the Torah, the Pentateuch, the five books of Moses, the Law, and all the remaining books of biblical scripture, the Midrashic, Talmudic, and rabbinic commentaries as well as the mystical and spiritual traditions of the Kabbala and Hasidism are centred upon it and extend it.[15] And at the heart of the Law is the Decalogue, the *aseret hadibrot*, the ten commandments. And at the heart of the Decalogue, the Law of the Law, as it were, is the first commandment, the commandment for which all the other commandments are themselves extensions, the law against substituting any other God for God, for the prophetic God, for the God of anti-idolatry: *anochi Adonai eloheycha asher hotzeitiycha meieretz mitzrayim mivayt avadiym* ('I am the Lord, your God, who delivered you from the land of Egypt, from the house of slavery').[16]

The Judaic genius, as readers of Maurice Blanchot and Emmanuel Lévinas will immediately recognize, is to have imagined a God completely external to the world, a God for which nothing in the world is finally sacred.[17] Judaism is '*la pensée du dehors*', a thought of the desert, a thought of exile and of exodus.[18] It is a thought of not confusing anything that is in the world for God, a thought of seeing to the end of the dramas in which human beings are engaged and learning when to stop, a thought therefore of learning to recognize yourself in the other.

Take, for example, the story Exodus 3 tells of the name of God.[19] Moses is a shrewd and canny dealer. He is willing to be a little cagey even with God. God says to him: go back to Egypt and take the Hebrews out of slavery (3:10). And Moses responds: Okay, no problem. Only, who shall I say sent me? (3:13). He tries to trap God into revealing Himself. But God is as cagey as Moses, even cagier. He says: when they ask you, tell them *ehyeh* sent you (3:14). That is, He does not necessarily reveal His name. He simply says: this is what you say when they ask you that. The Hasidic tradition which substitutes the word *Hashem* (meaning 'the name') in place of this word is, in this regard at least, as traditional as the mainstream, since they too assume that this is God's name, which is their very reason for not pronouncing it (in accordance with the third commandment).

What does *ehyeh* (or *jehovah*, which is the third-person form of the same word) mean? And here I turn to an insight offered to me by my colleague at Cornell University, Jonathan Bishop. It is clearly a form of the verb 'to be', a future form, and when it first occurs if does so in the first person in the form: *ehyeh asher ehyeh* (3:14).[20] Volumes, of course, have been written on this sentence. In fact, the Kabbalistic tradition takes it as a matter of principle that the unravelling of the name of God is the only important task in Judaism, the one which achieves for us what the Kabbalists take as the primary aim of exegesis: that of relating the heavens to the earth.

The task continues. For here again it may turn out that God is being a little bit cagey with us. Just a moment before Moses asks God His name, God has remarked to him: go down to Egypt and bring the Israelites out of bondage. And when you do, 'I will be with you' (3:12). The word employed by Torah is the same employed by God a moment later in the place of the name: *ehyeh*. The word slips by Moses, who of course has no reason to fix upon it. But in retrospect of God's next declaration we can return to it with renewed interest.

The phrase *ehyeh asher ehyeh* must in context come to mean: 'I will be with you in order that I will be with you.' Or, inserting the name itself within the name: 'I-will-be-with-you will be with you in order that I-will-be-with-you will be with you.' And one could go on in this fashion indefinitely. In other words, in the place of the name of God is a promise, the promise of a promise, a promise which is in the first place one of future being or presence. To be intimate with God, to know God's name as it were, is simply to follow the Law in order that God will be there so that you can announce that name, that promise. The Law of the Torah, the Law which is the Torah, the Law of God is thus the law of survival.

And that is precisely the meaning of the covenant. The covenant is the deal, the bargain, that God makes with man. You do this and I will do this. You follow my Law – which is the law of anti-idolatry – and you will survive, you will be there to testify to the power of this arrangement. Neither more nor less. Man's part is the law of anti-idolatry, learning when to stop, learning to recognize yourself in the other, and God's part is a guarantee of survival – if there is any survival to be had, which is not itself guaranteed.[21]

The Judaic God, who promises a future by virtue of this law, who reveals the way to go on in a world in which there are no gods, who reveals a way to go on in a world defined by the collapse of all possibilities of going on, is therefore by definition, as it were, the prophetic God: is, in fact, the prophetic itself. The notion of the Judaic God and the notion of the prophetic are, in this connection at least, one and the same.

To say, then, that Girard's thought is prophetic is to say that it is a reading from within the Judaic or Hebrew Torah which is the source of all prophetic thinking in our culture and the source in particular of the evangelical revelation. The Hebrew Bible, the Jewish Law, the Torah, is the first veritable text of demystification in our culture. And it is to the project of understanding this text as fully anti-sacrificial (in all the implications of that notion that Girard has made clear to us) that I see the future of Girardian research necessarily devoted.

But what, more precisely, is the Hebraic prophetic? What is the principle of anti-idolatry, of learning when to stop or of recognizing yourself in the other? And to what extent is Girard's anti-sacrificial reading of the gospels a Jewish reading? It is in the name of answering these questions – answers which will constitute the next step of Girardian research – that I turn now to the texts of Joseph and his brothers.

II

The Joseph story is something of an odd tale for Genesis to end with. It seems curiously misplaced in the Book of the Creation, the fall of man, the generations from Adam to Noah to Abraham, and the history of Patriarchs. It lacks the monumentalism of the *akeidah*, the story of the binding of Isaac, or of Jacob's wrestling with the angel. It comes, so far as we are able to tell, from the wisdom literature of the Solomanic courts and seems distinctly prosaic both in subject matter and in style. It seems, in short, little more than a domestic tale of the dotage of old age and the jealousy and naïveté of youth; on the whole a story little capable of sustaining the weight that its position within the biblical canon would confer upon it.

Moreover, the rabbinical commentary would seem to bear out this assessment. The Rabbis speak of the story as recounting how Israel came to sojourn in Egypt, and point out that Joseph's dream at the centre of the first part of that tale when he imagines that his sheaves of grain stood up and those of the brothers bowed down to his is literally prophetic of the end of the story, when Joseph will dispense grain as viceroy in Egypt.

I want to argue that within the confines of this marginal transitional piece is a genuine deconstruction of sacrificial thinking, all the more powerful for the quotidian and transitory context in which it is offered to us. For if we have traditionally read this story for the sake of the first part – where Joseph is expelled by his brothers, sold to the passing bands of Ishmaelite or Midianite traders – the most important part is really Part Two, where Joseph has become the right-hand man of Pharaoh in Egypt, the sacrificial actions of Part One are restaged (in the figures of Simeon and Benjamin), and the victim and his executioners are revealed as doubles. 'This is because of what we did to our brother Joseph', Judah remarks when things begin to go badly for them (42:21). And at the key moment when Joseph would take Benjamin from them, Judah steps forward and says, 'Take me for him', an offer which prompts Joseph, of course, to disclose himself with the words, 'I am Joseph', *aniy yoseif* (45:4).

Joseph's identification of himself as their brother – the identification, that is, of the Egyptian viceroy (who is currently their potential victimizer) and their sacrificial victim as one and the same – is indeed the fulfilment, then, of the prophecies of Part One as the Rabbis suggested but precisely as the complete demystification of sacrificial thinking itself, a demystification which has now become available to us within the text itself. Thus Part Two comes to serve as something of a model for an anti-sacrificial position for its readers, a model which highlights for us the sacrificial actions of Part One precisely in order that they may be rejected. And the Joseph story itself, as it comes at the conclusion of Genesis, can serve as something of a 'Part Two' to Genesis at large (a 'Part Two', therefore, whose very transitory quality has been no less apparent than that of the Part Two within the tale), a book for which sacrifice or expulsion defines for us its major themes. Even the Torah itself in this regard may be taken as a Part Two to the sacrificial cultures of Canaan and Mesopotamia from which it has come and from which it has taken its own exilic distance.

There is a story, a midrash, told by the Hasidic Rabbis (and told to me by Rabbi Aharon Goldstein of Ann Arbor, Michigan) which captures, it seems to me, this idea. A woman is sitting upstairs in an orthodox synagogue while the story of Joseph is being recited.[22] When they come to the section in Part One where Jacob sends Joseph to Shechem to find his brothers and Joseph ends up 'blundering in the field' as the Torah tells us, before someone directs him to Dothan, the woman cries out, 'Don't go down there! Don't you remember what they did to you last year there! They are going to sell you!' The joke, the misunderstanding of the story, presumably revolves around what the woman has failed to recognize, which is in the first place that it is only a story (so that Joseph could not 'hear her') and in the second that for Joseph this has not happened before, that for him this is a first time and he has not the hindsight she has.

But it may turn out that in laughing at her we unwittingly include ourselves in this very misunderstanding. For what if we consider the story of Joseph itself already in some fundamental way 'Part Two' to both Genesis and to the sacrificial practices of the culture from which it has emerged? Then is it not this story, the Book of Genesis as a whole, the Torah itself, that says to us finally: 'Don't go down there! Didn't you learn from last year? They are going to sell you!' And in laughing at the woman, in asserting that it is only a fiction and only after all a first time, do we not belie our own implication in the ignorance of such wisdom, a wisdom all the more powerful for its being presented to us within the context of a joke concerning someone who has been compelled to sit 'upstairs' and who has 'misunderstood'?

Nor has the power, it seems, of this 'Part Two' been lost on the many generations of Christian exegetes on the Old Testament who have found in it, from within the context of medieval typology, the prefiguration of the Passion. The betrayal of Joseph, his sale for twenty pieces of silver, the twelve brothers (the most pivotal of whom is named Judah), have all drawn the attention of the Church Fathers (and one need only check the *Patria Logia* or, more accessibly, the Douay Bible to confirm the acknowledgement of these parallels). Even the death and resurrection of Jesus finds its counterpart in the ascension of Joseph from the pit and his rise in Egypt to become the right-hand man of the Pharaoh, the dispenser of Israel's daily grain. The question I would raise is whether in opposing the Old Testament to the New, in reading the old God as the sacrificial God of vengeance or anger and the new as the anti-sacrificial God of love (a reading which, of course, is central to a certain Christian understanding of the two books), we have not unwittingly already slipped into the very structure we have wished to displace, believing in a new law or 'part two' which it has already been by definition, as it were, the goal of the Old Testament itself to reveal to us, an Old Testament which is thus that much richer by virtue of having foreseen our sacrificial misunderstanding of it.

To understand the power of Part Two, and in particular of Joseph's demystificatory disclosure, let us place the sequence in the context of Part One in which it occurs.

III

Jacob settles where his father sojourned, Torah tells us (a distinction which leads a number of rabbinical commentators to wonder whether here is not the source of his later misfortunes) and, moreover, that what follows are the chronicles of Jacob. The fact that the Torah then proceeds to tell us only the story of Joseph leads the Rabbis to suggest that this story is the most important in the chronicles of Jacob from this point on.

At seventeen, Joseph was a shepherd with his brothers (the sons of Leah) but a youth with the sons of Bilhah and Zilpah (the slaves of Joseph), and again the Rabbis wonder whether there is some distinction to be made in this regard (keeping in mind that Joseph is a son of Rachel, who was Jacob's favoured wife and whose only other son was Benjamin). The distinction between the sons of Rachel and the sons of Leah will become important later in Egypt when Judah proposes exchanging himself for his half-brother Benjamin.

The Torah tells us that Joseph 'brought evil report' of his brothers and Rashi, the foremost medieval French exegete, undertakes to tell us what these reports were – eating meat torn from living animals, treating maidservants as slaves, engaging in immoral behaviour, etc.: all the charges, in short, that will later be brought against Joseph in the house of Potiphar. Ramban, who represents another great exegetical tradition, suggests that we cannot even be sure it is the sons of Leah the Torah is talking about at this point; it may be the sons of Bilhah and Zilpah.

The Torah then goes on to note that Jacob loved Joseph more than any of the other children because he was a 'child of his old age' and that he made for him an aristocratic tunic. What is the meaning of the phrase 'child of his old age' (*ben z'kuneem*)? The rabbis are undecided. Is it the child of Rachel (Benjamin being too young to attend Jacob), or simply one who attends Jacob in his old age (as opposed to the others), or some special distinction that we are to confer upon Joseph from this privilege? Moreover, the words for fine woollen tunic are *k'tonet pasim*, which means a tunic suitable for royalty rather than specifically the famed 'coat of many colours'. The brothers saw the tunic, Torah tells us, recognized that it was Joseph whom their father loved most, and hated Joseph all the more for it.

All these details of the first few sentences of Part One are about to become important in the second part of this sequence. Joseph dreams a dream and says to his brothers: 'Behold, we were binding sheaves in the middle of the field when, behold, my sheaf rose up and remained standing and then, behold, your sheaves gathered round and bowed down to my sheaf.' And the brothers answer: 'Would you then reign over us?' and they hated him, Torah tells us, all the more.

Now there are traditionally two interpretations of this sequence, although I would like to argue that they are in fact two versions of the same interpretation – one, moreover, which is decidedly partial. The brothers say to him: 'So you would reign over us!' They see his dream as a sign of arrogance, that he would feel himself superior to them. What do the Rabbis say? Rashi, among others, says:

> Look, this dream is prophetic of the future – all dreams in the Jewish exegetical tradition have something prophetic about them – since Joseph's history will involve grain when he is viceroy in Egypt. Moreover, they will bow down to him since he will be the right-hand man of the Pharaoh and dispenser of that grain, and so in the long run they will have Joseph to thank for saving them.

In other words, each identically takes the dream as Joseph's assertion of his own superiority, the brothers simply translating that assertion into concealed arrogance or desire on Joseph's part while the Rabbis find in it a sign of providential intercession and read the brothers' anger towards Joseph as reflective of their own jealousy of that status.

Neither reading, however, relates it to the real dramatic or social context in which it appears. There may be another way to read this sequence, one that places it clearly within the ongoing contextual dynamics and therefore encompasses both of the earlier views.

And here I turn to an insight offered to me by my friend and colleague Professor Walter Gern, in New York City. The dream is prophetic, Gern suggests, but less of the very end of the history (although it may be of that as well) than of the more immediate situation to follow: in particular, of his expulsion by the brothers in the very next scene. The key, Gern suggests, is the reference in the dream to the sheaves 'rising up'. The action of making something into an uplifted thing, of course, is not foreign to students of Torah since it is the action which defines the very word used in the sacred context for sacrifice itself, for the burnt offering: the word *alah*, to cause to ascend, to rise up. It is the word used commonly in the Abraham and Isaac story, for example, when God asks Abraham to prepare Isaac as a 'burnt offering', an *olah*.

What is the significance of this connection? The word *alah* (or *olah*, which is the noun form) is not, in fact, used in the language of Joseph's dream. Rather the Torah offers us the much more prosaic and common everyday words *koom* (for rise up) and *naw-tsab* (for remained standing). In fact, for a story as clearly about an expulsion as the Joseph story is, the word *alah* would seem surprisingly absent. It is used only once in the story and then in an anti-sacrificial sense, at the moment when the sacrifice is to be aborted and the sale substituted when the brothers are lifting Joseph out of the pit, drawn up to be given to the passing bands of traders.

How then is this reference within Joseph's dream to an uplifted thing the key? If we had only the two final sequences of Part One – the dream sequence and the expulsion – I would have to argue that it was not, that Professor Gern's suggestion was only another reading of the traditional prophetic kind, finding a literalizing linkage not only to Egypt but to the action at Dothan as well, and not a very strong linkage at that. And yet I am going to argue that it is the very weakness of the linkage, the very dearth of references to sacrificial language, the very anti-sacrificial and quotidian quality to the story, that gives it its greatest power. But to do that I have to introduce another aspect of the dream: the context of Jacob's favouritism.

We recognize immediately, of course, that Jacob's view of the situation is important, because the Torah tells us that when Joseph repeats essentially the same dream, involving this time the sun, the moon, and the eleven stars bowing down to him, Jacob at first joins in the chorus of the brothers ('Would you have your father and your mother bow down to you as well?' he asks), but when the brothers 'hated Joseph all the more', the Torah tells us, Jacob 'kept this in mind'. Moreover, we know that Joseph made clear his dream to both his brothers and to Jacob, for in both tellings he repeats emphatically words meaning 'listen to what I say', 'behold' (*v'henay*, for example).

Why does Joseph do this? Joseph has seen that he is the apple of his father's eye, that he is the object of his father's desire. How do we know that? The Torah tells us specifically that Jacob loved Joseph more than all the other brothers, that he was the child of his old age, and also that he was the recipient of the special coat his father had given him. Joseph recognizes, in short, that his father sees him as aristocratic, as special, and wanting to please his father (he is, we recall, seventeen years old), he begins acting the way his father thinks of him. He puts on his father's 'coat of many colours', as it were; he thinks of himself as special just as his father thinks of him; he mimes or imitates his father's view of him.

Thus we come to understand his giving of 'evil report' to Jacob about the brothers. It is less important that we determine what precisely the brothers may or may not have been doing to deserve such report than that we recognize the action of giving it as a mimetic appropriation of his father's view of the situation. His father has already indirectly given evil report of the brothers by favouring Joseph to begin with, and Joseph is simply enacting Jacob's desire.

In the same way we come to understand Joseph's dream as similarly Joseph's dramatic representation of what Jacob's desire has been all along – to have the brothers bow down to him as one would before royalty. It is a prophetic representation, a going to the end of the road, of Jacob's desire. It is what Freud might call a rebus, a figuration of the total dramatic context in which Joseph, Jacob, and the brothers all identically find themselves.

Thus we also understand Jacob's hesitation when Joseph tells his second dream, his sense that there is something uncannily familiar about Joseph's narrative. Jacob is moved to 'keep it in mind'. We also come to understand the limitations of both the view of the Rabbis, who see only the literal representation of the dream, the end of the line as it were (ignoring totally the social situation in which it was produced and which it figures), and the view of the brothers, who recognize accurately that desire is behind the dream but see it uniquely as Joseph's desire rather than Jacob's, and equally ignore the implication of their own actions in the situation: that it is their very jealousy which will render that 'end of the road' possible. Neither, that is, has taken into account the 'excluded middle' sequence which is the mimetic appropriation of Jacob's desire by Joseph and the substitution – by Joseph first and later by the brothers – of Jacob's desire for their own.

And this excluded middle – these dynamics of mimetic appropriation and substitution – may now explain for us how the final sequence of Part One is linked to Joseph's dream and why Joseph's reference to an 'uplifted thing' is so powerful. In formulating his insights in the form of a dream Joseph has substituted, for Jacob's favouritism against the brothers, his own. Rather than saying Jacob is the author of this desire, he says that I, Joseph, am the author of this desire. Similarly, rather than condemn Jacob for what Joseph has said, the brothers condemn Joseph. Their condemnation of Joseph for what they perceive to be his arrogance is, moreover, but another substitution of the same kind as Joseph's. The dream sequence, in other words, enables us to read the first sequence by highlighting its structure through a controlled repetition of it. If there were no dream sequence and we proceeded directly to the expulsion (Jacob singles out Joseph for favouritism; the brothers become jealous and take action against him), the tale would be little more than the story of jealousy and dotage we have popularly taken it to be.

By the same kind of displacement we can now understand the relation of the dream to what follows. In the face of Joseph's sheaves which 'rise up and remain standing', those of the brothers now 'gather round and bow down'. What is 'bowing down'? It is, of course, sacralization – differentiation and exaltation. But in this context it is a repetition of the action of Joseph's sheaves. That is to say it is, by an inverse action, a gesture that makes Joseph's sheaves into an uplifted thing. In his dream Joseph imagines not only Jacob's desire but his brothers' response. In good rabbinical fashion he imagines the end of the drama – that the brothers will sacralize him. But he does so in the specific way in which the Torah has imagined us making something into an uplifted thing – and here is perhaps another example of the Hebraic demystificatory genius: we come to understand that action as an act of radical separation, of destruction, of violence, of sacrifice – a burnt offering.

And in the connection the Torah has offered us between the action of the sheaves within the dream and the action at Dothan that immediately follows (and which is linked in the text for us directly: the brothers see Joseph approaching and say 'here comes that dreamer. Let us kill him and then see what becomes of his dreams!'), we can now perceive how the final sequence links up with the first. The action of expelling Joseph is but a duplication of the same kind already imagined within the dream. Substituting Joseph's dream for his sheaves and Joseph himself for his dreams, they will simply intensify the same kinds of displacements to which we have already been witness. Joseph will himself be made into an uplifted thing – literally drawn out of the well – as a mimetic imitation of the dream language itself. Far from opposing Joseph's dreams (which are, after all, Jacob's dreams), the brothers (in expelling Joseph) violently enact them.

The notion of 'uplifting', within the dream, draws our attention less to the dispensing of grain at the end of the tale – as we have traditionally read it – than to the sacrificial victimage immediately to follow. Or, rather, it draws our attention to the dispensing of grain, but only as the result of that victimage. The dream sequence as a whole links for us the beginning and the end, mimetic appropriation with sacrificial victimage. It deconstructs for us the sacrificial thinking which constitutes Part One in its entirety. The final sacrificial substitution is but the violent culminating intensification of the mimetic displacements that have taken place throughout and of which the dream sequence itself is already a primary example. What the dream has revealed to us above all is that mimesis, sacrifice, and substitution are continuous with each other. The dream is prophetic, which is to say it offers us an account of the total dramatic context in which all are implicated. Just as the Joseph story does of Genesis that precedes it and Exodus that follows. Just as the Hebrew Torah does of the sacrificial cultures from which it has come and the Platonic culture to follow.

To answer, then, the questions with which we began, and to bring our discussion to a close, let us turn quickly to the end of Part One – to the sale of Joseph – and then briefly to Part Two of the story, in which Part One gains its greatest power.

IV

Joseph is sent by his father Jacob to Shechem to check on the welfare of his brothers. Does Jacob already perceive their intentions, and is he sending Joseph as a lamb to the slaughter? Joseph, of course, does not find them at Shechem and is spotted by another man, the Torah tells us, 'blundering in the field', and sent instead to Dothan. Why has the Torah substituted Dothan for Shechem? Is there a textual corruption here, as even the greatest of traditional biblical scholars have imagined? Or is there a principle of textual coherence, an editorial perspective, which sees fit to include these sequences within the 'story of Joseph', a perspective whose criteria of selectivity we can unravel?[23] In what follows we may perhaps begin to discern the answers to these and other such questions.

For what follows is in fact a series of extraordinary substitutions which constitute the entire fabric of the end of Part One. The sequence in which Joseph is sold may truly be described as substitution gone wild. They see him and conspire to kill him. 'Here comes the dreamer', they say. 'Let us kill him for his dreams and say a wild animal devoured him. And then we shall see what becomes of his dreams.' They would substitute, in other words, Joseph for his dreams, and murder for his language. Moreover, they would then substitute another story – that he was killed by a wild animal – for what they contemplate. Keep in mind that later, when they bring the bloodied tunic to Jacob, he will imagine that Joseph has been devoured by a wild animal. It is as if the brothers are already cognizant of what would count as a plausible explanation for Jacob of the fate of Joseph. Jacob and the brothers are in harmony on the topic of Joseph's death.

Reuben objects, and tells them to 'shed no blood'. Let us 'throw him into the pit but lay no hand upon him.' Reuben had the intention, the Torah tells us, to save Joseph and return him to his father. How are we to understand this remark? Is Reuben suggesting that they not kill him or only that they not shed any blood in killing him? Later, when they cast him into the pit and sit down to eat, Judah will say let us not kill him, as if their intentions were still to do so. In any case, we recognize that Reuben would substitute another solution for the one proposed. To suggest that the Torah may already begin to dissociate Reuben – or Judah – from the sacrificial behaviour of the others in Part One, a dissociation which will reach its culmination in Part Two when an anti-sacrificial position (the substitution to end all substitutions) comes to be substituted for the earlier one, is not, I would suggest, to weaken our thesis but to strengthen it. It is as if the kind of rabbinical commentary which looks forward prophetically to the end of the story (and reads from that perspective) has come to be inserted in advance and in a fragmentary form within the text itself.

Joseph arrives, and the brothers take his tunic and cast him into the pit. Then they sit down for a meal. That is, having substituted the suggestion of Reuben for their own, they make another. They substitute eating for dismemberment. What, after all, is eating itself but the substitution of food for the victim (sometimes they are one and the same) and ingestion for expulsion?

Then the Ishmaelites arrive and Judah suggests that they 'shed no blood' (has the Torah substituted Judah for Reuben?), but instead sell Joseph to the Ishmaelite traders, a sale that would thus substitute commercial transaction for murder, commercial transaction itself already being founded upon the possibility of equivalency or substitution. The brothers agree and suddenly there are Midianite traders rather than Ishmaelites, the Torah having substituted the former for the latter. And then, the Torah tells us, they drew Joseph out of the well and sold him to the Ishmaelites for twenty pieces of silver. Who drew him out of the well? The brothers? The Midianites? The Ishmaelites? And who sold him to the Ishmaelites? The Ishmaelites, it seems, have been substituted for the Midianites (who were substituted for the Ishmaelites to begin with). The text leaves the matter undecided as if what were important were less who was substituted for whom, who the specific agencies of action were, than that substitution itself were on display. The long traditions of biblical scholarship that have read in this passage an example of textual corruption may reflect this situation more than resolve it for us, substituting in turn the notion of textual 'corruption' for the sacrificial substitutions the text may already be revealing to us.

In any case, Joseph is handed over in exchange for twenty pieces of silver and comes to be brought to Egypt. But the sequence does not end there. The chain of substitutions will return to Jacob, where it all began. Reuben returns to the pit, notices that Joseph is not there (a moment which echoes Joseph's earlier trip to Shechem), and tears his garments. He substitutes self-mutilation for mutilation of the other and garments for himself. He says 'He is gone! Where can I go now?' as if in some fundamental way the fate of Joseph were a stand-in or substitute for his own.

The brothers then proceed to kill a goat (in place of killing Joseph). They smear the blood of the goat (which substitutes for the goat itself) upon Joseph's tunic (as a substitute for smearing it upon Joseph) and then return this same tunic to Jacob (in place of returning Joseph). And they ask him, 'Do you recognize this tunic? Is it Joseph's?' Just as Judah will be asked later by Tamar, with whom he consorted ('Do you recognize whose pledge this is?'); just as Joseph will recognize the brothers later in Egypt but they will not recognize him, and similarly disclose himself to them: 'Do you recognize me? I am Joseph.' Do you recognize, in other words, the brothers say to Jacob, Joseph through this series of substitutions? Do you recognize your coat, your aristocratic tunic, the object of your desires as the origin of this substitutive violence?

The bloodied tunic, in other words, is the return to Jacob of his own violence, of their violence against Joseph, of their violence against Jacob. Do you recognize your own violence? Here it is. This the end of the road of sacrificial violence on which you are travelling, the death of your favoured son. The Joseph story is a counterpart in Genesis to the story of Abraham and Isaac.

And Jacob's response to this prophetic presentation? 'A savage beast must have devoured him.' Far from recognizing himself in the other, his own violence in the violence of the other, he externalizes it, he dehumanizes it. A savage beast did it. He repeats the explanation the brothers imagined originally. Like father, like sons. And then he tears his clothes (as Judah did) as if he would rather go on with the traditional substitutions than demystify them, even at the cost of his own son.

The conclusion of Part One of the Joseph story, in short, brings us back to the beginning. It demystifies sacrifice for us. It reveals the substitutive nature of the mimetic displacements with which the story began and the sacrificial violence in which it concludes. It shows us the end of the road we are travelling in order that we may give it up. It says to us 'Do you recognize yourself, your own violence, in this tale?' in order that we may put an end to sacrificial substitution, that we may give up idolizing sacrifice.

Why, then, is Part One insufficient? Why does there need to be a Part Two? Is Part Two just a repetition of what is already available to us in Part One?

In a sense, yes. In the sense that all the Hebraic biblical narrative is structured as a replaying of the same drama. The whole was already contained in the first sequence of Part One when Jacob favoured Joseph, Joseph gave evil report of his brothers, and they acted against him, they hated him all the more. All traditional Jewish writing, I would suggest, is so structured; which is why, in a sense, we can begin anywhere.

At the same time, Part Two is necessary. For, to this point in the story, the anti-sacrificial position we have suggested the text presents for us, the demystification of sacrificial thinking, has occurred to virtually no one within the text. There are hints of it in the words of Reuben and Judah, but no more than that.

And yet the Hebrew biblical text exists – and here is perhaps my main point – to make it available to the characters themselves within the text (which is what makes it what I have called a text of demystification). It has, of necessity, to do this since what it asks of us primarily is whether or not we recognize ourselves in the text – whether we recognize, in other words, that the text is already the world in which we live. We have never been outside the text. Rather than a parallel to our lives (which is analogous, perhaps, but never contiguous with it), the text is an authentic extension of our experience. The inside of the text is to the outside as the two apparent 'sides' of a Moëbius strip which are really extensions of the same idea. The text is the prophetic future of the dramas in which we ourselves are already engaged. In watching characters come to find themselves implicated in their own sacrificial gestures, their own texts, the text is demystified for us. And it is this gesture of demystification which offers us a way out of the crisis. Part One deconstructs sacrificial violence for us. It enables us to recognize ourselves in the other, to recognize that the other is only the future or the past of the same, of where we are. Part Two will offer us a model for what to do about it: namely, to fictionalize it, to regard our sacrificial violence from a distance in order that we might abandon it. There is, unfortunately, no time left in the present forum to pursue this inquiry very much further, certainly no time to pursue the intricacies of Part Two by which the knowledge of the identification of sacrifice with violence becomes available to each of the major characters. Judah learns it when he consorts with Tamar (after denying her his third son by the rites of Levirate marriage), and she identifies the man with whom she has played the harlot as Judah himself. He says, 'She is right. She is more righteous than I. This is because I denied her Shelah, my youngest son.' Joseph learns it in the house of Potiphar, where he is subjected to the same kinds of unjust accusations concerning morality to which he presumably subjected the brothers initially (he is treated 'measure for measure', the Rabbis note). And the brothers as a group learn it, of course, in the sequence in Egypt when they come to ask for grain.

What happens in this final scene of Part Two? There is a famine in Israel and Jacob sends the brothers to find grain in Egypt, where Joseph has, of course, become the chief dispenser of that grain and the right-hand man of the Pharaoh. Joseph recognizes them, but they do not recognize him. It is as if Joseph has become himself the text in which they must learn to recognize themselves, their own brother. He takes Simeon as hostage and demands Benjamin – Jacob's youngest and only other remaining son of Rachel – before he will give them grain. On their way home they discover that the money they paid Joseph has been returned to them, that they too are now potential victims of the unjust accusations.

They relate to Jacob what has happened and he says: 'First I lost Joseph; then I lose Simeon; and now you tell me you want me to send with you Benjamin!' But Judah intercedes: 'If I don't return with the boy, let the lives of my two sons go as ransom for him.' Finally Jacob agrees and they return to Egypt.

Joseph now prepares for them a huge meal, with Benjamin getting the largest portions, and sends them away for a second time. Now he has guards intercept them, accuse them of thievery, and when they look in their sacks the money is back, and this time so is the cup Joseph gave to Benjamin. They return, and Joseph asks them for Benjamin. At this point Judah steps up and says: 'If we return to Israel without Benjamin, it will kill my father. Take me for him.' At which point, of course, Joseph discloses his own identity to them, all rejoice in the discovery, and Jacob comes to Egypt with the remainder of his family and blesses the two twin sons of Joseph.[24]

In short, what has happened is that Joseph, from his position as Egyptian viceroy, has restaged the sacrificial activity of the earlier sequence in its entirety. The unjust accusation, the money in the sack, recall the silver for which he himself was sold. The taking of Simeon and the threatened appropriation of Benjamin recall the sale of Joseph. And this time the demonstration is not lost on the brothers. For they say, when things begin to go badly, 'This is because we sacrificed our brother Joseph.' They link the troubles into which they have fallen to human behaviour, to their own violence.

And at the key moment everything converges upon Joseph's disclosure: 'I am Joseph', *aniy yoseif*. The Egyptian viceroy who is their lord, who controls the stage, as it were, turns out to be the same as their victim. 'I am Joseph,' he says to them, 'who you would sacrifice.' Moreover, their victim (who is also their lord) is also their brother, identical to them by family origins and identical to Benjamin, the other son of Rachel, for whom Judah would now exchange himself. The disclosure of Joseph's identity is a demystification, in short, of sacrifice: the identity of victim, master, and sacrificers, all as doubles, all as brothers. And in context of Judah's offer it shows us the way out: to acknowledge our identity, which is to say our identicality with the other, that the other is the same, that the other is us.

Does Joseph recognize this dynamic? Has he staged this earlier sacrificial activity deliberately? Not necessarily, I would argue. I would even suggest that there must not be total recognition if Joseph is to be fully like us. Joseph's disclosure is still to some extent an echo of his new masters (we recall that the Pharaoh said earlier, in calling Joseph from the prison, 'I am Pharaoh'). Even in the act of disclosing himself, he takes away their responsibility for the sacrificial gesture.

> I am Joseph your brother – it is me, whom you sold into Egypt. And now, be not distressed . . . for . . . God has sent me ahead of you to insure your survival in the land and to sustain you for a momentous deliverance . . . It was not you who sent me here but God. (45:4–8)

Demystifying the text for us, and perhaps for Judah, Joseph remains to some extent still within it, as he must. What is important is that the possibility of a demystification of sacrifice has become available within the text, which is thus a perfect mirror of our own world, in which the possibility of a demystification of sacrifice has become available to us by the same process in the form of the Hebrew Bible.

Joseph, that is, in the last account is not dissimilar to the Torah itself, the Hebrew Law, the very biblical text. And in that Law we must come to recognize ourselves. The texts says to us: here is the bloodied tunic which is the end of the road that you are on. Do you recognize yourself in it? Do you recognize this as your own violence so that you may give it up? Joseph, the Torah, Jewish culture itself, asks no less of us.

Let me conclude, as I began, with a midrash. There is a story, told by Gershom Scholem, of the medieval Jewish prophet Abulafia, who describes the culminating moment of the prophetic ecstasy in the following way.[25] He says that the Talmudic scholar is sitting in his study reading Talmud and he suddenly sees himself sitting in his study reading Talmud. He comes, in other words, to see his own double, to recognize himself in the other, to recognize the other as himself. Moreover, he understands that other as his own past or his own future, the road he is already travelling. And having had this vision, he comes finally – at the critical moment – to distance himself from it. He fictionalizes it. He tells a story about it, a midrash. The substitution to end all substitutions, as Michel Serres has said.

The Judaic Law, the law of anti-idolatry, the prophetic law, is nothing else. And if today the thought of René Girard strikes us as trenchant, it is because it functions in the same way as the Joseph story does, as a Part Two to the sacrificial qualities of our own critical thinking, as the text which says to us 'I am Joseph'.

Totalization and Misrecognition

JEAN-PIERRE DUPUY

(Translated by Mark R. Anspach)

> . . . By associating itself more and more closely with linguistics, so as one day to constitute with it a vast science of communication, social anthropology can hope to benefit from the immense vistas opened up to linguistics itself through the application of mathematical reasoning to communication phenomena. At the present time, we know already that a great number of ethnological and sociological problems, whether they concern morphology or even art or religion, await nothing more than the goodwill of mathematicians who, in collaboration with ethnologists, could propel them decisively forward – if not yet towards a solution, at least towards that preliminary unification that is the condition for their solution.
>
> Claude Lévi-Strauss, 'Introduction à l'œuvre de Marcel Mauss', 1950[1]

I Introduction

1. The Girardian theory is a theory of origins – it is a *morphogenetic* theory. Anti-structuralist therefore, but it would be better to say that it brings forth what structuralism carried within itself, but was prevented by its very method from delivering. To appreciate the scope of this assertion, it is appropriate to return to what Vincent Descombes, in a remarkable text, dubs 'the equivocal character of the symbolic' in the discourse of structural anthropology.[2]

Equivocal, for there are two definitions of the symbolic. According to the first, the symbolic is a 'signifying convention' (Lacan). This means two things, simultaneously: on the one hand the conventional establishment of a sign that is perfectly arbitrary, like an algebraic symbol; on the other precisely what an algebraic symbol is not: the symbol of this convention. In this first sense the symbol is a sign of recognition, the prototype of which is the password. It is the token and the effect of a collective *will*, of a *social contract*.

The problem is that the password, the will and the contract cannot produce society as a whole but only a plot, a conspiracy or an intolerant sect. Hence the second definition of the symbolic:

'structuralism here proposes a paradoxical reversal: when the symbols are not the effects of the convention, they are its source. If they do not come after the social bond, it is because they come before and produce it.'[3] It is the symbol which makes the social, not the other way round. One recalls the fearsome reproach levelled by Lévi-Strauss against Mauss: 'Mauss still thinks it possible to elaborate a sociological theory of symbolism, when it is clear we must seek a symbolic origin of society.'[4]

In our work over the last several years we have shown how and why, at the formal level, the Girardian theory provides a way to move beyond the two alternatives to which political thought has always confined itself and which the oscillation of structuralism between the two meanings of the symbolic merely reproduces: either the social is an artifact, produced by men's conscious will, or it is a structure: that is to say a totality that is outside history and therefore pre-exists its realization.

We have isolated the formal and logical problem which no morphogenetic theory of society can fail to confront: how to conceive of a process of totalization where the totality, far from dominating and guiding from the outset its own realization from the heights of its ontological presence, engenders itself in the very movement in which it is actualized. That is the very thing which we have been able to show the Girardian theory succeeds in conceptualizing. What is more, Girard formally resolves the difficulty in the same manner, exactly, as theories of self-organization resolve a formally identical problem in biology: the passage from the simple to the complex, from the undifferentiated to the differentiated.[5]

This formal resonance between approaches that belong, by their contents, to such different fields is something we have been able to verify in reference to the two principles which constitute the framework for self-organization theories.

First, that of 'order, or rather complexity, from noise' (H. Atlan), according to which every living organization has to be understood as an alloy of antagonistic principles: differentiation and undifferentiation, variety and redundancy, diversity and repetition, separation and reunion, difference and identity. Now it is precisely the figure of the model-obstacle which makes mimesis simultaneously a principle of separation and a principle of reunion. As for the figure of the sacrificial crisis, it can be analysed as production of redundancy by a mimetic effect and production of variety by a random effect (the 'choice' of the surrogate victim).

The principal of 'operational closure' (Varela) is no less active in each of the mimetic and sacrificial figures – and that is what explains why these figures so often take the form of a self-referential paradox. Thus the figure of 'pseudo-narcissism' – here mimesis, which is flight towards the Other – finds itself capable of engendering its opposite or, more exactly, of becoming indistinguishable from its opposite: self-sufficiency. He who desires himself – or rather, presents the illusion of doing so – does not escape, for all that, from imitation: he imitates the desires of the Others that are focused on him precisely because they are attracted by his apparent desire for himself. The illusion of self-sufficiency is therefore *produced by the very thing that it produces*: the fascinated gaze of the Others.

This loop connecting levels to make them seem at once distinct and identical is present in all other figures as well, whether it is the loop between cause and effect, between operand and operator, or between the individual and the collective. Its most spectacular forms are certainly – apart from pseudo-narcissism – those we call pseudo-masochism, self-exclusion (i.e. the 'strategy of the sulker': this is Girard's inspired reading of Camus's *The Stranger*[6]) and negative imitation.

I do not intend to take all this up again here, even if the pathways for research that we have thus opened are far from being adequately explored. I simply wished to remind you at the start that much has already been done in this direction, enough in any case to convince us that in itself the formal model that constitutes the framework of the Girardian theory is of the greatest interest: mathematicians and logicians should get as much pleasure out of making it work as they got not long ago from setting in motion the now somewhat rusty engines of structuralism. Nor have I yet mentioned parallel endeavours. Lucien Scubla, for example, has drawn on catastrophe theory to elucidate Girardian sacrificial logic.[7] This variety is not the sign that 'anything goes'* (as in anarchist epistemology *à la* Feyerabend), for all these tools were basically conceived to resolve the same logical problem: how to conceptualize morphogenisis and therefore differentiation springing from undifferentiation, discontinuity from continuity, etc.

* Translator's note: in English in the original.

2. I should like to address here a complementary question: the *epistemological* question.

The totalization processes Girardian theory brings to light have in common that they can be actualized only through *misrecognition* (*méconnaissance*). Men know not what they do; it is unbeknownst to them and without their willing it that their history unfolds. Were they to understand, it would all be over for this story, in so far as its mechanisms are those of violence and the sacred. The misrecognition of these mechanisms is an 'indispensable' condition for them to be productive: 'this is the most crucial but also the most delicate point' of the Girardian theory.[8] It is this point which I would like to discuss here.

Apparently, the preceding affirmations flow logically from the theory itself. The possibility condition of mimetic and sacrificial forms does indeed seem to be that their *arbitrariness* should remain concealed from the people who act within them. This is true of triangular desire. The circle that viciously joins the Other as model and the Other as obstacle exists only because the Subject, or rather his 'desire', interprets in terms of intentions and values what is merely the operation of a mechanism. It is true of the victimage mechanism and of the social and cultural differentiation that results from it. The moment the arbitrariness of the victim is exposed to the light of day, the reconciliation through unanimous violence falls apart and its mythopoeic effects weaken until they disappear altogether. Girard formulates this with precision: 'The efficacy of the mechanism and the richness of ritual production are inversely proportional to the community's aptitude at identifying this same mechanism in operation.'[9]

In every case, then, the mimetic and sacrificial forms are unable to reflect upon themselves without dissolving into nothing. Differentiation turns into undifferentiation when it becomes the object of its own thought. Any true theory of these forms is therefore knowledge of the self's radical opacity to the self, recognition of this misrecognition. Hence a twofold question: how can such a knowledge erupt upon the scene of human history? We know Girard's answer to this first question. And: what will be the effects of this knowledge as it spreads? Does it necessarily imply, as Girard believes, a disagregation of ritual mechanisms?

It seems very important to me that we discuss here the theses René Girard has developed in this regard. I think that one can in fact choose without incoherence to refuse them while still accepting the rest of the theory. More precisely, we ought to put to ourselves the following two questions:

1. Is it certain that recognition of misrecognition suffices to destroy the misrecognition?

2. Does such recognition render totalization impossible, does it merely displace it, or could it even be that it has no effect at all?

The point is not a purely epistemological one; it commands the whole 'prophetic' dimension of the Girardian message. What Girard affirms of modernity, of its nature and its future, rests precisely on the thesis that with Christian revelation working away at it to undermine it from within, it can only culminate in something radically *other*: either terminal violence or the Kingdom of Love. Some reproach Girard's Christianity for its violence: rendering for ever ineffective all the devices that men have always invented to fight 'bad' violence with 'good' violence, it would leave them unarmed before an irreversible outpouring of their own violence. And it is true that one finds this in Girard:

> Every advance in knowledge of the victimage mechanism, everything that flushes violence out of its lair, doubtless represents, at least potentially, a formidable advance for men in an intellectual and ethical respect but, in the short run, it is all going to translate as well into an appalling resurgence of this same violence in history, in its most odious and most atrocious forms, because the sacrificial mechanisms become less and less effective and less and less capable of renewing themselves.[10]

But others reproach this same Christianity of Girard's for its heavenly etherealness. And it is true that his conception of love as perfect revelation is 'not of this world'. Now these two criticisms, stated separately, are contradictory – and Girard, when he defends himself against them, does not fail to point this out. But they must be considered together, for it is together that they pin down the paradox with which Girard concludes his work. This paradox is that if the knowledge of mechanisms has as its horizon absolute knowledge, which is Love,[11] the process that leads to it (we call it 'modernity') – i.e. partial but irreversibly growing knowledge[12] – seems to take the opposite direction: it unlooses violence. But that is because violence, in abolishing differences, digs its own grave and prepares the ground for Love. We have here, then, an authentic example of the *cunning of History*. 'All the great modern theories', Girard writes, 'labour, without suspecting it, for the revelation of that which they think they combat.' The toilers of modern thought 'do not even know why they smooth out the mountains and fill in the valleys with so strange a frenzy. Barely have they heard of that great king who will pass in triumph over the road they are readying.'[13]

In short, knowledge, so long as it remains incomplete, is a snare. Girard asserts this directly: 'Science appears more and more to us as a kind of trap that modern man has laid for himself without realizing it.'[14] And, further on:

> . . . the impression that we have of falling deeper into a trap, the springs of which we ourselves forged, is going to come into focus. Humanity in its entirety already finds itself confronted with an ineluctable dilemma: men must reconcile themselves for evermore without sacrificial intermediaries, or they must resign themselves to the coming extinction of humanity.[15]

One may find this conclusion undesirable, in that it takes the form of all theodicies and, for that very reason, seems to leave no place for praxis.[16] Then one needs to turn back to that which founds it, and so question the Girardian theory of knowledge.

3. It is not directly this critique which I am going to present to you in what follows. Some first reflections have been developed elsewhere: thus it is that within the epistemological framework of self-organization theory, Henri Atlan denies that the misrecognition of mechanisms is a necessary condition for their functioning: observing at two different levels the social system of which they are a part, the actors can very well see, from the 'exterior', the arbitrariness of the process of social differentiation, while still giving it meaning from the 'interior'.[17]

My ambition is certainly not to propose definitive theses on such a difficult question, but simply to contribute some material for our common reflection. Therefore I have preferred, rather than frontally attacking the Girardian problematic, to present three case studies, three debates which relate to today's social sciences and which, even if they have not been treated directly by Girard, have an evident connection with his work. Now in each of these cases, diverse as they are, the question of misrecognition is central. That should not surprise us. The two questions we have raised concerning Girard are questions that apply to all the social sciences. All, in effect, start out from the postulate that the true significance of social processes eludes those who none the less act within them.[18] The understanding the social theorist has of the actors' lack of understanding is therefore a key component of his model. He cannot help wondering, then, about the effects of a universalization of this understanding.

I will take up successively:

a) the 'paradox' of panic in Freud, and the distinction between 'exogenous' fixed points and 'endogenous' fixed points;

b) the question of reciprocity in primitive exchange and Bourdieu's critique of Lévi-Strauss's critique of Mauss;

c) the question of a certain return to liberalism in present-day political philosophy.

II The 'Paradox' of Panic, According to Freud (Of the Distinction between Exogenous Fixed Points and Endogenous Fixed Points)

1. Few commentators have to my knowledge pointed out that the theory of the crowd Freud gives us in his *Group Psychology and the Analysis of the Ego*[19] presents a double paradox, apparently unresolved. Let us recall briefly the basic elements of the problem.[20] The crowd is in general characterized by three features:

– Its principle of cohesiveness, of a libidinal nature. For a collection of individuals to form a unity, the antisocial force *par excellence* must be conquered: that force is egoism or 'narcissism'. This, affirms Freud, is what one observes in a crowd: 'While with isolated individuals personal interest is almost the only motive force, with crowds it is very rarely prominent.'[21] In the midst of the latter, it is common to see individuals sacrifice their personal interest and their self-love to a collective ideal which transcends them: 'Such a limitation of narcissism can, according to our theoretical views, only be produced by one factor, a libidinal tie with other people. Love for oneself knows only one barrier – love for others, love for objects.'[22] It is therefore 'Eros, which holds together everything in the world',[23] that gives the crowd its cohesiveness.

– The focal point of these libidinal ties, namely the person of the leader. For each member of the crowd, the 'ego ideal' finds itself replaced by the *same* 'external libidinal object', the leader, so that everyone identifies with everyone else. To be sure, Freud recognizes the existence of crowds that do not have anyone at their head, but those that do are perhaps 'the more primitive and complete'.[24] If one traces the history of crowd psychology through the landmark works of Le Bon, Tarde and Freud, one will in fact observe a displacement of the centres of interest: from the spontaneous and short-lived gathering to the 'artificially' constructed crowd and, in a parallel shift, from the group to its leader. With Freud, the crowd is no longer the anarchic product of social decomposition; it is on the contrary, by the grace of its leader, the archetype of all durable social formations. The leader is the totalizing operator of the collectivity, or rather its *fixed point*.

– The dialectic of identification and the libido explains finally why the crowd should be the quintessential medium for contagion phenomena. Freud alludes to that 'emotional contagion' through which the 'affective charge of the individuals becomes intensified by mutual interaction. Something is unmistakably at work in the nature of a compulsion to do the same as the others, to remain in harmony with the many.'[25]

Now, this topology is marked by a double *singularity*, in the sense mathematicians give this word.

There is first of all the figure of the leader, that nodal point at the group's centre which I have already discussed. Moscovici defines this figure's 'paradoxical' character in the following terms:

> Crowds are in principle composed of individuals who, in order to participate, have conquered their antisocial tendencies or sacrificed their self-love. And yet, in the middle of them stands a figure who is the only one in whom these tendencies are kept up, not to say exaggerated. Through a strange but not inexplicable effect of the bond which unites them, the masses are not disposed to recognize that they have renounced what the leader maintains intact and which becomes their centre of attention: precisely that self-love . . . All leaders symbolize the paradox of the presence of an antisocial individual at the apex of society. For whosoever lacks narcissism also lacks power.[26]

I will not insist any further on this first point, since you will already have noticed that if one merely replaces the Freudian *couple* of identification and the libido with the *sole* Girardian mimeses, this paradox resolves itself into one of the latter's 'attractors', the figure of 'pseudo-narcissism' whose functioning I outlined above. Let us move on then to the second 'paradox' – and this time, it is Freud himself who utters the term. The phenomenon in question is that of panic.

What in fact happens in a panic, when the crowd loses its leader, its fixed point? One is witness to nothing other than a powerful resurgence of narcissism, self-love and egoistic interests, where 'each individual is only solicitous on his own account, and without any consideration for the rest.'[27] The emotional bonds which assured the cohesiveness of the crowd are broken: 'the mutual ties between the members of the crowd disappear, as a rule, at the same time as the tie with their leader'.[28] Each individual then finds himself to be 'by himself in facing the danger'.[29] Freud is emphatic: 'It is impossible to doubt that panic means the disintegration of a crowd' and brings with it the 'cessation' of all attachments among its members.[30] Deprived of any regulatory centre, made up of an *anarchic* composition of atoms who look only to their private advantage: with these two traits, panic seemingly realizes the utopia of market society; it presents itself as the negation of the organized crowd. And yet Freud acknowledges that, as indeed we all know, it is at precisely this moment, when everything that makes a crowd a crowd is gone – the leader, the emotional bonds – it is at this very moment that the crowd appears the most to us as a crowd. One thus arrives at 'the *paradoxical* position that this group mind does away with itself in one of its most striking manifestations.'[31]

There is something stranger still. For once the emotional bonds among all the members of the crowd, including the leader, are destroyed, there no longer exists in theory any circuit for the transmission of contagion, which therefore should not be in evidence. Now – as, once again, we all know quite well – it is nevertheless, Freud admits, in situations of panic that contagion can attain 'enormous proportions'.[32]

So how does the current get through?

To invoke, as Moscovici does, a 'contagion' of withdrawal into the self, a 'narcissistic infection',[33] is hardly serious. What good is it to demonstrate, in page after page, that the primary notions of contagion, imitation, suggestion and hypnosis merely dissimulate the underlying action of identification and the libido if one hastens to fall back on the first concepts as soon as the second ones stop being operational?

I therefore ask once more: how does the virus transmit itself?

2. To unravel this paradox – something Freud does not even try to do – one must abandon the clear-cut division between spontaneous crowds and artificial crowds, between anarchic masses and masses assembled around their leader. One must leave behind the paradigm of the *exogenous fixed point*, programme and producer of the crowd, in order to envisage the paradigm of the *endogenous fixed point*,

produced by the crowd even though the crowd imagines itself to be its product. In short, one must conceive of the capacity of every group in 'effervescence' to project itself outside itself, and its propensity to take for *external* guideposts these projections from the *interior*. One must finally see that these last can assume very diverse forms between which *substitution* is possible: leader, victim, idea, movement, trend . . .[34]

Thus, in a panic, when the leader has taken flight, there emerges in his stead another representative of the collectivity, one that is transcendent in relation to its members: it is none other than the collective movement itself which becomes detached, distances itself and takes on an *autonomy* in relation to individual movements, without ever ceasing, for all that, to be the simple composition of individual actions and reactions. As Durkheim sensed so well, the social totality displays in such moments – above all in such moments – all the qualities that men attribute to divinity: exteriority, transcendence, unpredictability, inaccessibility. 'The crowd needs a direction', writes Elias Canetti, a goal that is given '*outside* the individual members and common to all of them': it matters little what it is, so long as *it is 'unattained'*.[35] In the flight of panic, that is exactly what is realized by the sole action of the totalization process itself.

Panic therefore takes the form of a communication among the elements of a totality through the intermediary of this same totality considered as transcendent. The fixed point here is the whole itself – for example, the direction of the collective movement – engendered by the composition of individual acts which, however, take the former as their guide, as if it bore an orientation that were not already present in its elementary components. The holistic credo according to which the whole is greater than the sum of its parts proves then to be singularly relevant.

Thus unravelled, the paradox of panic has the same form, you will have noticed, as that of the leader. In the latter as well, the social unity is achieved in the very moment it is lost by putting itself at a distance from itself. The crowd needs the leader in order to perceive its own Oneness, but this tragic redundancy, this fatal redoubling, is simultaneously what confirms its division. A division on the *interior* of the crowd in the case of the leader, a division *between* the crowd and its transcendent Other in the case of panic: one moves from the figure of the leader to that of panic by a simple operation of substitution.

3. There is evidently, in all these figures, misrecognition. The theorist recognizes the misrecognition of the agents. For them, the fixed point remains exogenous. It is endogenous only for the theorist. The latter's privileged viewpoint is intimately tied to his position of *exteriority* in relation to the phenomenon he is studying.[36] But if I have chosen to talk about panic, it is, as you may suspect, as a metaphor for modernity, that 'decelerated' or 'slow-motion' mimetic crisis of which Girard speaks. Who can call himself an external observer of its dynamic? Or rather, in so far as the knowledge of the mechanisms is continually growing, everyone finds himself at once on their interior and on their exterior.[37] Hence the relevance of the question posed at the outset: what might be the effect of a recognition of one's own misrecognition?

In order to put forward some elements of a response, I will turn to another metaphor of panic: the market. I have shown elsewhere that the logic of panic according to Freud is that of the market according to Walras.[38] I will content myself here with recalling that, in the model of general economic equilibrium, prices change their status according to the logical level at which they are considered: exogenous for the social actors, they become endogenous for the model-maker – and this property is often deemed a 'contradiction' by the model's critics. The set of prices, which for the theorist is the fixed point of an operator of totalization, appears to the agents as a transcendent given – quite an unusual trace of the sacred in a theory that wishes to be purely rational.

Now there is a theorem in game theory that establishes a certain equivalence between this transcendence and this rationality. Under some rather general hypotheses, it affirms approximately this: the set of 'equilibria' in a market economy (it's 'fixed points') tends to coincide with the *core* of the game by which it can be represented, when the number of agents increases indefinitely.[39] What is the core of a game? It is the set of the only possible states that can withstand the vetoes of all conceivable coalitions. These states are therefore the only ones that are rational *at every level*: individual, collective and intermediary.[40]

Suppose the core is limited to a single state: if the agents are infinitely numerous, this will be the only fixed point in the economy. One will then be able to consider the system of corresponding prices, and the behaviour which it induces, as the products of a perfect rationality and of a total circulation of information. This can be expressed as follows: the rationality associated with large numbers produces an effect of transcendence. In this case, therefore, the knowledge of the mechanisms has no effect on them.

Here we have, then, a first response which has the force of mathematics going for it. Unfortunately, things very quickly become muddled as soon as one renounces the hypothesis of the fixed point's uniqueness which, problematical enough in economics, is utterly unrealistic in a panic situation. For transcendence multiplied – that is to say divided, splintered, set against itself – is no longer truly transcendence. The presupposition of totality, a necessary condition for the process of totalization, is transformed by its indeterminacy into a source of conflict, which can unleash dangerous instabilities. How should the question of recognition and misrecognition be reformulated in these conditions?

To tell the truth, it is only recently that economic theorists have begun facing the possibility that their models, inasmuch as they represent processes which are 'operationally closed' in Varela's sense, engender a great variety and a great complexity of *eigenbehaviours* ('self-determined' behaviours), or fixed points. The epistemology of these models for the most part still remains to be worked out. I will content myself with referring you to the little that has already been done in this area, in addition to André Orléan's contribution to this volume.[41]

III Logics of Reciprocity: Bourdieu's Critique of Lévi-Strauss's Critique of Mauss

1. In his celebrated *Essai sur le don*,[42] Marcel Mauss observes that in a good many archaic societies, 'contracts are fulfilled and exchanges of goods are made by means of gifts. *In theory such gifts are voluntary but in fact they are given and repaid under obligation*.'[43] He insists on the presentations' having a

> voluntary character, so to speak, apparently free and without cost, and yet constrained and interested . . . They are endowed nearly always with the form of a present, of a gift generously offered even when in the gesture which accompanies the transaction there is only a *fiction, formalism and social deception*, and when there is, at bottom, *obligation and economic interest*.[44]

Acts that are separate – giving, receiving and giving in return – present themselves as so many gestures of generosity or cordiality and in reality obey strict imperatives from which no one is exempt. What then is the nature of this 'obligation'? Mauss, having once posed the question, adds, as though he were merely repeating the same question in another form: 'What force is there in the thing given which compels the recipient to make a return?'[45] The native informant will soon convince him that 'in the things exchanged . . . there is a certain power which forces them to circulate, to be given away and repaid.'[46]

Lévi-Strauss, in his no less famous 'Introduction', reproaches Mauss with allowing himself here to be 'mystified by the native'.[47] Mauss's error, in his view, is to have stayed at the level of a phenomenological apprehension that breaks exchange down into its different moments, creating the need for an operator of integration to reconstruct the whole – which is where the *hau* or 'soul of things' comes in, providentially filling this very role. But that is going at the problem from the wrong end, asserts Lévi-Strauss. And turning Mauss's own words against him – 'The unity of the whole is more real still than each of its parts' – Lévi-Strauss affirms: 'It is exchange which constitutes the primary phenomenon, and not the discrete operations into which social life breaks it down.'[48]

'The *hau* is not the ultimate reason behind exchange: it is the conscious form in which the men of one particular society, where the problem was of special importance, apprehended an *unconscious necessity* whose reason lies elsewhere': this 'underlying reality' is to be sought in 'unconscious mental structures' to which access can be had through language.[49] And it is language which betrays the natives, as Mauss's own observations demonstrate: in these societies, the same word designates purchase and sale, borrowing and lending. 'The whole proof is there', Lévi-Strauss proclaims triumphantly, 'that the operations in question, far from being "antithetical", are but two modes of a single reality. The *hau* is not needed to produce the synthesis because the antithesis does not exist.'[50]

And he concludes: 'Exchange is not a complex edifice, constructed from the obligations to give, to receive and to make return with the help of an emotional and mystical cement. It is a *synthesis immediately given* to, and by, symbolic thought . . .'[51]

It must be recalled that this same text, which Vincent Descombes rightfully considers the manifesto of French structuralism, is the one in which Lévi-Strauss writes that the universe 'has signified, from the very beginning, the totality of what humanity can expect to know.' It is a 'closed totality, complementary with itself' which, as a system of systems of objective relations, is always already constituted, outside of and overhanging history.[52] Descombes makes the meaning of this clear:

> . . . the signifier and the signified are given in their entirety from the very first appearance of an opposition of signifiers . . . Just as a language has to precede the experience which it will permit to be expressed, so the laws of social life have to precede the events [. . .] which they order.[53]

Among those who criticize Girard's theory for its totalizing and totalitarian character, there are some who would do well to remember in what terms the birth of structuralism was announced.

2. Let us turn now to Pierre Bourdieu, who in one of his best writings, the *Outline of a Theory of Practice*, denounces Lévi-Strauss's 'objectivist error'.[54]

Bourdieu distinguishes three modes of *theoretical* knowledge of society:[55]

– the *phenomenological* mode, which 'sets out to make explicit the truth of primary experience of the social world' as a world that seems 'self-evident, natural': this primary experience is by its nature not self-reflecting; it 'excludes the question of the conditions of its own possibility';

– the *objectivist* mode, which constructs the objective and structural relations of the social world and establishes 'the objective truth of primary experience as experience denied *explicit* knowledge of these structures';

– finally, the mode embodied by the *theory of practice*, which breaks with the objectivist mode without, however, returning to the phenomenological mode of knowledge and bowing to the demands of certain humanist critics who want to stick to 'lived experience'. This second break results from inquiry into the conditions of possibility, and therefore the limits, of the objective and objectifying point of view which 'groups practice from outside, as a *fait accompli, instead of contructing their generative principle by situating itself within the very movement of their accomplishment*.'

One will have recognized in this last formulation the very characteristic by which we distinguished at the beginning the totalization processes that are the object of our research: neither artifacts nor the executions of a structure/programme always already there – processes, therefore, of morphogenesis and of self-organization. That is reason enough for us to take an interest in Bourdieu's problematic. Here is how he sums up the double *Aufhebung* which he advocates:

> Just as objectivist knowledge poses the question of the conditions of the possibility of primary experience, thereby revealing that this experience

> (or the phenomenological analysis of it) is fundamentally defined as *not* posing this question, so the theory of practice puts objectivist knowledge back on its feet by posing the question of the (theoretical and also social) *conditions which make such knowledge possible*,

objectivist knowledge thus being revealed in its turn as fundamentally defined by its exclusion of this question.[56]

We may observe parenthetically that Girard's theory does not exclude the question of the conditions which make possible the objective knowledge it claims to offer. To this question it gives an answer that is singular but clear: the revelation. Yet one could not describe the knowledge it brings as a 'theory of practice'. Indeed, it will be perceived that from here on, the roads taken by Bourdieu and Girard rapidly diverge.

The critique of objectivist knowledge is also a critique of the ethnocentrism of the ethnologist, certainly the subtlest and best-hidden form of ethnocentrism. As Marcel Gauchet writes in a text to which we will return later,[57] it manifests itself in the ethnologist's refusal

> to analyse his work as dependent on its own social background, which amounts not only to putting oneself above any sociological determination at the same time that one strives in general to show the grip of collective determinations on the action of individuals in another universe, but also to positing ethnological knowledge as an intrinsically necessary project of the human mind – of which the absence in any society can in consequence only be labelled as a lack.

The idea here is not so much that the objectivist point of view is a point of view like any other, just as *relative* as the others to a situation of observation – in this case the point of view of the totality, implying its completion and univocality. It is to express something quite different from mere relativism: namely that the knowledge proper to primary experience should not be conceived as a knowledge in a state of lack, as a lack of knowledge, but rather as a knowledge that has its own necessity, which can be appreciated only in relation to the society in whose logic it participates.

This idea is all the more convincing when one is in a situation where – as in Bourdieu's portrayal of the problem at hand – the 'misrecognition' proper to primary experience is a mode of knowledge that socially institutes itself *against* objectivist knowledge, following a logic which is that of lying to oneself (lying to oneself: a paradoxical notion which implies an indirect self-reference, a doubling, since if to lie is to know that one lies, to lie to oneself is, at a certain level, not to lie).

'. . . Even if reciprocity is the objective truth of the discrete acts which ordinary experience know in discrete form and calls gift exchanges,' Bourdieu affirms, '*it is not the whole truth of a practice which could not exist if it were consciously perceived in accordance with the model.*'[58]

Let us now consider the obligation to receive and the obligation to make a return for what is received. Taken together in the theoretical schema of reciprocity, they lead to a contradiction. For he who returns without delay the very object that is given to him has in fact refused to receive. The exchange of gifts can therefore function as an exchange of gifts only on condition that it dissimulate the reciprocity that is its objective truth. All the space, or rather the time, of practice is needed to undo this contradiction. Temporal elongation – by separating the moment of the gift and that of the return gift, by making each gift appear as 'an inaugural act of generosity, without any past or future, i.e. without calculation'[59] – *defers* reciprocity in such a way that the return gift, by being at once *deferred* and *different* relative to the initial gift, does not appear as included in the project of the latter. Gift exchange thus stands in opposition to the two-way trading of interested exchange, but also to the loan, the legal title of which freezes, as though it were outside time, the moment of reciprocity.

It must be understood that the foregoing argumentation demonstrates only one thing: that the scheme of gift exchange and that of reciprocity cannot be present *simultaneously* in the consciousness of social actors. 'If the system is to work,' writes Bourdieu, 'the agents must not be entirely unaware of the schemes which organize their exchanges, and whose logic the anthropologist's mechanical model makes explicit, while at the same time they must refuse to know and to recognize this logic.'[60]

But this argumentation does not tell us why it is the scheme of gift exchange that shapes practice and that of reciprocity – which is, however, its 'objective truth' – that remains hidden. A supplementary explanation must therefore be provided. The one furnished by Bourdieu disappoints us a little even if, in a sense, it is already present in Mauss. It is that the 'law of interest' governs the world[61] and that this law is not pretty to see, nor to put on display. One sometimes gets the impression, reading Bourdieu, that his savages are *petits-bourgeois* hypocrites, skilful at dissimulating their 'haste to be even, to owe nothing' under the glitter of genuine courtesy and strained disinterest.

3. However that may be, on the misrecognition/recognition question with which we are concerned it would seem, on reading the following lines from Girard, that the distance between Bourdieu and Girard is not so great:

> In a society which is not in crisis the impression of differences results both from the diversity of the real and from a system of exchanges which *defers and in consequence dissimulates the elements of reciprocity* which it necessarily contains, on pain of no longer constituting a system of exchanges, which is to say a culture.[62]

Nevertheless, an abyss separates our two authors. For Bourdieu, it is not so much knowledge (of objective structures or mechanisms) that destroys totalization as the *form* of this knowledge: the explicit, articulated form which is proper to what we call theory and which implies a distance in relation to practice. It is not the irruption of knowledge which destroys totalization because, in fact, the knowledge is *already there*. As Bourdieu says – referring to the example of a Kabyle worker who proclaimed the convertibility of the meal traditionally given at the end of the job into money, with which he demanded to be paid instead – the worker was only 'betraying the best-kept and worst-kept secret': the one that is in everyone's keeping.[63]

In this way the fellow who pipes up with the 'objective truth' appears as a naïf, who articulates what everybody knows already, and a lout, who upsets the apple cart and spoils the party.

To sum up: misrecognition being not a lack of knowledge but an institution that implies the knowledge that is dissimulated, it is not knowledge which is incompatible with totalization, but its explicit expression and institutionalization.

One is reminded of those rules that are formulated in rigid fashion even though everyone know not only that they can be transgressed but that efficiency demands that they be transgressed, as long as nothing is said about it. Think of the airport check-in deadline set by airlines: the objectivist is the one who insists on being told whether he must *really* be on time!

This is the naïveté of the 'new economists' who are bent on demonstrating, with the triumphant manner of those who believe they are disclosing disturbing truths, that the law of the market differs not a whit from the *lex talionis*.[64] It is also the naïveté of the anthropologist Remo Guidieri when he discovers that what Mauss calls a 'gift' is in truth a *loan*, the aim and effect of which are to *obligate* the recipient and to make him suffer the torments of *indebtedness*.[65]

Question: here is an object of which the stability and the very existence demand that its 'internal' truth differ from its 'external' (i.e. 'objective') truth and dissimulate it. Can the latter claim any kind of priority? Any greater truth value? Lévi-Strauss and Girard, it seems, answer yes (even if the second author takes shelter behind the facts, refusing any value judgement). Bourdieu and many others answer no.

4. It is interesting to note that this point, quite precisely, is the object of one of the most fearsome attacks ever to be launched against Girard, the one by Pierre Manent in the journal *Commentaire*.[66] The attack comes in the form of a critique of Machiavelli, a critique with a double charge of meaning and a double charge of ammunition, and with Girard's theory as the ultimate target.

Machiavelli, too, declares that humanity is founded on violence and that the nature of the polis is inseparable from its violent origin. But, Manent inquires, does not Machiavelli's 'revelation', which obliges men to look in the eye the role of violence in the constitution of their world, leave them even more blinded than the myth which transfigures or erases that violence? To conclude: '*The founding "myths" are more knowing than "realistic" science*.' For men have 'good reasons' for repressing violence: 'They sense [. . .] that the *ends* of social life are irreducible to its violent *origins* . . . Men need to hide from themselves those origins if they want to live in accordance with their conscience.'

Manent thus goes beyond even Bourdieu: superior value is claimed for the 'internal' truth, quite simply because it is this, and not the 'external' truth, which makes possible the very existence of society. The geometrical metaphor should moreover be inverted, for it is not the external truth that encompasses the internal truth but rather the internal truth that encompasses the external truth, since it *contains* it: it has it inside itself and keeps it dammed up there.

This is where Manent intends to deliver the *coup de grâce*. Machiavelli, for his part, at least knows what he is doing: he needs to get a jump on Christianity, for it is propagating a utopia that will render terrestrial cities illegitimate. Its non-violence is a violence against nature. If Machiavelli reveals the violent nature of the human order, it is to protect it from this second-degree violence. Girard stays within the same framework as Machiavelli, but he reverses the valuations. That is absurd, concludes Manent: for 'if human "culture" is essentially founded on violence, then Christianity can bring nothing other than the destruction of humanity in the fallacious guise of non-violence.'

5. I compared Bourdieu with Girard in order to show that their common critique of structuralism led to opposite conclusions. It is negatively that I would like to associate them one last time: neither one of them, I think, follows through completely his anti-structuralist epistemology.

For if they both truly admit that social totalizations are not outside history and overhanging it, always already constituted, but that on the contrary they are engendered in the very moment of their accomplishment, then they ought to recognize that properties of *undecidability* result from this – which should keep them from placing themselves at the level of the finished totality to speak of the 'objective truth' (one could persuade oneself of this using arguments of a 'Gödelian' or, if one prefers, 'Borgesian' nature). Now, our authors do not seem ready to accept this; not Girard, though his view would have to be shaded carefully,[67] and certainly not Bourdieu, who *knows* that the objective truth of all societies, 'the true soil of their life' (Lukács) and their potential finality are those of 'a system governed by the laws of interested calculation, competition, or exploitation'.[68]

The problem is that there have been as many 'objective truths' disclosed as authors who have dealt with primitive exchange. We cannot leave unmentioned here one of the most interesting, the one offered by Marshall Sahlins based on his rereading of Mauss in *Stone Age Economics*,[69] which has the added advantage of taking us closer to the Girardian interpretation. For Mauss, as read by Sahlins, the reality which the appearance of gift exchange conceals and denies is that of *Warre* (an archaic spelling of 'war' which Sahlins takes from Hobbes): not so much war itself as that lawless state of nature where everyone knows that his neighbours are always ready to turn to violence to defend their honour and property, and anticipates that they are about to do so. Superimposed over this unsupportable threat, the empirical level of gift exchange appears as the 'primitives' social contract'. By exchanging goods rather than blows, savages make war on war; every trade pact is a peace pact. Primitive exchange is not guided by the pursuit of private interest but by the necessity of ceaselessly reproducing the social bond.[70]

Throughout these famous pages, Sahlins is on the verge of saying something he never actually expresses. What he does not tell us outright is that between the reality of *Warre* and the appearance of the gift there is not only a relation of negation, but also one of *identity* – or rather, of near-identity: the *difference* that exists is the one we have discussed, the non-equivalence between the gift and the return gift, the lapse of time that separates them . . . This distance from pure reciprocity is enough to transform the identity into negation.[71] When the distance shrinks to the point of disappearing, 'the reciprocity', Girard writes, '[. . .] becomes visible by growing shorter, so to speak, [it] is no [longer] that of fair but of sharp dealings, the reciprocity of insults, of blows, of vengeance and of neurotic symptoms. That indeed is why traditional cultures want nothing to do with this overly immediate reciprocity.'[72] Such is the formidable ambivalence of reciprocity, its irreducible undecidability.

Bourdieu has hardly convinced us that his primitives had to dissimulate the true nature of their exchanges – if this nature is reduced to the 'law of interest' – and still less that they had to mask the *obligation* they were under to proceed with them. (Notice that Bourdieu, following Mauss in this respect, puts moral and social constraints into the same basket as the egoistic interest of the *Homo œconomicus*, which is curious to say the least.) Sahlins, illuminated by Girard, subtly resolves this enigma. What the gamble on *difference* serves to dissimulate is not what reciprocity is supposed to reflect (for example, economic interest) but reciprocity itself, inasmuch as reciprocity *is* the very form of violence and *Warre*.

With Sahlins, we find ourselves singularly close to Girard once more. But this, I think, takes nothing away from the force of my argument. Is not the multiplicity of possible interpretations the sign of their own undecidability? By recognizing this one provides oneself with a new means of dealing with the issue that concerns us, the recognition of misrecognition. I will advance the following conjecture: if the agents are aware of this undecidability, that can only increase the chances for stability on the part of the totalizations composed by their actions, *vis-à-vis* injections of supposedly external 'objective truths'. You will find arguments in favour of this conjecture in Pierre Livet's work on the 'autonomy of the social'.[73]

IV Political Philosophy: of a Certain Return to Liberalism

It is clear that we are not providing a simple or direct answer to the two questions with which we began. What we are actually doing – which is probably more interesting – is bringing out the real complexity of the issues involved, raising new questions as we go along: the multiplicity of fixed points in organizationally closed systems, the form in which the knowledge of mechanisms presents itself, problems of undecidability, etc. It is with the question of political philosophy that we will provisionally bring our explorations to a close. The schema of 'all/one' evidently links the Girardian theory, *on a formal level*, to the great systems of political philosophy that our modernity has constructed over the last three centuries. It is natural, therefore, to ask ourselves about the meaning of this formal homology. The subject is a vast one which several of us have begun to study.[74] I will limit myself here to a few glimpses by which we may discern the outlines of another kind of recognition of misrecognition.

At the price of being undoubtedly too schematic, we will take as our starting point the following opposition. If primitive and traditional societies imagine, in obedience to the logic of the sacred, that they owe their order and meaning to a will that is more than human, what we call modernity is the knowledge that men owe the laws of the polis to none but themselves. Can the law remain the law if there is no longer, between it and men, that distance once guaranteed by the sacred? Putting the laws above men, even though men make their laws and *know it*, is a problem Rousseau compared to squaring the circle.

Modern political philosophy has responded in diverse ways to this challenge, which is the challenge of the self-institution and self-regulation of society. We have studied three paradigmatic schemas, all of which proved to duplicate the same abstract form they work so hard to keep at bay: that of the exteriority, not to say the transcendence, of society in relation to itself.[75] Hobbes, Rousseau, Smith: three contrasting ways of isolating society's *fixed point*, its principle of cohesiveness, once this has shifted from an *exogenous* to an *endogenous* one (cf. Section II). This fixed point is, respectively, located in a singular element of the social whole, coextensive with this whole or finally – and this is the 'economic' solution of market society, perhaps the most paradoxical – removed once more from men's grasp and placed *between* them, where it is incarnate in the operation of a mechanism (cf. the role of prices in the Walrasian model of general equilibrium as analysed above).

The endogenization of the fixed point was in some sense the promise of its progressive disappearance into the social space. The state's withering away is as much a part of the liberal utopia as it is a part of the Marxist utopia. As we know, the history of democratic states has moved in the opposite direction. The endogenous fixed point became the administrative state, which is perhaps even more 'exterior' to society than the sacred itself in its claim to institute society totally from a separate position of power and by its aim thereby to put an end to that same separation.

The immanence-transcendence of the principle of cohesion, its interiority-exteriority, take us back to the dimension of the symbolic, and we are faced once more with the problem of defining its nature. Lacan, who was fond of 'mathematical paradoxes', one day made use of the following parable. An old Arab, realizing that his end was near, made out a will dividing his fortune among his three sons: half would go to the eldest and a fourth to the middle son, while the youngest would make do with a sixth. Now it turned out that the inheritance was composed of eleven camels. Mightily annoyed and unwilling to sacrifice several animals, the three brothers were about to come to blows when they decided to solicit the judgement of the local qadi. After a moment's reflection, the qadi pronounced these words: 'Take the camel you will find in my tent, I am giving it to you to add to your legacy. Allah willing, you will bring it back to me faster than you think.' In effect, the eldest was pleased with the share of (11 + 1)/2, or six camels that now fell to him, just as the next in line was content with his share of three camels and the youngest with two. Six plus three plus two makes eleven, and the twelfth camel was then free to return to its original owner, a return gift that immediately cancelled out the qadi's initial gift. The twelfth camel is the *symbolic* camel, the one that is at once useless and indispensable, since it is what permits the social compact to come into being.[76]

How are we, in this context, to frame the question of misrecognition and of the effect of the recognition of this misrecognition? Here, I am mainly going to take up the 'liberal' schema, by which I mean the *political* model inherent in the representation of society as a *market* society. I might note that this model is studied seriously, which does not mean uncritically, in France today, particularly in those circles now reflecting on the roots of totalitarianism and on the constitutive fragility of democracies.

In his text cited above, 'Politique et société: la leçon des sauvages (II)', Marcel Gauchet treats us to a very instructive exercise in comparative epistemology.[77] Primitive peoples manifestly possess a knowledge of the social bond, observes Gauchet, after so many others. How else can we explain the fact that they go to so much trouble to stage it, acting it out with an emphasis that to us seems excessive? Do they want to show that they are making peace? First they mime war, then reconciliation. 'Everything takes place', Gauchet writes,

> as if the ritual behaviour were a way of *explicitly* thinking out, confronting and conjuring away the threat [that hangs over] the collective order. Everything takes place as if there were a *knowledge* at work as to the necessity of taking into account the ever-possible vacillation of the symbolic guideposts that give the social space its identity, and of reaffirming the existence of the social bond.[78]

One could doubtless add that this knowledge, expressing itself in words and gestures but not in abstract symbols, in an object-language but not in a metalanguage, here runs into the difficulty of signifying an operator of negation. Thus it is that the ritual includes that which it aims to exclude. It knows no way to put out the fire other than by playing with fire. There we come upon the dangerous proximity of affirmation and negation. Some will see in this the key to the 'hierarchical' form which Louis Dumont characterizes as the encompassing of opposites.[79] It will make others think rather of a sort of collective unconscious and of the mechanism of Freudian *denial*. Others still, finally, will prefer to all that the Girardian interpretation.

But no sooner have we posited this 'knowledge' on the part of primitives than we must stipulate that they are not in command of it. Otherwise we would be in contradiction with the thesis stated earlier according to which archaic societies believe themselves to be conceived and regulated by an Other than themselves. It is a knowledge incarnated in a practice, but radically incapable of attaining the distance from itself by which it could constitute itself into a theory. In order to express this 'essential unreflectiveness', Gauchet resorts to strange formulations: primitive society 'thinks itself thought', it refuses 'to recognize itself as the scene and agent of the thinking that determines it', 'it founds itself in the exclusion of self-consciousness.'[80] Primitives do not know that they know, and they do not know what they know.[81] The awkwardness of these expressions results perhaps from attempting to state in terms of essences that very thing of which Girard, for his part, speaks in terms of mechanisms.

Now for Marcel Gauchet, with the coming of social division – that is to say, of the existence of a separate power and of the open display of civil conflict – one is witness, so to speak, to an inversion of this picture. The process of instituting society, so manifestly explicit among the primitives, becomes *invisible*, submerged as it is in the society's overall functioning. On the other hand, this process becomes in that very manner the possible object of the type of knowledge, separated from practice, which we call theory. Everything takes place as if the distancing in relation to self introduced by social division rendered possible that reflexivity forbidden to societies that conceive of themselves as undivided while dooming it, by the very fact of that separation, to an essential incompleteness. 'The unthinkable character of the instituting of society in the savage world is intrinsically linked', Gauchet conjectures,

> to its explicit status, as conversely the possibility of aiming to elucidate it through an effort of understanding is linked in our society to its being covered over in collective experience . . . There thus would be a correlation in primitive society between the direct grasp of social practice on the truth of social being and the constitutive unreflectiveness of that practice, as in our society between the occultation of the truth and the overt aim to get at the truth through theory.[82]

On one side knowledge, but the lack of knowledge of this knowledge; on the other side misrecognition, but the possibility of a recognition of this misrecognition.

Armed with this symmetrical inversion, Gauchet is going to be able to execute a veritable reversal of Louis Dumont's theses on modernity.[83] Not that he is opposed – quite the contrary – to the analysis the latter gives us of what makes for the perfect singularity of this modernity in the history of humanity. For the first time, the ontological precedence of society over the individual is inverted. The illusion of the individual's self-sufficiency, which is the core of economic ideology, masks on the plane of values the elementary sociological truth that the individual is always a social creation. With the advent of individualist and egalitarian societies, it is therefore the self-misrecognition of society that is instituted. But it is the value judgement that Dumont makes regarding this evolution which Gauchet is led to contest. For Dumont, it manifests a degradation of the social bond and of its representation. Society, in its essence a 'fact of consciousness', 'something willed or thought by men',[84] ends up being reduced to the status of a natural automatism whose harmonious functioning proceeds very well without either their will or their consciousness.

And what if, on the contrary, asks Gauchet, we were to consider the recognition of this self-misrecognition of society to constitute an important step forward, both on the plane of knowledge and on that of freedom? Was not the advent of the individualist fiction paradoxically necessary for men to become aware of the *autonomy* of society in relation to their consciousness and their will? For 'where society is a fact of consciousness, . . . it is removed from the operation of understanding, at least in the sense of an operation of exposure of the mechanisms regulating collective phenomena unbeknownst to their agents.'[85] The very idea of a social science is correlative with the discovery of the *self-organizing* properties of society: of the fact, that is, that society is neither the product of an 'external programme' (the will of a radically Other) nor of an 'internal programme' (General Will, social contract, fabricating activity of a state).[86] Now this discovery could not have been made where the social order is 'willed', 'known', where the idea of an 'unbeknownst' is inconceivable.

It is doubtless something of a paradox to present as the 'discovery' of society a representation which assimilates society to a natural object. But behind the inadequacy of the metaphor must be grasped what it aims to express: a certain *objectivity* of the social order, the recognition that it is anterior to the actions and will of individuals. We know, moreover, that these themes will be taken up again with renewed vigour by the liberals of the nineteenth century and the conservative critics of the French Revolution, but this time the metaphors will partake more of sociologism than of economism.[87]

As Marcel Gauchet writes, these are 'far-reaching theses, and it assuredly is not enough to anathematize their reactionary inspiration in order to rid ourselves of them.'[88] It is a considerable emancipation for men to know they need not constantly concern themselves with social cohesiveness, manifesting with all their will and all their consciousness their acquiescence and their subordination to the collective order. Here liberty is attained through a certain renunciation of control, through confidence in the 'invisible' mechanisms which shape 'spontaneous social orders'. We know that in our day Hayek has made himself the champion of these theses and that he has drawn unacceptable ethical and political conclusions from them: the systematic critique of all 'constructivism', even of all reformism, and the denunciation of preoccupations with social justice.[89] One could show that these conclusions in no way follow from the premises, but that would be another debate.[90] I simply wanted, for my part, to offer up for your meditation a new form, in which it appears that the recognition of misrecognition is the recognition of a real object, not of an illusion, so that the object is not destroyed by the knowledge of it which we acquire.

Money and Mimetic Speculation

ANDRÉ ORLÉAN

(Translated by Mark R. Anspach)

Neoclassical economics is largely founded on the following utilitarian postulate: individual preferences, whether in regard to goods or to strategic objectives, are already determined before any exchange takes place. They are the object of an *a priori* calculus 'of pleasures and pains' which the subject carries out in the isolation of his own consciousness. This proposition seems to us poorly adapted to the context of a society which has made the revolution of use values the mainspring of its development. Paradoxically, it corresponds 'better' to the situation in archaic societies in which consumer goods are submitted to a social control that determines their quantity and quality. Market society, however, obliges us to theorize the perpetual transformation of consumption and production norms. Our thesis is that the utilitarian postulate is a fatal obstacle to such an analysis. The problem must be posed the other way round: rather than supposing the subject to be constituted before the exchange, exchange should be seen as the source of individual desires.

This is the methodological revolution urged on us by A. O. Hirschman, in his book *Shifting Involvements: Private Interests and Public Action* (Princeton, 1982), with the concept of disappointment:

> The world I am trying to understand . . . is one in which men think they want one thing and then upon getting it, find out to their dismay that they don't want it nearly as much as they thought or don't want it at all and that something else, of which they were hardly aware, is what they really want. (p. 21)

Thus there appears, between expectation and reality, an irreducible distance in the midst of which is played out a constant redefinition of objects. It is not a question of a learning process at the end of which the economic agents would accede to the knowledge of their own preferences, but of a process without end in which old commodities are eroded and new ones invented. If the utilitarian theory is able to ratify 'changes in taste' *a posteriori*, it is incapable of rendering their genesis intelligible. Now it is precisely these *endogenous* transformations of social meanings which are, we think, at the heart of the logic of the marketplace. The formalization of this dynamics of disappointment is a stumbling block in the path of every economic heterodoxy.

A. O. Hirschman proposes that we follow Harry G. Frankfurt,[1] who distinguishes first-order desires and second-order desires, or desires about desires. The latter bring into play a 'capacity for reflective self-evaluation'. Amartya Sen's concept[2] of a 'meta-ranking of preference orderings' belongs to a similar perspective. These approaches do not satisfy us. They do capture one dimension of the problem: the fact that individual preferences evolve as a result of a process of internal criticism. But in their effort to analyse this criticism as the consequence of a second-order choice or meta-choice, they evade the fundamental point: at no level of consciousness does the opacity of desire dissolve away.

It is the analysis of this situation which leads us then to René Girard's theory. In effect, the Girardian individual and the subject in the marketplace are characterized by the same *radical incompleteness*: a desire whose law they do not know, one which does not resolve itself into a more or less lengthy list of objects. Like the Girardian individual, the subject in the marketplace never views his desire head-on; he always reads it obliquely in the gaze of others. This suffering from his lack of closure is something which the producer-exchanger experiences in the unforseen conjunctures that are forever upsetting his production or consumption plans. Social demand characteristics, efficient technologies, organizational forms and all the other things which condition his life as a producer are revealed to him only *ex post facto*. They impose themselves with the inexorability of upheavals of nature.

This tension that runs through the economic agent leads to the emergence of a specific desire, the desire for *wealth*. Wealth is that principle that Girard calls desire's ultimate goal, the possession of which would finally allow the subject to accede to self-sufficiency. It is what all things are measured against; it is the very substance of social evaluation. The determination of wealth is thus the fundamental economic problem. The dominant strategy in political economy (whether it be neoclassical, Marxist or Ricardian) consists in deriving the definition of wealth from a law at the basis of exchange: Value. There would thus reside, at the foundation of the social order, a principle of coherence manipulating the agents without their knowing. This value is identified with Labour or with Utility, depending on the school of thought. The originality of the Girardian approach, however, is to present itself as the systematic refutation of every objective reference anterior to exchange relations. If a social bond is constituted, it can emerge only from the contradictory encounter of individual desires for fullness. Wealth is but a hypostasized form of individual needs, not the expression of a natural complementarity linking the members of society. Individuals only ever pool together what they do not possess.

The primal scene on which René Girard invites us to reflect is particularly exemplary; the slate of social meaning has been wiped clean; one can see only a crowd of individuals defined by their desire for wealth alone, without merchandise, without money, without government, in the middle of a formless mass of natural contingencies. The desire for wealth, as we have defined it, does not possess any *a priori* point of resolution. It is indefinite, floating. It is proportional to the uncertainty that gnaws away at the economic agents. One must emphasize the rigour of the Girardian logic, of the theoretical enterprise which consists in eliminating every form of transcendence in order to render the social alchemy in all its purity. It culminates in this primal scene which poses in all its magnitude the central economic question: how can the order of the market emerge from an undifferentiated structure of rivalries?

Before turning to the analysis of exclusion, let us note that there is nothing exotic for the economist about this primal scene. It corresponds to the speculative pressures that periodically overheat the financial markets or currency exchanges. Indeed, at the root of all speculation one finds a sudden distrust of the central currency, due for example to significant public debts or to an excessive balance-of-payments deficit. At issue in this distrust is the legitimacy of the monetary sign's representation of wealth.

In this context wealth becomes once again an indeterminate object. Since, at the same time, the economic conjuncture becomes greatly uncertain, the producer-exchangers are going to try to preserve themselves from unpredictable fluctuations by seeking all the more avidly this problematical wealth. But once it ceases to be identified with the instituted money, they no longer know behind which mask it is hiding. Stocks, real estate, gold, foreign currencies, primary commodities, etc. attract the anxious attention of individuals looking for likely refuges from 'the terrible oscillations of chance'.

When the monetary convention was strongly established, everyone was distinguished from everyone else in that he was a concrete producer, attached to specific use values. In speculation monetary mediation vacillates, suspicions arise as to its stability; the system of roles is transformed; distinctions fade away. Individuals are then reduced to their minimal definition, possesors of wealth. This process of undifferentiation transmutes the economic society and its structuring hierarchies into a speculative mob.[3] Not knowing which god to worship, each makes of his own unpredictability the measure of the unpredictability of the others. The mimetic hypothesis will allow us to analyse this situation and its evolution. To do this we are going to use a simple model that incorporates certain contributions of Girardian thought.

The Fundamental Girardian Theorem

The central question is how, in the situation of original undifferentiation, individuals determine their choice of objects. This problem is all the more thorny in that our approach can be read as the methodical negation of all guide marks, whether they be internal to the logic of needs or proper to the objects. How then in this state of radical uncertainty, of the disappearance of every reference point, do the agents orientate themselves? Imitation constitutes this rationality 'in the final instance'. It reflects the following elementary logic: if the person I copy has some information on the determinants of wealth, I will improve my performance by imitating him; if, as luck has it, he knows nothing, my situation will remain unchanged. For this reason the mimetic strategy is superior to the one which consists in repeating an initial choice marred by a great uncertainty.

There is therefore not the least conflict between imitation and rationality. This is, incidentally, seen very clearly in the fact that imitation is indivisible from learning processes. When one finds oneself confronted with the emergence of phenomena about which one possesses no knowledge at all, imitation is a means of adaptation. But the nature of imitation is ambivalent: as an adaptation of isolated groups to a given situation, it is a performance factor; as a generalized process, it induces an enigmatic drift of individual choices. In fact from the moment when everyone bases his decision on that of his neighbour, supposing that nobody knows what makes up wealth, the mimetic dynamics closes in on itself.

The strangeness of this phenomenon in which the intelligence is employed not to evaluate the intrinsic quality of objects, but to discover what others imagine their quality to be was captured clearly by J. M. Keynes. It is for him a characteristic expression of speculative behaviour. Thus he writes:

> professional investment may be likened to those newspaper competitions in which the competitors have to pick out the six prettiest faces from a hundred photographs, the prize being awarded to the competitor whose choice most nearly corresponds to the average preferences of the competitors as a whole; so that each competitor has to pick, not those faces which he himself finds prettiest, but those which he thinks likeliest to catch the fancy of the other competitors, all of whom are looking at the problem from the same point of view. It is not a case of choosing those which, to the best of one's judgement, are really the prettiest, nor even those which average opinion genuinely thinks the prettiest. We have reached the third degree where we devote our intelligences to anticipating what average opinion expects the average opinion to be. And there are some, I believe, who practise the fourth, fifth and higher degrees.[4]

The operation of this mechanism produces the decomposition of the bonds that might have tied the collective evaluations to any objective basis beyond the market itself. How then is the group going to behave? Will it not be led ineluctably to dissolve under the pressure of rivalries surrounding the definition of wealth? The Girardian thesis is that at the convulsive climax of the crisis of undifferentiation, 'the resolution of the dilemma is at hand. The whole community now hurls itself into the violent unanimity that is destined to liberate it.'[5] This polarization is born of the amplifying properties of imitation:

> The slightest hint, the most groundless accusation, can circulate with vertiginous speed and is transformed into irrefutable proof. The corporate sense of conviction snowballs, each member taking confidence from his neighbour by a rapid process of mimesis.[6]

With the help of a model inspired by a certain number of studies of a sociological sensibility dealing with the transmission of opinions among the members of a group,[7] we intend to specify the conditions of emergence as well as the properties of this kind of founding unanimity.

Consider a population of N agents indexed by i, i varying from 1 to N. The mimetic hypothesis implies that at the moment (t+1) the agent i chooses his strategy, s(i, t+1), by copying the choice adopted by an agent j in the preceding period, t. Since we have assumed that stable, objectified relations do not exist among the crowd of speculators, the agent i does not always copy the same agent j. He chooses his model at random from the group of speculators. To be exact, [p(i, j); j=1, . . ., N] will designate the law of the random drawing effected by i from the population under consideration.

We thus have:

$$\forall\, i, \sum_{j=1}^{N} P_{ij} = 1$$

It follows that s(i, t+1) = s(k, t) with the probability P_{ik}. We do not necessarily assume all laws P_i to be equal. One can have $P_{ii} \neq 0$, which expresses the self-repeating component, or self-confidence: i reiterates his previous choice, s(i, t), with the probability P_{ii}. One can also have a certain number of individuals to whom i is not directly linked, corresponding to the case $P_{ij} = 0$. Generalized imitation then appears as a stochastic process, since each elementary choice brings chance into play. The process can be completely defined by bringing together all the probability relations obtaining for each individual, which can then be written in matrix form:

$$P = \begin{bmatrix} P_{11} \ldots P_{1j} \ldots P_{1N} \\ \ldots\ldots\ldots\ldots\ldots \\ P_{i1} \ldots P_{ij} \ldots P_{iN} \\ \ldots\ldots\ldots\ldots\ldots \end{bmatrix}$$

P is a Markov matrix. The question is how the set of choices prevailing at each moment evolves: what does {s(1,t), . . ., s(i,t), . . ., s(N,t)} converge to? We will call {s(1,0), . . ., s(i,0), . . ., s(N,0)} the initial choices, at the moment t = 0. s(i,0) has the form of an opinion, whether bearing on objects, on presumed causes for the disorders that rock the crowd, or on the victims. One can then demonstrate the following result, or 'fundamental Girardian theorem': under certain conditions to be specified later, *the imitation process converges to the unanimity of the group*. Here we have the logical basis of the victimage dynamic: unanimity of the members through mimetic contagion.

The first property this model yields us is *the indeterminacy of the opinion* on which the unanimity focuses. It can by any one of the initial opinions, s(i,0). One can none the less assign to each potential final state, {s(i,0), . . ., s(i,0), . . ., s(i,0)}, a probability q(i) of its being achieved. This varies according to the agents i whose initial opinion is adopted, at the end of the process, as the general opinion. The probability measures the power of the agent i; that is to say, his ability to influence the group as a whole.

The second property is *the self-fulfilment of the unanimity*: as soon as the members share the same strategic vision, s(i,0), reciprocal imitation no longer disturbs the consensus but instead contributes to its reproduction. This property is entirely independent of the specific content that makes up s(i,0). It springs from the general configuration of the relations among the members of the group. This circumstance has an important effect on the social fabric. The whole subjective dimension of the community's choice fades away: no longer is it shifting, changeable; rather it is stable, no longer a pretext for conflict but a renewed basis for agreement. The individuals are then led naturally to assign the origin of these emergent characteristics to a foundation more stable than the individual or the community; they see in them the effect of objective forces of nature. In the dizzying glare of this social catharsis is thus forged the misrecognition of the real conditions for its appearance, the exacerbation of competitive rivalries. The polarization process itself comes to be cloaked by this misrecognition. When the partiality, the indeterminacy of the chosen object disappears, when the group explains the polarization by certain qualities proper to the object, the basis for unanimity becomes firmer. Imitation ceases to be the dominant strategy; the recurrence of the belief in the chosen object takes its place. There is no more widespread belief in economics than the one that makes prices the expression of inviolable objective realities. J. M. Keynes distinguishes himself once again when in his study of the logic of speculation he underscores *a contrario* the conventional character of certain economic variables. Thus he writes regarding the interest rate:

> its actual value is largely governed by the prevailing view as to what its value is expected to be. *Any* level of interest which is accepted with sufficient conviction as *likely* to be durable *will* be durable . . . [It] may fluctuate for decades about a level which is chronically too high for full employment; particularly if it is the prevailing opinion that the rate of interest is self-adjusting, so that the level established by convention is thought to be rooted in objective grounds much stronger than convention . . .[8]

For the unanimity theorem to be valid, an essential condition must hold: the graph associated with the Markov matrix P has to be strongly connected aperiodic. Here it is a question of a very intuitive condition. It means that there is an effective interdependence among all the agents; in other words, that there are not 'too many' zero P_{ij}'s.[9] It is, in particular, a question of assuring that every agent k can influence every agent j, not necessarily directly in the form $P_{jk} \neq 0$, but through a chain of indirect influences:

there exist $i_1, i_2, \ldots, i_n$ such that $P_{ji_1}, \ldots P_{i_1 i_2}, \ldots P_{i_n k} \neq 0$.

To put it in another way: if one assigns to each probability $P_{ij} \neq 0$ a directed edge, the property of strong connectivity means that for every j and for every k there exists a path, the union of directed edges, that links them together.

In order to make this clearer, let us consider a situation that does not satisfy this condition. Take the case where the matrix P is decomposable and is therefore written:

$$P = \begin{bmatrix} A & O \\ O & V \end{bmatrix}$$

There exist then two sub-matrices, A and V, which have no relation between them – which are autonomous. In this situation there is evidently no chance of producing unanimity. But that is not at all in contradiction with the Girardian analysis. Indeed, this analysis associates the formation of unanimity with undifferentiated systems. But the decomposability of the matrix P signifies the existence of structural heterogeneities that inhibit imitation. For example, if one considers the group of operators intervening in a commodity market, the differentiation buyers/sellers renders their respective strategies irremediably distinct. They cannot give rise to reciprocal imitation. We will label as differentiation any social topology, whatever its roots – institutional or economic – which serves to block the mimetic process. One can therefore identify undifferentiation mathematically with the property of strong aperiodic connectedness. Our fundamental theorem can then be stated as: *undifferentiated structures converge to unanimity*.

Speculative markets (exchange or financial markets) are precisely structures highly subject to undifferentiation: each speculator is potentially a simple individual in search of wealth; he can be alternately buyer or seller; he is but tenuously bound to the concrete dimensions of productive activity. A holder of steel stocks can at any time exchange them for automobile bonds. In this way these distinctions can easily dissolve, leaving the operators to relate to one another as doubles. Thus is the influence of imitation powerful. The avoidance of mimetic polarization – on the rise or the fall – and its devastating effects on the real economy explain, then, the rigorous regulations to which these markets are frequently submitted.

Thanks to this model we have been able to bring out the essential properties of mimetic logic: *undifferentiation* of the agents, *unanimous polarization* of choices, *indeterminacy* of the chosen object and *self-fulfilment* of the final state. Here we have characteristics which radically distinguish this analysis of speculation from the habitual corpus. It seems to us that they are entirely confirmed by the empirically observed facts.[10] Moreover, the mimetic hypothesis has fulfilled a certain number of theoretical requirements formulated at the outset. The subject in the marketplace is not closed in on himself; he does not know perfectly what he desires. Use value does not pre-exist the exchanges but is established through the confrontation of rival schemes. The model presented summarily in this text none the less displays a certain number of weaknesses. In particular, since it assumes that the P_{ij} are fixed, it misses the process by which the undifferentiation is intensified. Growing undifferentiation means the formation of new connections between agents: that is to say the passage from P_{ij} zero to P_{ij} strictly positive. For this reason the dynamic formalized here is only weakly cumulative compared to a pure mimetic process.

For utilitarian political economy, bogged down in the metaphysics of the rational subject, there is no possibility of contagion: the individual always decides his private choices with full autonomy according to rigid preferences, decision rules fixed *a priori* without regard for the social configuration. The postulated naturalness of individual desires corresponds to the state of maximum differentiation that can be represented by the following matrix:

$$I = \begin{bmatrix} 100\ldots00 \\ 010 \quad\;\; 00 \\ \\ 000 \quad\;\; 10 \\ 000 \quad\;\; 01 \end{bmatrix}$$

One could argue that it is in the formation of prices that these separate subjects come to be interdependent, that they oppose one another. But as is shown by the concept of the auctioneer,[11] the neoclassical market is merely a passive location for registering individual preferences. The principle of decreasing marginal utility ensures *a priori* the existence of a single equilibrium. There is no genuine feedback from prices to preference orders, only a mechanical process of trial and error for obtaining the equilibrium or natural price. This is a result of the fact, already emphasized, that this theory assumes the use value to be defined unambiguously before any exchange. The price only serves to bring to light a pre-existing social coherence. It plays this revelatory role thanks to a property deduced from the postulate of decreasing marginal utility: when prices rise, demand decreases.

In the analysis advanced here the situation is quite different. Use value – or wealth – is indeterminate; it is the quest for it that provokes speculation. In this case (according to René Girard's analysis), by a reversal 'that is both eminently logical and self-defeating', violence becomes the signifier of the 'supreme goal'.[12] It is the intensity of the rivalries an object arouses among those who would possess it that becomes the gauge of its capacity to represent wealth. *In a highly uncertain market, price is the indicator of quality.* There thus appear anti-Walrasian effects: as the price increases, the object becomes more desirable and the demand for it grows in consequence. The logic of imitation then introduces positive feedback tied to this new price function. The difficulties in analysing prices stem from their ambivalent nature, at once a plastic form moulded to the contours of the global coherence and a measure of quality.

The Development of Money

Our analysis took as its point of departure the undifferentiated crowd, a crowd in a state of panic where every individual is in search of wealth: that is, in search of identification. This scene, to whose elaboration our whole conceptual endeavour has been directed, has a fundamental theoretic importance: it reveals in all its intensity the violence proper to the market order. The institution of private property provokes the isolation of the producers. For the manifold discussions among men involved in setting up production and distribution in previous societies, the market relationship substitutes separation. The incompleteness of the subject is derived from this. In studying the logic of the dynamic of undifferentiation, we have demonstrated that it leads to a unanimous polarization on a random object. This choice is none other than the engendering of money. This event has major repercussions; it introduces *a morphogenesis*, a qualitative transformation of social relations. It is the emergence of a meaning, of a language, of a representation through which the community torn asunder constitutes itself as a social totality.

The institution of money can be identified with the formation of market society. Money is first; it is the nexus from which all economic meanings proceed: the panicked crowd gives way to an organized crowd – a society. The strength of this approach is to postulate nothing as to the substance, the content of wealth; *to make meaning spring from an amorphous structure* because it conceives of meaning as proceeding from a formal property, unanimity, and not a substantial one. In economic terms, we substitute for theories of value a theory of money. Whereas the first see the complementarity among members of society as the effect of natural constraints, we analyse it as the product of the monetary relationship, partial and precarious as it is.

In this analysis it is clear that *money has no intrinsic value*. It is the mimetic choice that confers this property on it *a posteriori*: money becomes the basis of social evaluation because the whole community identifies with it. Therefore what is at stake in the subjects' relation to money is not conformity to a hypothetical nature but the approval of society itself. The new social language that is instituted, thanks to which men henceforth can understand each other, is the discourse of prices, the arithmetic of profits and losses. The law that founds it is the rule of payment in cash.

Through the good graces of mimetic convergence, the principle of wealth is able for a time to escape its own indeterminacy: it is identified with money. Thus is engendered a sign radically distinct from all others. By this process difference is born where before was only a formless mass of objects, only the infinite variability of human rivalries. From this founding differentiation, sovereignty, flows the legitimacy of all secondary mediations. As soon as they have been rendered intelligible, then, social arrangements are analysable as an algebra of this original quality. It is a question of dividing, of cutting up. Such is the essence of technocratic practice. Control always proceeds by establishing a network of regulations, of norms, of classifications that aim at carving up the social space. In so far as a given money represents the supreme goal, the states' practice is validated.

Money encounters no limits to its field of action; it speaks the language of infinite persuasion; there is nothing it cannot purchase. That is the theory of money as superpowerful. But it is a misapprehension of the real nature of the process which made this particular sign into the representation of wealth. There can be no question of an identity such as would be justified by a relationship between similar logical categories, but of a transitory coincidence: what mimetic convergence has made, it can just as easily unmake. In other words, the monetary choice does not radically cancel out the subjects' lack of being; it does not destroy the separation of the market. For this reason the handling of sovereignty is a delicate art.

The monetary crisis is to be interpreted as a resurgence of the desire for wealth. It corresponds to that moment when the central monetary institution ceases to be transcendent but is seen for what it is: one particular sign, contingent, the management of a certain form of economic domination. The conflictiveness proper to the market universe resumes its place at the front of the social stage. Like a gangrene it attacks individual expectations; a new period of instability sets in. Speculation is the mode of expression that most exemplifies this crisis. Our analysis makes it possible to situate with accuracy the stakes: the redefinition of the monetary relationship and its conditions of operation turns on the outcome. Thus one witnesses the constitution of an historical cycle, easily discovered, of creation/destruction of the monetary relationship, with destruction engendering forms that are qualitatively new. Because it establishes the irreducibility of the crisis of undifferentiation, our approach is opposed to technocratic thought: it denies that there can exist a *theory* of social control. Mimetic contagion is what social engineering strategies always end up tripping over; in other words, it is the concept best suited to analysing 'the autonomy of the social'.

Demystification and History in Girard and Durkheim

PAISLEY LIVINGSTON

Although a certain debt to Durkheim is characteristic of any number of contemporary sociologists and anthropologists, the work of René Girard displays a special affinity to Durkheim's project. One way to express this affinity would be to note that if it is fairly common for contemporary thinkers to retain some Durkheimian motifs, it is unusual for them to maintain Durkheim's realist epistemology and his confidence in the possibility of a true science of mythology and ritual. Inspired by Heidegger and by Winch's reading of Wittgenstein, many contemporary theorists reject above all else Durkheim's project of a scientific demystification of cultural beliefs and practices.[1] Structuralism, they claim, makes the same error by wrongly seeking to cut beneath a culture's self-understanding in search of the hidden and unconscious determinants of action and representation.

Yet Girard boldly supports this very project, and does not believe that the failures of a certain structuralism in any way incriminate the larger ambition. In fact, an important element in his critique of Lévi-Strauss is that it was this structuralist's cultural relativism that prevented him from carrying on with what was important in Durkheim's project: because they are the product of an analysis not controlled by criteria of realism, the various binary oppositions remained little more than gratuitous constructs or theoretical fictions. Girard, then, agrees with Durkheim's attitude – if not with all his claims – precisely to the extent that the sociologist attempted to discern the real causes behind symbolism. It is for this reason that Girard has written that Durkheim's perspective is 'the only one from which the problem of culture, or the problem of language, or, if you prefer, the problem of symbolic thought, becomes concrete'.[2] Durkheim's approach to the sociology of religion amounts, he adds, to a 'precious legacy' that later theorists have 'obscured and pushed aside'. Girard's own anthropological hypotheses should be seen as an attempt to return to this legacy, as well as an effort to move beyond the specific shortcomings of Durkheim's work.

In order to grasp Girard's relation to that legacy, it is necessary to focus on some basic questions about Durkheim's conceptions of the source of mythology and the nature of anthropological knowledge. In this manner it should be possible to make explicit some of the conceptual or epistemic problems within the Durkheimian 'perspective', problems with which Girard in turn has had to contend. One of my goals will be to suggest the extent to which the work of both theorists manifests several different strains, some of which represent extremely valuable insights. Although I shall be offering criticisms of some of both thinkers' points, these remarks are motivated by the overarching view that Girard is right in preferring Durkheim's ambitions to the false choice presented by structuralism and the various anti-structuralisms.

My first question, then, concerns the two thinkers' reasons for deeming a science of society necessary and possible. This question is central to both theorists in that both assume that in archaic societies the predominant systems of symbolism or 'collective representations' were not accurate depictions of social reality: mythology and ritual, it is held, essentially misrecognize their own objects and aims. The anthropologist is not a believer of the cults that he or she studies, and to 'think native' is to cease being an anthropologist capable of explaining religious beliefs and practices. Thus in reference to archaic beliefs Durkheim claims that 'the reasons with which the faithful justify them may be, and are most often, erroneous; but the true reasons do not cease to exist, and it is the duty of science to discover them'.[3] A true knowledge of the sacred, a real knowledge of the social bases of collective representations, is possible, then, only after a fundamental demystification. If the *arche* of 'archaic' social systems is in general a belief in the existence of sacred forces or entities, any scientific demystification of such a system must replace this illusory *arche* with a valid foundation.[4] Only in this manner could the sociologist's discourse justify its pretension to externality and ground its claim to replace the illusion of myth with the truth of scientific knowledge. My question, then, concerns the nature of this *arche* or foundation of the science of the social.

Yet this question is intimately related to a second one, which is that of the source of the error which it is the social scientist's goal to correct. The manner in which the demystifier defines this source of error has many implications for his own claim to truth, for the validity of this claim requires that one specify how it is that a discourse could have freed itself from conditions that were formerly the cause of only erroneous representations of social reality. A failure to respond to this question results in the familiar spectacle of the sociological theorist who, with a strange efficacy, reduces other knowledge-claims to their sociological conditions, without once being troubled by the possibility that this demystification itself must also be the product of a given social condition.[5] Thus, in posing the question of the status of the demystification of archaic beliefs in Girard and in Durkheim, it will be necessary to speak of several *archai* at once: first of all, there is the foundation of the anthropological discourse that purports to explain the beliefs of another society; secondly, there is the illusory or symbolic *arche* that the 'faithful' imagine to be the source of truth, power, authority, etc.; and again, there is the *arche* the anthropologist discovers lurking behind the symbolic one, as its hidden and previously unknown cause. Our two questions, then, are as follows:

Q1: Why, according to the anthropological discourse, did an illusory *arche* conceal the true cause of symbolism in the first place?

Q2: How does the anthropological discourse ground its own claim to truth? Why was it not also conditioned by the causes of error it has discovered behind other representations?

Let us turn now to Durkheim's manner of defining the sources of myth and of its demystification, noting first of all that it is impossible to derive from his writings a single, systematic position. Indeed, as many of the major commentators have already observed, one can discover in Durkheim wholly contradictory statements about the validity of religious representations, about their relation to those of science, and about the process of social change that led to the emergence of a scientific world-view.[6]

We may begin by noting that Durkheim is properly viewed as the grandfather of structuralism in that he insists upon distinguishing sharply between the subject's lived experience of social reality and the underlying and hidden bases of that experience. In *The Rules of Sociological Method*, this distinction is voiced when Durkheim comments that science must not 'flee from paradox'.[7] By this he means that his own scientific discourse will not hesitate to contradict the 'doxa' or commonplace opinions. Thus if Durkheim brilliantly critiques all scientific reductions of symbolism to some psychological or biological level of description, thereby arguing strongly for the autonomy of the social, he advocates the most efficacious reduction possible at this level: it is the task of sociology to explain social thought and action in terms of laws, causes, constraints, and functions which can be wholly unknown to the actors. Society is viewed as a *systematic totality* in which the whole has a hierarchical priority and domination over the individual parts, just as a set and its members are said to belong to logically distinct levels or types. We will have occasion to return to this basic assumption.

Now, for Durkheim, the essential error of archaic representations is that this systematic social totality is misrecognized: the real social 'force' that touches the individual during the effervescence of a ritual gathering is the 'emergent property' of the group, a property that owes nothing to the natural or supernatural entities through which it is symbolized. Divinity, society, and totality stand for the same thing: the transcendent power of the system over the individual. To recognize the force of the social totality in the symbols of divinity is to progress towards the truth. Hence the *nature* of the error is that sacred collective representations displace the social causes on to a purely symbolic plane.

Yet when Durkheim needs to carry this argument one step further by identifying the *causes* of this erroneous displacement, he falters disastrously.[8] What is most astonishing is the extreme paucity of Durkheim's comments on this issue, for his direct statements on the matter really amount to only a few lines. Nor are these comments consistent. At one point, he offers a purely circular argument by suggesting that the force of the social totality was originally misrecognized in a religious form 'because' science did not yet exist. At the same time he tends to hint at psychological and/or physiological reasons, as is suggested by the following passage:

> It is undoubtedly true that if they were able to see that these influences which they feel emanate from society, then the mythological system of interpretations would never be born. But social action follows ways that are too circuitous and obscure, and employs psychical mechanisms that are too complex to allow the ordinary observer to see from whence it comes. As long as scientific analysis does not come to teach it to them, men know well that they are acted upon, but they do not know by whom. So they must invent by themselves the idea of these powers with which they feel themselves in connection, and from that, we are able to catch a glimpse of the way by which they were led to represent them under forms

> that are really foreign to their nature and to transfigure them by thought.[9]

This passage reveals the extent to which Durkheim lacks anything approaching a detailed or coherent account of the basis of mythical error. Moreover, it is striking to observe here how much recourse the champion of an autonomous science of the social ultimately has to what he has earlier called an 'obscure psychology'.[10] Paul Hirst has made this point forcefully, and notes that 'Durkheim's conception of the source and function of ideology is not in any sense sociological. Ideology is an effect of the existence of human subjects *per se. It is an effect of the nature of the human mind*'[11] (Hirst's emphasis). Yet we shall see that this conclusion is only partially correct: although it is important to note that Durkheim 'explains' the origin of mythology in psychological terms, he does not consistently state that the 'human mind' remains unchanged in this regard. There is, of course, an important vein of naturalist thought in Durkheim's work, yet this vein is combined – sometimes quite uneasily – with other elements, beginning with a form of historicized Kantianism. These other elements allow Durkheim to claim that history, conceived as a process of real social change, does make a fundamental difference to the conditions of knowledge, a difference which cannot be derived from the invariants of an individual psychology. Durkheim's understanding of the possibility of demystification can be grasped only by attending to the diverse strands of his ideas on historical change.

It is well recognized that Durkheim does not have a single, systematic theory of change, and in what follows I shall be attempting to isolate a few distinct lines of thought that appear in his work. The first tendency that must be mentioned is the notorious mechanistic approach presented in *The Division of Labour in Society*. What remains interesting about this attempt to elucidate a causal dynamic of change is the way in which Durkheim clings tenaciously to his thesis that society is a single, systematically organized mechanism. Durkheim plays at being the Newton of sociology and discovers the laws of social gravitation, laws that have only two variables: 'mass' and 'density'. Now Durkheim wants to argue that the early, 'mechanical' solidarity gives way to social organizations in which there is a progressive 'indetermination' of individual consciousness in relation to the global constraints imposed on it by the social mechanism. In an apparently paradoxical gesture, Durkheim states that this 'loosening' of the earliest social mechanism is determined by this same mechanism: 'Thus it is wholly mechanical causes that make the individual personality be absorbed within the collective personality, and it is causes of the same nature that make it become disengaged from this collective personality.'[12] Nowhere does Durkheim explain how it is that a closed and mechanical system is supposed to be capable of engendering its opposite: a real indetermination and complexity.

The same sort of problem recurs in the study of suicide, yet here Durkheim avoids this paradox in an interesting manner. He must ask himself how the laws of social interaction can determine their own opposite: the absence of law, or 'anomie'. It would seem that if anomic suicide were the effect of social causes, then an increase in its frequency would be the result not of an absence of constraints, but of the operation of a different sort of constraint. Thus Durkheim introduces a type of constraint that does not belong to his privileged level of description: he transgresses his methodological rule by having recourse to a psychological hypothesis. Evoking the 'authority' of Chateaubriand, Goethe, and Lamartine, Durkheim proposes that the human personality suffers from an irreducible lack or infinite desire which, if it is not contained by some sort of social norm, can give rise to suicide. The element that introduces indetermination within the social mechanism is in this case a certain kind of desire, a 'lack' that is not socially constituted.[13]

We have noted two ways in which Durkheim tries to explain social change (and, by extension, the social conditions of demystification). The first is wholly paradoxical in that it amounts to claiming that a closed social mechanism changes its own laws. The second avoids this paradox by 'opening' up the social mechanism to another sort of cause, situated within an individual psychology. A third tendency that can be traced throughout Durkheim's writings amounts to a cancelling of the very question. By this I mean to refer to the many passages in which Durkheim attempts to diminish the tension between religious and scientific modes of representation, the passages where he downplays the problem of the historical emergence of truth by suggesting that science and religion ultimately share the same 'categories'. The conclusion of *The Elementary Forms of the Religious Life* is the primary locus of these equivocations in which Durkheim retreats from the consequences of his own adherence to a form of scientific realism.

Now if these three tendencies were fully representative of Durkheim's thinking about social change, Paul Hirst's impatient condemnations would be somewhat justified. Yet I believe there are other tendencies to be discerned in Durkheim on the subject. Contrary to Hirst's claims there is an important strain of Kantianism in Durkheim, yet it is to the Kant of the historical writings that one must look in order to discern this, not to the First Critique. Even the hesitations between a faculty psychology and a theory of historical process are essentially Kantian.[14]

It may be noted in passing that this aspect of Durkheim's Kantianism is no mystery to such a thinker as Jürgen Habermas, who has recently offered his own reconstruction of a logic of historical demystification that he finds 'hinted at' in Durkheim. Although I shall not set forth the details of Habermas' 'thought experiment' here, it may be useful to point out that the central Kantian notions that figure in both Habermas' and Durkheim's vision of demystification are 'publicity', 'autonomy', and 'cosmopolitanism'. When Habermas speaks of the *Versprachlichung des Sakralen*, he has in mind a communicational process through which an unquestioned sacred *arche* and the institutions that it grounds become the object of discussion and critique. It is precisely upon such a process that Habermas relies in his rejection of the positivist claim that the only rationality is an instrumental form of reason – Habermas' goal being the conception of a historical process of desacralization that would amount to the realization of a communicational and normative rationality.[15]

How, according to Durkheim, would this progress have become possible? That it is a matter of *history* is evident in the following statement, where we can also note Durkheim's effort to adapt the Kantian notion of a regulative idea: 'Really and truly human thought is not a primitive fact; it is the product of history; it is the ideal limit towards which we are constantly approaching, but which in all probability we shall never succeed in reaching.'[16] Yet how does such a process begin, given that the 'primitive fact' is that of mythological illusion? One of Durkheim's answers is that a germ of truth is already contained within the religious representations, and it is this element of Durkheim's thought that Eric Gans has developed in his own work on this problem.[17] Mythology offers 'a first intuition of the realm of truth' because it carries the individual mind outside itself and gives thought a 'stability' and an 'impersonality' that will be necessary to the cognition of objective realities. If religious thought amounts to a profound misrecognition of social structures and events, it does not dictate a *complete* misunderstanding of the natural environment. With the right changes in social organization, the cognitive abilities that have been elaborated will eventually return to illuminate a previously misrecognized social and cultural reality. Durkheim points to this possibility in the passage immediately preceding our last citation:

> If logical thought tends to rid itself more and more of the subjective and personal elements which it still retains from its origin, it is not because extra-social factors have intervened; it is much rather because a social life of a new sort is developing. It is this international life which has already resulted in universalizing religious beliefs. As it extends, the collective horizon enlarges; the society ceases to appear as the only whole, to become a part of a much vaster one, with indetermined frontiers, which is susceptible of advancing indefinitely. Consequently things can no longer be contained in the social moulds according to which they were primitively classified; they must be organized according to principles which are their own, so logical organization differentiates itself from the social organization and becomes autonomous.[18]

This passage brings forth the importance of a concept of autonomy within Durkheim's view of desacralization. Durkheim's point is that in time, the scientific method of thinking and of inquiry won a *significant* (but by no means total) autonomy from its social conditions and thereby became capable of revealing rather than concealing the nature of social action. Durkheim does *not* claim that this occurs in one fell swoop, or that a complete, absolute, and eternal Truth is obtained. That is only the position that the critics of his project attribute to him so as to be able to discount him as naïve. In fact Durkheim here explicitly situates perfection as an ideal limit, an abstractive concept that serves as a model. The essential part of Durkheim's claim is that the historical process in question became possible because the individual religious systems of thought could not maintain their illusory closure. Durkheim's point is that something new emerged as a result of the exchanges and collisions between different cultures, which did not always simply assimilate external influences to their own terms. On the contrary, the interactions of societies may have led to a questioning of the individual culture's belief that its own system could represent the totality. Yet Durkheim is not wedded to the view that the source of radical historical change is only extrinsic to society; he would in any case have to describe how the shock of cultures is translated as a change of the internal relations within a society. It should be obvious as well that some forms of 'international' contact do serve primarily to reinforce local beliefs.

Here we touch upon a second aspect of Durkheim's emphasis on autonomy. He always links the emergence of truth to his idea of the development of the morally and intellectually autonomous individual. The co-operative labour of science requires individuals who are socialized in this manner: that is, who are capable of incorporating certain norms and of subordinating subjective impulses to abstract and impersonal criteria. Thus it is possible to see that more recent attempts to reconstruct the norms of scientific inquiry have a foreshadowing in Durkheim, who already points to the same kinds of idealized norms that Merton, for example, will develop in some detail: individualism (science is anti-authoritarian), universalism, freedom of epistemic considerations from other factors, self-criticism, and so on.[19]

Moreover, Durkheim sees in individualism a new type of freedom as well as a source of creativity. This link between a certain type of psychological development and the emergence of science is stressed in the study on the division of labour, yet in that context the 'progressive indetermination' of the individual in relation to collective representations remained the mechanical result of demographic factors. A more promising way of talking about this indetermination is that of Durkheim's article 'Individual and Collective Representations', where the 'relative autonomy' and causal efficacy of thought are described as potentials inherent within the development of conscious representations as such. The key point is that Durkheim does not always insist that the individual's thought and action are determined by social constraints and by social constraints alone; in arguing that consciousness is not reducible to automatism, he conceives of a generative and creative potentiality within consciousness:

> An agent endowed with consciousness does not behave like a being whose activity could be reduced to a system of reflexes: he hesitates, feels his way, deliberates, and it is by this distinguishing particularity that he is recognized . . . This relative indetermination does not exist where there is no consciousness, and it increases with consciousness.[20]

To sum up briefly this discussion of Durkheim, it is possible to see that in his effort to conceive of the possibility of radical historical complexification, including the emergence of rational inquiry and truth, Durkheim loosens up his systematic view of the social order in two main directions: first of all, instead of speaking of *the* social totality he refers to individual cultures' illusory claims to totality; the only 'totality' is an ideal of cosmopolitanism having 'indetermined frontiers'. No real societies in history were really closed or autonomous systems in so far as their interaction with other societies were an important factor of change. Secondly, Durkheim loosens his systematic view of social order from within when he suggests that the fact of individual consciousness as such contains a potential for reflection and responsible action (a *relative* yet significant autonomy). Durkheim clings to the idea that the historical development of individualism certainly has social causes, but these could have been effective only through their interaction with the capacities of the individual mind. Now, these two perspectives are in principle quite interesting, even if Durkheim does not in practice offer much more than a sketch of an argument. For example, he never really makes explicit the sociological conditions that facilitate an individual psychological development. It will be useful to return to this issue later in relation to the notion of imitation within Girard's thought.

How, then, has René Girard responded to the problems inherent in Durkheim's project? We may begin by noting that unlike Durkheim, who says precious little about the ultimate source of mythological error, Girard presents a far-reaching hypothesis concerning the process of hominization and the emergence of religious symbolism. It is no exaggeration to say that as far as Girard is concerned, properly human representations and consciousness begin with an illusion: the first 'non-instinctual attention', he writes, is that excited by the vision of a victim killed by the rest of the group.[21] Although Girard describes hominization as a lengthy evolutionary process during which the instinctual patterns of behaviour were altered, he also characterizes it as a process that was really completed only as a result of an *event* (or series of structurally similar events). This is Girard's radical reworking of the Durkheimian notion that an 'effervescence' occasioned by ritual gatherings was the source of religious sentiments and symbolisms.

Girard lauds Durkheim for having sought such a causal event within the domain of interaction, yet points out that it is circular to characterize the crucial gatherings as either rituals or ceremonies. Ritual cannot really be explained – that is, given a concrete basis – by referring to other rituals.[22] His own founding events – 'spontaneous' collective murders – are not said to have occurred as ritual enactments; they are not yet 'sacrifices'; rather, they are the result of a dynamic that is at this point 'social' only in the sense that several hominoid creatures were involved. It is a spontaneous and real event, not a ceremony, that constitutes the earliest cultural groups. And these groups are formed through their unanimous sharing of a single illusion, that of the mythical transformation of the victim. Now although this illusion finds its specific forms and contents in different ways of misrepresenting the victim (execration, idolatry), its ultimate basis is defined by Girard as the system or mechanism of mimetic interaction, which alone caused these original murders to occur. The specific determination of the victim is, according to Girard, 'arbitrary', but the murder itself is not; there is nothing accidental about the collective murder, which stands as the universal starting point of all world cultures. No diffusionist speculations are necessary, for in each instance a structurally similar beginning or origin was engendered by what Girard refers to as 'the mimetic machine', by which he means the redundant patterns of interaction resulting from a mimetic or imitative propensity.

If the foundation of cultural representations and of social action is a mechanism that was hidden from the consciousness of the actors whose motives and experience it determined, how did it become possible to become aware of this mechanism? It should be pointed out that the concept of a 'mechanism' of interaction typically suggests a strong determination of thought and behaviour: individual and group actions and representations are to be understood as the results of a process governed by a set of essential laws. Such a mimetic machine would indeed be another *arche*: a controlling system that dictates the essence, logic, and end of a process. Girard calls this human 'mimesis' a propensity, yet it may also specify a *nature* in the sense of this latter term that was made explicit by Kant when he stated: 'Nature is the existence of things in so far as they are determined following universal laws.'[23] Now, if the sacrificial error was dictated by human nature, then there is no difficulty in making its worldwide recurrence plausible; yet the emergence of something radically different from this error will as a result require some explanation. Girard's work contains, I think, two very different ways of responding to this problem. He believes that the two are wholly compatible, yet I have doubts on this score.

One of Girard's explanations of the historical emergence of truth was set forth after the publication of *Violence and the Sacred* in his massive *Des Choses cachées depuis la fondation du monde*. Essentially the same response is given in his two subsequent books, both of which contribute valuable clarifications and additional exemplifications of the hypothesis.[24] Girard claims that the real undoing of the sacred system of misrepresentation resulted from the true revelation offered by the Judaeo-Christian Scriptures. Scientific explanations may very well contribute to the demystification that has been in process for two thousand years, yet such efforts depend upon – and often retard – the work of the real agent of demystification, the Logos that became immanent in Christ. Girard:

> Men did not stop hunting witches because they invented science; they invented science because they stopped hunting witches. The scientific spirit, like the spirit of economic enterprise, is a by-product of the deep subterranean influence that has been exercised by the evangelical text.[25]

Now it is not wholly new to suggest that Western science is not entirely the result of Greek civilization and of the Enlightenment, or that it is essentially conditioned by aspects of Christianity. Yet Girard revives this notion at a propitious moment, and does so in his own unique way. Properly speaking, Girard's point concerns not the natural sciences as such but the possibility of a rigorous and complete cultural apperception, beginning, he would insist, with the possibility of recognizing the innocence of scapegoats, an innocence that was never fully unmasked before the Judaeo-Christian revelation. Despite the claims that may be made for certain Greek tragedies, only the Scriptures go all the way in demonstrating the manner in which a community achieves its unanimity and order through a violent exclusion of victims, whom it systematically misrecognizes in the forms of the sacred.[26]

Also original in Girard's account are some of the arguments he offers to support it. For example, if he contends that sacrificial cultures could never have attained self-reflection without the influence, from without, of a divine revelation, he adds that this would be so because the system of mimetic interaction really functions as a closed dynamic or 'machine': 'No system of thought can truly think the thought that is capable of destroying it.'[27] Although I disagree with Girard's argument here, I believe the latter statement to be wholly consequential. If a system is defined as a *closed* totality or whole, the states of which are governed, generated, and produced by an overarching set of laws, it indeed follows that these laws will be invariant across the diversity of the states. In other words, nothing completely new or contrary to the laws will be produced by such a system; if the system is said to be that of mimesis as a totality, it will hence include and govern everything essential in mimetic interaction and representation – for Girard, the very essence of the human. This sort of mimetic 'machine' may very well generate 'disorder' in the form of what Girard calls a mimetic crisis, but the processes and eventual resolution of such a crisis remain orderly in so far as they are essentially governed by the laws of mimesis.

To prevent misunderstandings, it should be pointed out that Girard is in no way perpetuating here some kind of Durkheimian 'functionalism' whereby social systems would always be 'cohesive' and 'in order', Conflict, violence, and a partial stability through violent domination are at the centre of Girard's attention; indeed, his emphasis on the problem of rivalry and conflict have led to some of his finest analyses (e.g. his remarks on exogamy in *Violence and the Sacred*). It must be noted, however, that at an epistemic level – that is, from the viewpoint of an external observer – conflictual interaction may manifest *systematic* patterns of great redundancy; it is only in this latter sense that it could be properly spoken of as 'orderly'. We should also understand that as far as Girard is concerned, the very functioning of the mimetic machine depends upon and dictates the misrecognition of its nature by those caught up in it. Should the mechanism of victimization become fully known to the participants, it would cease to achieve its goal. One of the 'laws' of its operation, then, is that the group must be oblivious to the innocence of the victim.

We have already seen how Durkheim's insistence on the 'holistic' or systematic nature of the social order has made it difficult for him to explain radical change in history, and we have seen him encounter the paradox of a closed system that alters its own dynamic or 'programme'. One way in which Girard avoids making the paradoxical claim that the mimetic system changed its own rules is by saying that the radical change of the system in fact had its provenance wholly outside the system. In this sense the origin of change transcends the purely human and social domain, for it is a divine being – the Christ – who announces, in word and deed, the innocence of the victim and the falsehood of violent accusation. Girard does *not* say that mythology was from that moment on effectively or practically debunked, for he admits that Christendom in many ways functioned as a sacrificial institution having a fully sacrificial misunderstanding of itself. Schwager's contribution to this volume also bears witness to this point.[28] However, Girard suggests that in principle the mythical illusions were debunked by Christ's message, which has continued to exercise its 'subterranean influence' in spite of and alongside the sacrificial distortions. Even the accounts of the evangelists are tinged by certain sacrificial or mythical elements (the emphasis on Christ's miracles, for example); yet the truth passes through none the less. In this sense Girard recalls Kierkegaard, who insisted on distinguishing between the institutions of Christendom and the true spirit of Christianity. Yet at the same time, Girard speaks in the name of a certain 'orthodoxy'.[29]

It is my opinion that Girard's references to a subterranean 'influence' leave many questions unanswered. What is lacking is a more specific statement about the kinds of social and/or psychological conditions that must be satisfied for essentially mimetic human beings to be capable of being subject to this influence; similarly, it would be necessary to inquire into the kinds of conditions that lead people, in their mimetic or 'satanic' nature, to oppose this influence and to cling to their illusions. The fact that the majority of humankind today continues to cling tenaciously to the sacred illusions – or in Girard's words, to the 'gods of violence' – would seem to suggest the pertinence of these questions. Nor is this persistence of illusion to be identified only in the most obvious phenomena of warfare, witchcraft accusations, and persecution. If we accept André Orléan's brilliant analysis of the 'sacrificial' dynamics inherent in the monetary system, it would seem that a displaced sacrificial misrecognition remains the operative condition of one of the most basic and central social institutions of the modern world. As this system is described by Orléan, it is certainly a matter of a collective belief in the existence of a transcendent substance that is in fact only a fiction created by the mimetic convergence of the believers' own actions; the mystification is none the less very real and effectual.[30] In what sense is this monetary system, as described by Orléan and Dupuy, to be taken as a by-product of the Christian revelation? In what *concrete* ways did the Christian revelation effectively make possible a scientific demystification of this monetary system?

Yet questions of this nature come after an even more fundamental difficulty: if we do not accept Girard's notion of a truly Divine revelation, how can change be accounted for within his system? A second approach to this issue can be discerned here and there in his writings, yet he does not seem to consider at present that there is a valid response that could be separated from the perspective we have just discussed. It is primarily in *Violence and the Sacred* that these elements can be found; it is here, for example, that he refers to the partial knowledges that develop directly from the founding sacrificial institution. The following passage is characteristic:

> The surrogate victim, as founder of the rite, appears as the ideal educator of humanity, in the etymological sense of *e-ducatio*, a leading out. The rite gradually leads men away from the sacred; it permits them to escape their own violence, removes them from violence, and bestows on them all the institutions and beliefs that define their humanity.[31]

Girard certainly does not really mean to say that the institution of sacrifice truly *is* the ideal educator; nor does he think that sacrificial institutions truly can eliminate violence from society (they are, at some level, necessarily violent themselves). In other words, the knowledge that was achieved within sacrificial cultures was always limited by a crucial blind spot. For this reason Girard goes on to warn that such a knowledge, which was born in myth and remains linked to it, cannot prevent the possibility that mankind will return full circle to the original violence. Even so, Girard acknowledges that a certain truth is already obtained from within the 'mimetic' system, for its rites 'gradually' lead men away from the sacred. But how can this agent of demystification be the product of the mimetic system itself? How is the 'rupture' brought about?

I believe that an answer to this question can be formulated within the general framework of Girard's theory of mimesis; such an answer needs to be approached first of all in an analytical manner, and then to be given psychological and historical depth. The first step follows upon an idea proposed by Jean-Pierre Dupuy, who claims that the mimetic model can best be understood as being analogous to a 'self-organizing system' (as such machines are understood, roughly speaking, by both Atlan and Varela).[32] Such a system is not, in fact, 'closed' (it exists only through an ongoing interaction with its environment); nor is it a simple dynamic, for its internal order generates real complexity – or, in short, a veritable history. Now, although it is an open question to what extent the mimetic patterns of interaction described by Girard are accurately characterized by the theory of self-organizing systems (a theory not without its own conceptual problems), there is a crucial point behind Dupuy's move: namely that it is incorrect, and creates unnecessary problems, to posit a *closed* dynamic at the heart of mimetic interaction. Dupuy sees no problem with the notion of mechanism, and speaks of a 'neo-mechanicism' in which the mechanisms modelled are capable of generating the complexity of an unforeseeable history (the self-organizing system is said to maintain only an 'informational' closure).

Dupuy and Pierre Livet understand Girard's theory of mimesis as falling within a certain class of interactive mechanisms: those in which the agents' behaviour is conditioned by their reciprocal anticipations of what the others will do. Livet argues that while such mechanisms of interaction will certainly engender the patterns Girard describes they are also capable of generating more than this, while remaining in some sense 'closed'.[33] This point seems crucial to me, but I think it could also be useful to follow Durkheim in a further 'loosening' of the notion of social 'totality'. Whether or not the term 'mechanism' is used is surely not the essential point: what matters is the extent to which a single set of patterns of interaction are posited as being the causal nexus out of which all thought and behaviour are generated. Is it not more prudent to suggest that although certain sequences of interaction can indeed be 'programmatic', they are not *the* programme, if by this we mean the unique causal dynamic responsible for the history of the system(s).

The mimetic system, mechanism, or machine that Girard describes is *coupled* to something else, and this coupling, described as an 'internal indetermination' or absence of a 'fixed point', generates an evolution that is not simply the repetition of a cycle of crises and resolutions. A variety of communicational frameworks, patterns of interaction, and cognitive capacities becomes possible, including the emergence of a significant degree of accurate social apperception. To adopt Girard's terms, mimetic processes, in conjunction with the other kinds of processes and factors involved in human existence, would be capable of generating an open-ended history that would indeed lead mankind away from the sacred – at least far enough to permit some individuals to look back and observe some of its essential features.

To pursue this line of inquiry, it is necessary to explore the Girardian theory of mimesis with an eye to the possibility of its incorporation within such a historical framework. It is our viewpoint that the mimetic figures Girard has described amount to a fundamental discovery, because they indeed model important features of patterns of social interaction. Yet we are reluctant to understand these figures as comprising a mechanical system that is 'closed' (either at the level of 'information' or at the level of 'matter/energy'). In other words, Girard is right in pointing to the mimetic 'propensity' of human beings, a propensity which he contrasts to the instinctual control of behaviour in the animal kingdom. He is also right in identifying some of the behavioural, affective, and ideational sequences that tend to be generated as a result of this propensity – for example, that of the 'double mediation' or 'obstacle-model' form of reciprocal imitation. Girard's analyses brilliantly demonstrate the errors of a philosophical anthropology that seeks to define the human as an immediate and infinite 'freedom' or complete 'indetermination'.[34] Is it not possible to maintain Girard's descriptions of certain mimetic patterns while differing with aspects of his interpretation of their range?

It may be useful to begin to explore this alternative by concentrating on the different shades of meaning included within the semantic fields of such terms as 'mimesis' and 'imitation'. In this regard Durkheim's critique of Gabriel Tarde could be instructive.[35]

Rather than seeing in imitation a single phenomenon, Durkheim responded to Tarde by specifying three possible kinds of imitation: 1) a levelling of thought and of behaviour as a result of social interaction; 2) an agent's conformity to customs and manners exemplified by a model; 3) the immediate copying of others' behaviour. Durkheim's strategy in his polemic with Tarde was to contend that only the third type is, properly speaking, a variety of imitation since only in this instance is it a matter of an automatism. The other kinds could very well seem 'imitative', yet it would be useless to try to explain them in these terms because such actions are determined not only by imitation but by a significant degree of choice, reasoning, and even creativity. For example, the sentiments of respect and trust that could lead someone to 'do the same thing' as someone else do not seem to be necessarily reducible to some form of spontaneous imitation; many other factors may have been involved in a decision to assume that this model is the most advantageous one to follow.

Durkheim's distinctions are of course rudimentary and somewhat incoherent, but his more basic point seems promising in so far as it underscores the value of distinguishing between the different conditions that can lead human agents to share similar ideas and to perform similar actions. It is not a matter of denying that human behaviour can sometimes be determined by a seemingly spontaneous unconscious, and mechanical process of imitation; it is, however, important to question whether other apparent 'copyings' can be reduced to this same model of causation. Durkheim claims, *contra* Tarde, that it is sometimes a process of 'reasoning' that leads a subject to consent to follow another's example, and that this type of case is not reducible to that of a spontaneous mimetic 'contamination'.

If we turn to Girard's views on imitation with these issues in mind, we find that his concept of 'mimetic desire' embraces the full range of Durkheim's spectrum, yet tends to reduce the different types of copying and representing to one level which is held to generate the others. Girard complains that the Western philosophical tradition has operated almost exclusively with a mutilated notion of human mimesis, one from which the elements of desire – and, 'more fundamentally', of 'appropriation' – have been excluded.[36] At the same time he examines those literary masterworks in which these excluded dimensions of humanity are revealed – those works in which the individual characters are clearly depicted as leading lives determined by a network of mimetic interactions. These interactions involve relations of 'desire' in a variety of senses, for the latter term is not construed narrowly as involving only sexuality or the erotic. In fact, the notion of 'desire' in Girard seems to embrace all action: when a character acts, consciously or unconsciously, in a manner so as to bring about one state of affairs instead of another, he is said to 'desire' this former state of affairs. Thus 'object of desire' is synonymous in Girard's analysis with 'state of affairs that is the goal, conscious or unconscious, of an agent's behaviour'. His statement that all desire is 'imitative' therefore amounts to saying that subjects find their aims or goals only by copying them from others.

Another aspect of Girard's sense of 'imitation' is revealed when we ask how it is that a subject is directed to imitate one model as opposed to another. Clearly the mimetic subject tends to be focused on one model to the exclusion of other possible mediations. Yet is it proper to say that a subject 'desires' to imitate a given model? Either this would lead to a regress, or it would be necessary to say that this 'choice' is not the result of mimetic desire. In other words, Girard's utilization of the notion of imitation excludes the possibility of the following sort: agent X *desires* the state of affairs S, where S is 'X imitates only agent Y's desires'. Now Girard does not in fact believe that a model or mediator is necessary for the desiring subject to make a 'choice' of a model, for no such 'choice' is made *by the subject*. Rather, subjectivity and desire are effects of a deeper and more spontaneous level of reality. The 'subject' always has a model already, which is why Girard speaks of an 'interdividual psychology', one in which there is no individual subject before relations of mimicry. Thus we see that Girard's theory of mimetic action indeed takes as its starting point the kind of 'automatic' or 'spontaneous' and irreflective imitation that Durkheim discussed.

Although Girard has never explicitly pronounced his views on the philosophy of mind, it should be clear that his rejection of the romantic view of the self implies a critique of all psychologies in which the individual consciousness is conceived as an autonomous and wholly reflexive source of teleological action. Desire is not based upon reasoned convictions, nor is it a matter of deliberative choice. What remains to be developed, however, within this theory is a conception of the conditions under which mimesis can engender significant degrees of 'autonomy' and 'responsibility', where these terms do not designate myths of pure spontaneity, absolute reflexivity, and metaphysical freedom. In other words, it should be possible to develop a model in which the mimetic propensity allows the constitution, through the introjection of certain concepts and norms, of a certain type of agent whose desires and decisions bear little relation to the mimetic enslavement to some individual human mediator. The model in question, then, would be of a mimetic subject capable of qualitative choices, a subject capable of learning. In fairness to Girard, it should be noted that the difficulty of arriving at such a model is anything but a problem found only in his work.[37]

Girard claims that his fundamental variety of mimesis is 'appropriative'. This means that the subject of desire, while copying a model's aims or goals, also desires to make this object of desire his or her own *proper* and unique possession. Girard contends that rivalry will typically ensue as a result of the reciprocal imitation in which two or more agents 'feed' each other's desires for some object. A sharing of the object would seem to be excluded from the nature of the 'propensity', for the rivalry is not the result of any contingent object's real scarcity. In his earlier, more 'metaphysical' terminology, Girard clarified this by saying that the subject desired the 'being' of the mediator, and that the desire to copy was also a desire to supplant.[38]

An analogous pattern remains implicit in the structure of his later views of this fundamental type of mimesis. 'Appropriative' does not mean only 'appetitive', and it still entails that the subject of imitative desire seeks to replace the model. The original mimesis is emulation, not co-operation. It is for this very reason that this precultural process of imitation generates a highly unstable situation within the hominoid group, a situation where the instinctual checks on intraspecific violence (dominance/submission patterns) are loosened and replaced by a 'propensity' for rivalry and violence.

In this manner Girard sets the scene for his culture-producing events, a crisis of violence followed by an equally mimetic convergence upon the pattern of 'scapegoating', or more generally, the pattern of the 'one and the many'. In this first 'non-instinctual' moment of attention, the group perceives its victim as the source of order and unanimity. Within this configuration, the 'many' can indeed share the same 'desire', perhaps because their 'objects' (which are beliefs and practices as well as material objects) are now tinged with the symbolic meanings of the sacred. What the 'many' share, then, is their common difference from the 'object', a difference that diminishes or even precludes the possibility of their engaging in an appropriative rivalry over the object. Thus rivalry is 'wired into' the system of appropriative mimesis – the mimesis that Girard says is 'most fundamental' – yet its system of interaction also contains a partial solution to rivalry, a violent basis for co-operation.

Girard contrasts this sort of model of human (and protohuman) action to the philosophical tradition's tendency to work with an isolated subject whose mimesis engages him largely in an immediate cognitive relation with an external 'reality'. Clearly, in Girard's view, this kind of asocial and 'disinterested' cognition of reality is probably the *least* fundamental variety of 'imitation'. Girard shares with the pragmatic tradition, as well as with psychoanalysis, a tendency to reinscribe descriptions of such 'cognition' within the network of 'interests', 'drives', or 'desires' within which they arise, and where they are most frequently overdetermined by these other sorts of relations. The desire 'to know', along with the love of 'sophia', would be imitated, not spontaneous or original forms of human endeavour. Yet clearly the possibility of the emergence of knowledge requires that we envision how 'accurate cognition' became the object of a desire which, however 'mimetic' it may have been, did not prohibit its realization.

Now Girard grants that within sacrificial cultures there was already a certain development along these lines relating to the investigation of physical reality. What mimesis cannot fully come to know, however, is its own workings. Why? Girard admits that the individual subject can acquire large amounts of knowledge about the nature of its own *former* imitations; the great texts show us the moments of 'disillusionment' when one mediator, revealed not to be the source of all truth and spontaneity, is replaced by another, and it is at such moments that the character may begin to have an inkling about the nature of his own illusions. Yet the myth that some other model truly possesses the sacred difference may persist.[39] It is this myth, and its ultimate sources, that must be revealed for the full truth of mimesis to become available to the subject. At the level of the individual subject, and within the context of modernity, this would mean the end of the slavish relation to human mediators and the ambivalent and violent emotions this form of mimesis inspires. In regard to social and cultural history, it would be a matter of giving the lie to the mythical differences mimetic interactions have generated, starting with the stereotypical symbols that serve to label victims of persecution – symbols Girard categorizes rigorously in *Le Bouc émissaire*.[40]

As I have already suggested, it seems incorrect to me to pretend that any *total* demystification has in fact already occurred; it seems more accurate to say that the sacrificial illusions have only been displaced in the modern world, which means that they certainly persist and maintain a certain efficacity but also that there has been a certain, albeit localized, progress away from them. Consequently it seems useless to look for the divine, social, or psychological conditions that are supposed to have made a total revelation possible. It seems to me that such a search is motivated by a reliance on the dubious assumption that societies exist as a 'totality' – by which is meant a single, unified, interlocking system where each part is rigorously subordinated to the order of the whole. To the extent that the sociologist describes a humanity governed totally by a single social mechanism and hence cast into error, it is difficult for him to explain how the error was ever discovered. Yet no one has truly demonstrated that some totalizing mechanism governs the history of the interaction between cultures; nor is there good reason to think that the individual's relation to the group is that of the purely logical model of the relation between part and whole. To believe in the existence of a transcendental *arche* is the very essence of archaic thought, which has its vestiges in any epistemology that seeks to subordinate the complexity of thought, nature, and culture to a single system of determinant laws.

The naturalist attitude in sociology perpetuates the logic of the sacred by erecting symbols of totality where no such total system of laws has ever rigorously been established. This kind of scientism rejoins myth when it imposes a realm of necessity, expelling chance, creativity, and individual autonomy, all of which could have a place in a conception of the 'nature' of society as *natura naturans*. In this sense mankind's 'education', which is clearly incomplete, could very well have been a process in which mimetic interactions have contributed to the development of cognitive capacities leading to local 'revelations', but not to any definitive and absolute endpoint. These capacities, it should be added, often remain harnessed to the most 'archaic' impulses, so that it is not always obvious that their development is necessarily an element of the real demystification that is lacking.[41] In this regard Girard's thinking surpasses by far that of Durkheim, for Girard never encourages us, in the name of a positivist value-neutrality, to treat social facts as mere things. Girard never loses sight of the fact that the ultimate goal of a 'truly human' science is a knowledge that gives the lie to the 'reasons' with which we justify our violence. The demystification of this spurious reason is a crucial activity, and in exhorting us to choose to abandon the gods of violence Girard is surely addressing himself, at least implicitly, to our potential for a more perfect reason, a reason that has as its goal a genuine freedom from violence and servitude.

Fetishism and Form: Erotic and Economic Disorder in Literature

ANDREW FEENBERG

> In a sort of way, it is with man as with commodities. Since he comes into the world neither with a looking glass in his hand, nor as a Fichtian philosopher, to whom 'I am I' is sufficient, man first sees and recognizes himself in other men. Peter only establishes his own identity as a man by first comparing himself with Paul as being of like kind. And thereby Paul, just as he stands in his Pauline personality, becomes to Peter the type of the genus homo.
>
> Karl Marx, *Capital*

> The laws of the capitalist free market, like those of eroticism, arise from underground pride.
>
> René Girard, *Dostoïevski*

The work of René Girard would seem to be quite remote from the concerns of Marx, and yet on two independent occasions his theory of mediated desire has inspired Marxists to rethink important problems in the fields of literary criticism and economics. Lucien Goldmann initiated the first of these encounters between Girard's thought and Marxism twenty years ago in an article comparing Girard's theory of the novel with that of the early Lukács.[1]

Goldmann pointed out the similarity between Girard's theory of mediated desire and the theory of the 'degradation' of values in Lukács' pre-Marxist *Theory of the Novel*.[2] Goldmann attempted to explain the underlying unity of these two approaches to the novel in terms of the Marxist category of commodity fetishism. He argued that there is a 'rigorous homology' between the position of 'authentic values' in the novel and the position of use values on the market: both become 'implicit' as they are subordinated to exchange value. The individual who attempts to pursue authentic values in a world where they have become inaccessible is possessed by a demon and lives by illusions that bring about his destruction. Yet his struggle indicates by implication what has been lost in the reification of society. Such an individual is a 'problematic hero' because of the contradictions between his aspirations, their expression and society. According to Goldmann, it is the interposition of a debased social relation between the individuals and the objects of their desires that generates the universe of inauthenticity described by Girard and Lukács.

Goldmann's comparison is intriguing, but not entirely persuasive. The fetishistic substitution of exchange value for use value can be related to the Lukácsian idea of 'degradation' and to Girard's concept of 'mediation', but it is identical with neither. In Lukács' theory the 'problematic hero' of the novel is engaged in a degraded search for authentic values in a degraded world. The market is one, but not the only structure corresponding to Lukács' image of the novelistic world as a dead 'second nature' against which the hero struggles for meaning and value. The mediation of use values by exchange values is of a different kind from Girardian mediation, which describes the relations of rivalry of two individuals who unconsciously designate each other's objects of desire in a competition based on mutual imitation and jealousy. Furthermore, there is something distinctly naïve about Goldmann's identification of use value with authenticity in the context of a discussion of Girard, for whom the very category of use value is subject to a radical critique.[3]

These problems may explain why Goldmann's theory had little impact on the study of the novel and none at all on the second encounter between Marxism and Girard to which I now want to turn. Quite recently, Girard's writings have come to the attention of a number of French economists – some of them Marxists – with surprising results. No doubt this encounter could not take place until Girard himself had developed the theory of sacrifice that supplies the bridge between his theory of desire and his reinterpretation of the human sciences.[4] Then it became apparent that Girard's work had suggestive implications for economics, specifically for the theory of conspicuous consumption and the Marxist theory of monetary exchange.

It is as a theoretician of *desire* that Girard can interest economists who have become sceptical of utilitarian attempts to found economics in need. Girard's theory of mimesis provides the basis for a critique of substantialist illusions in economics because it offers an alternative to the conventional notion that desire is a direct relation to something desirable in objects. He proposes instead a theory of 'triangular' desire which reduces all object relations to prior social relations of competition and imitation. This position supports a rejection of three of the bases of traditional economic philosophy: the belief that scarcity is a natural phenomenon, the belief that consumer behaviour can be derived from competition for a falsely hypostatized substance called 'prestige', and the belief that prices 'represent' another hypostatized substance such as utility or labour.[5]

In *La Violence de la monnaie*, Aglietta and Orléan follow Girard in suggesting that the basic relation of exchange can be interpreted as a conflict of 'doubles', each mediating the desire of the Other. Like Goldmann, they see a connection between Girard's theory of mimetic desire and the Marxian theory of commodity fetishism.[6] In their theory, the market takes the place of the sacred in modern life as the chief institutional mechanism stabilizing the otherwise explosive conflicts of desiring subjects. But the identification and critique of theological residues in apparently secular institutions was precisely the basis of the theory of alienation Marx learned from Feuerbach and refined in his later work. His application of the term 'fetishism' to the economic problem of the commodity was no accident. Thus Goldmann's attempt to link Girard and Marx is not so arbitrary as it may at first seem.

Girard's literary theory has inspired a reflection on economics, and on precisely that aspect of economics which, for Goldmann, explained the structural similarity of the theories of the novel of Girard and Lukács. But if economic exchange is in principle identical with mimesis, which in turn elucidates the structure of novelistic desire, are we not justified in pursuing Goldmann's insight into the relation of fetishism and literary form? Perhaps the economic reflections inspired by Girard's theory can contribute to concretizing that insight and render it fruitful for the study of literary texts.

The aim of this paper is to call attention to the critical implications of the economic application of Girard's work. To that end I propose to re-examine several texts, one of which Girard himself discussed before the development of his theory of sacrifice and its application to economics. The texts I have chosen include two stories by Borges and Dostoevsky's short novel, *The Gambler*. I will show that the curious intermingling of economic and erotic relations in these works can be understood from the standpoint of a mimetic theory of fetishism, such as that proposed by Aglietta and Orléan. From this standpoint it is also possible to extend considerably Girard's original analysis of the Dostoevsky text, and the new analysis in turn suggests a new interpretation of Goldmann's comparison of Girard and Lukács.

Borges wrote two stories, called 'The Zahir' and 'The Aleph', which show the influence of H. G. Wells' 'The Crystal Egg.'[7] Curiously, when juxtaposed these titles represent a visible figure of the infinite. In fact, Borges informs us that '*Zahir* in Arabic means 'notorious', 'visible'; in this sense it is one of the ninety-nine names of God . . .';[8] and 'Aleph' is, of course, the mathematical sign for 'infinity'.

These two stories of Borges resemble drafts of a single story, and somehow, retrospectively, they suggest that Wells too was working towards the production of the same ultimate text. In each of Borges' versions there is a first-person narrator in love with a dead woman who was always indifferent to him, and fascinated by a fetishistic object which has the attributes of infinity. In 'The Zahir', this object is finally revealed to us as . . . money. The story can be considered as a fantastic reflection on the paradoxes of the marketplace and the mysterious power of symbols. Borges' story offers a remarkable illustration of Aglietta and Orléan's thesis concerning the sacred character of money. A careful reading of his tale can liberate us from the assumption that *we know what money is* when we encounter it in fiction.

Wells' story does not at first suggest such metaphysical complexities. It concerns a 'crystal egg' within which it is possible to see a view of Mars, and through which, presumably, Martian observers see earth. Mr Cave, the antiquarian owner of the crystal egg, becomes obsessed with it (it becomes 'the most real thing in his existence'[9]), and eventually dies with a smile on his face holding the egg in his hands. After his death the egg is mysteriously lost.

In constructing his own stories out of the material supplied by Wells, Borges dropped the Martian element and concentrated instead on the implicit sacred significance of a ubiquitous object that serves as a mysterious medium, and which becomes an obsessive focus of attention for its owner.

The 'Aleph', in the story of that name, is 'the place where all places in the universe can be found together, without confusion, seen from every angle.'[10] The narrator learns of its existence from Carlos Daneri, the cousin of his friend Beatriz Viterbo, whom he loved hopelessly in her lifetime and to whose memory he has dedicated himself. Daneri, it transpires, is writing an immense and silly poem in which he attempts to express the experience of the Aleph. At the end of the story it turns out that this cousin is the narrator's successful competitor in both literature and love, and his triumph is somehow connected to his secret knowledge of the Aleph.

The narrator concludes the tale of his discomfiture with some speculations on the word 'Aleph' which, in its cabalistic application, signifies 'pure and unlimited divinity', while in its mathematic usage it signifies the transfinite numbers 'in which the whole is no larger than one of the parts'.[11] The Aleph, like the crystal egg, contains a mysterious spatial representation that defies ordinary logic. Its possessor is possessed by it and elevated above his fellows. The Aleph is a figure of God inexplicably revealing Himself to the narrator's triumphant double.

'The Zahir' covers much the same ground as 'The Aleph' in a still more revealing way. The narrator of 'The Zahir', 'Borges', received this commonplace Argentine coin in change in a bistro he entered after leaving the funeral of a woman he confesses to having loved long ago, 'moved by that most sincere of Argentinian passions, snobbery'.[12] Teodelina Villar was an elegant and disdainful fashion plate whose ever-changing image once adorned innumerable advertisements for creams and cars. The narrator describes her devotion to fashion as a kind of religion: 'She was in search of the Absolute, like Flaubert; only hers was an Absolute of a moment's duration.'[13] In his last glimpse of her corpse, the narrator sees her face again as it was when he loved her, frozen once and for all in the cold mask of perfect indifference and snobbery.

Who can doubt that the old love story, were it told, would be the record of Borges' unrequited passion? But instead of the expected romance we are offered a bizarre variant on the crystal egg theme, a narrative of obsession with a common coin, a 'Zahir'.

The narrator's obsession is apparently unmotivated. The coin seems perfectly ordinary and yet, even after he has spent it, his thoughts return to it again and again until finally it blots out the rest of his existence. Eventually, he finds a book which explains his plight. The book recounts the history of the various 'Zahirs' of times past, objects which completely absorb the consciousness of those who look on them. The Zahir is typically expelled from society, but not before it has found victims. Once a blind man of the Surakarta Mosque was the Zahir, but he was stoned by the faithful; once it was a copper astrolabe thrown into the sea by order of the King of Persia, 'lest men forget the universe'.[14] Although everything can become a Zahir, God in his mercy creates only one at a time.

The narrator observes that the Zahir represents a radical simplification of existence: from a multitude and variety of sensations, he is passing to a single one: 'Whatever is not the Zahir comes to me fragmentarily, as if from a great distance . . .'[15] He seeks consolation in the thought that the secret of the entire universe may be revealed in a flower; every thing is a 'symbolic mirror' of the whole, even the Zahir.[16] His last hope, inspired by a certain *Libro de Cosas que se ignoran*, is that by sheer concentration of awareness he will pass beyond the Zahir itself to the ultimate substance that underlies it: 'perhaps behind the coin I shall find God'.[17]

The interpretative problem posed by these stories consists in finding the connection between the parallel erotic and metaphysical fascinations of the characters. In 'The Aleph' this problem is obscured by the doubling of the subject and the allocation of some important elements of the structure to a third person in the story. 'The Zahir' is on the contrary crystal clear: in it the infinity of consciousness returns to the alienated subject as an infinite destructive power first in the form of the beloved and then far more radically as a paradoxical monetary obsession which has nothing to do with economic gain and in which nevertheless money plays a peculiarly appropriate role.

'The Zahir' is a story about fascination, represented in various degrees and kinds but always as an emblem of overpowering objectivity very much along the lines of Sartre's remarkable description:

> In fascination . . . the knower is absolutely nothing but a pure negation; he does not find or recover himself anywhere – he is *not*. The only qualification which he can support is that he *is not* precisely this particular fascinating object. In fascination there is nothing more than a gigantic object in a desert world. Yet the fascinated intuition is in no way a *fusion* with the object. In fact the condition necessary for the existence of fascination is that the object be raised in absolute relief on a background of emptiness; that is, I am precisely the immediate negation of the object and nothing but that.[18]

The narrator, Borges, is predisposed to fascination, and Teodelina was for him just such a fascinating object. His enslavement to her is barely hinted at in the reference to a love based on snobbery. In what does this love consist? Borges gives us little evidence, but what we have speaks plainly. Teodelina is a worshipper of the God Fashion; her eyes are always turned away from Borges towards Paris and Hollywood. Teodelina's whole activity consists in becoming a perfect object: that is to say, in the exercise of the fascinating power of the fashionable model of the moment. As a snob, Borges is sensitive to her appeal.

The relationship is not so one-sided as it may seem. The seductive power of Teodelina is no accident but derives from her struggle to constitute herself as a fascinating object. Sartre notes that fascination is 'the non-thetic consciousness of being *nothing* in the presence of being. Seduction aims at producing in the Other the consciousness of his state of nothingness as he confronts the seductive object . . . To accomplish this I constitute myself as a meaningful object.'[19] Fashion is the code through which Teodelina so constitutes herself. Her ultimate triumph is to enter the code as a model in her own right, to become an advertising image. Thereupon she withdraws from the world to avoid making concessions and competing 'with giddy little nobodies'.[20]

Despite her successes, Teodelina's life is a profound failure. She too is the victim of a fascination that brings no satisfaction, that can never be fusion with the object but only a 'consciousness of [her] state of nothingness'. 'Her life was exemplary, yet she was ravaged unremittingly by an inner despair. She was forever experimenting with new metamorphoses, as though trying to get away from herself.'[21]

These worldly phenomena of fascination with fashion and the fashionable form a triangle of desire. Teodelina is both object and mediator for Borges the snob. She is object in so far as she is the model of his rivals, the readers of the fashionable reviews in which her picture appears. In this respect Teodelina is like any other 'star' of modern consumer society. She is offered to society as an idealized model, a lesson in desire. Her admirers participate in a consumer culture in which possession of Teodelina's attributes can be immediately decoded by others as the sign of desirability. The skilled consumer knows how to free herself in time from the fascination with Teodelina's image while carrying away the lesson:

> In the world of commodities, the imitation of the Other's desire does not necessarily propel the Subject headlong towards the obstacle which serves as his model. Open conflict can be avoided by a simple lateral shift. To avoid experiencing the torments of desire, it is enough for the Subject to find the EQUIVALENT of the object possessed or desired by the Other.[22]

In her social function Teodelina is a currency, a common coin in the transactions of desire, not an active party to the rivalries and loves she inhabits anonymously. Teodelina is a medium of erotic exchange and as such has in principle no 'use value' in the sexual marketplace.

However, Borges knows Teodelina personally. Thus for him, her status as star belongs to her personally. Through her total absorption in this status she becomes a mediator to Borges, who is fascinated by her fascination with her own objectivity. It is not her beauty that interests him, but her relation to an ideal of perfection which he conceives as a kind of religion. This second-order fascination corresponds to a sense of self which is the secret inner world of symbols, a religious world, a fetishistic world, always pointing beyond towards a source in the absolute. It is this inwardness of symbols which fascinates Borges. The form of his love for Teodelina thus adumbrates the disorder represented by his fascination with the Zahir, through which he hopes to reach the absolute.

The narrator's terminal fascination is with a piece of money, a still more universal equivalent than his beloved's face, and certainly a far colder object than the most heartless coquette. The universality of money is clearly its attraction, making it an ideal 'Zahir'. It can stand for everything and yet it is nothing in itself, just a thin piece of metal with a few scratches to distinguish it from other thin pieces of metal of the same value. The Zahir is like the Aleph in being virtually infinite. Both are the pure potentiality of everything and just for that reason neither has a content, a 'use value', in itself. Both represent the universe – the one in space, the other economically. The chief difference between them is one of viewpoint: we learn of the Aleph only indirectly and as a prop in a banal competition of doubles, whereas Borges places us directly inside the consciousness of the Zahir's victim.

The relation between the Aleph's ubiquity and God is clear enough, but the monetary metaphor to the divinity is more subtle. The paradoxical status of Teodelina as a goddess of desire placed beyond all human contact exactly describes the position of money in the fetishistic system of economic exchange. Aglietta and Orléan explain the peculiar position of money as a function of the primitive mimetic crisis in which the desires of the entire community are focused on a single object:

> Although this paroxysmic situation can lead to the destruction of the community, it also offers an escape: *the exclusion* of this object from the private sphere, its divinization or, in other words, its institutionalization . . . It is only because mimetic contagion makes possible this transcendence that society is able to free itself for a time from the destructive effects of violence.

> The 'monetary thing' provokes a respect and fear in the individuals which suggest the attitude of believers towards the divinity.[23]

In this description of the quasi-sacred character of money we recognize the Zahir, object of universal fascination and scapegoat expelled from the community 'lest men forget the universe'. However, the Zahir is not merely money, it is money gone mad, money that no longer plays its part as a medium of exchange but which has become the absolute object in itself, a sacrificed god returning for vengeance. Recognizable in this description is a particular form of monetary disorder, thesaurization, which converts the medium of exchange into an object of desire: 'Although money as a medium of exchange is a sign of life, its pursuit for its own sake in the accumulation of treasure is deadly.'[24]

The narrator of Borges' story cannot, of course, be described as economically interested in money. He is engaged in a kind of metaphysical thesaurization rather than in the ordinary accumulation of wealth. Similarly, it is difficult to believe that his passion for Teodelina was ever consummated. In both cases, the narrator is fixated on the sacred function of mediation and cannot pass beyond to what is mediated by the sacred. He cannot free himself from the intermediary in order to transact the business of living. His is a case of arrested circulation.

The theme proposed by Wells has undergone a remarkable transubstantiation in Borges. Wells' crystal egg can be in two places simultaneously, a curious feat no doubt, but one that still suggests naturalistic explanations. The Aleph carries the principle of the egg beyond all natural possibility to its logical conclusion by being everywhere in the universe simultaneously. However, the power of the Aleph is still relatively weak: it can be forgotten, because 'Our spirit is porous in the face of forgetfulness.'[25] The Zahir, finally, overcomes even forgetfulness: time, after all, is money. The Zahir not only represents the universe, as does the Aleph, it obliterates it. Money, which in principle can stand for anything at all, here actually replaces everything: 'the whole is no larger than one of the parts.'

These stories by Borges are particularly clear – because fantastical – expressions of the interaction between erotic and economic fetishism in literature. But a similar structure can be found beneath the 'realistic' surface of many novelistic works. Money, which seems to be part of the social background of the story, is often an object of demonic passions inexplicable in narrowly realistic terms. Dostoevsky's novella *The Gambler* is a particularly clear example of the non-economic relation to money in the novel.

The Gambler concerns the household of a spendthrift and profoundly humiliated General, who unwittingly transfers a great Russian estate into the hands of a pair of schemers. At the beginning of the story the estate still belongs to 'Granny', an imperious old lady whose anxiously awaited demise forms the background to the intrigue. The General has lost his own money and that of his children, and he cowers before Granny, before the Count de Grieux, to whom all his own estates are mortgaged, and before Mlle Blanche, the *grue* with whom he is desperately in love. It is clear that as soon as the General inherits, all his wealth will be confiscated by these two parasites.

There are two individuals in the General's household who have a certain independence and strength of character. They are his stepdaughter, Polina, and the hero, Alexey, an impoverished nobleman who serves in the humiliating position of tutor – *outchitel* – to the General's children. Polina has been de Grieux's mistress, a fact which torments her because de Grieux offered her money in a parting gesture she cannot forgive. Alexey's abject passion for Polina masquerades at times as a tragicomic attempt at chivalry. Alexey is determined to win immense sums at roulette, convinced that this will make a man of him, gaining him the respect and, more importantly, the self-respect he requires to be worthy of Polina.

In *The Gambler*, more than in most novels, money is an obsessive object of interest literally from the first page to the last. Its ubiquity receives apparently realistic explanations: the hero is poor, his employer is bankrupt, and so on. However, behind this façade of ordinary financial exigency, the reader soon detects another more basic relationship to money: money is required not so much to buy things as to settle power struggles between lovers. Erotic and economic relations are inextricably intertwined.

Girard's analysis of the story is based on 'l'identité secrète de l'érotisme et du jeu'. [26] He shows how the struggles for domination between lovers are mirrored precisely in the imaginary struggle of the gambler with the roulette wheel. In the psychological underground of the doubles, victory is assured to the individual capable of hiding his desires behind a veil of proud self-sufficiency. The idolator can become the idol if only he can hide his passion. Applied to gambling, this mentality yields a 'system' which 'consists in extending to the domain of physical nature the influence which self-mastery is able to exercise in the underground world'.[27] Alexey lives by these rules and is destroyed by them.

Girard's analysis illuminates the love affair between Alexey and Polina and helps us understand its bizarre reversals and its relationship to gambling. However, something important is missing: an account of the role in the story of the strictly economic relationship to money. For *The Gambler* cannot be understood by focusing exclusively on the demonic triangle formed by these two principal characters and the roulette wheel. The story takes place in Germany, identified contemptuously by Alexey as the epitome of the capitalist spirit, and it contains characters like de Grieux and Mlle Blanche who are engaged in quite ordinary money-grubbing. The heroic quality of Alexey and Polina stems from their refusal of the commercial ethic which surrounds them. It is in distinguishing themselves from what Lukács called 'the world' that they achieve the status of 'problematic' characters possessed by an 'ideal'.[28]

A careful examination of the story reveals the importance of this theme. The confusion of the erotic and economic realms can be traced in the structure of all the relationships: each couple is made up of one party for whom it is an economic exchange, while the other perceives it as a passionate relation of doubles. The resulting confusion of economic and erotic orders leads inexorably to catastrophe. It is necessary to sketch the variety of ways in which the relationships are structured by the conflict of economic and erotic motives.

Mlle Blanche is a professional coquette in search of a price for her favours. She is a hard bargainer, like a peasant seeking a good price for his cow, and does not hesitate to point out the (exaggerated) value of what she has to offer. Her coquetry consists in a narcissistic self-absorption which signifies her 'object' as desirable to the General. From her standpoint, the General is a buyer on the marketplace. However, he is no ordinary buyer; he is passionately and miserably in love, and he suffers terribly because his beloved is a commodity which he must buy or see sold to another. To make matters worse, his fate is contingent on a chance event, Granny's inheritance, and this drives him literally crazy with frustration and helplessness. And, since the General is truly in love, he is in no position to bargain for Mlle Blanche's favours. She is literally 'everything' for him and sets her own price, essentially his entire fortune.

The relationship has a pathetic quality because while the General is enslaved by the laws of desire, Mlle Blanche relates to him as a prudent *petit bourgeois*, trading on her person while she is young and attractive to constitute a capital to protect herself in old age when she will no longer have anything to sell. Characteristically, she does not gamble herself but loans money to gamblers. The affair has a sad end: by the time the General can afford her he has been reduced to a shadow of himself and soon dies, leaving behind a prosperous widow.

Polina's case is more complex. The General wanted to buy only what he needed, while Polina wants something much more difficult: to prove that she herself is beyond all price.

Polina has been de Grieux's mistress, but their relations were infected by a mutual suspicion of mercenary afterthoughts. De Grieux fears that Polina intends to trade her love for the mortgaged estate of her stepfather, the General, in which her own property has long since been confounded. Polina is appalled at de Grieux's suspicion, which seems to signify her as a mere commercial object. She is a romantic young woman who can imagine nothing more degrading than this misinterpretation of her passion. She therefore withdraws in her pride, becomes cold and indifferent to de Grieux, and attempts to escape the role in which he has cast her.

This escape is finally blocked by a diabolical gesture: de Grieux offers her a way of recovering her own money from the wreckage of the General's estate. The sum involved is 50,000 francs, precisely the amount of money Mlle Blanche will later demand of Alexey for a month's delights in Paris. Polina now knows her price and a first exchange has been completed, that of her favours for de Grieux's money.

The humiliation she experiences drives her into Alexey's arms. He is poor and can apparently offer her nothing for her love. By giving herself to him she once again signifies herself as beyond price, as a creature of passion rather than calculation – as a person, in short, rather than a commodity. But this is not enough for Polina. She wants to fling de Grieux's money in his face to prove that she is not for sale and that their earlier relations were in no sense a commercial transaction.

Once Polina yields to Alexey, the sadomasochistic relationship of doubles in which they are locked is reversed. Alexey immediately interprets his victory over her as the beginning of a run of gambling luck and rushes from her side to the roulette tables, where he wins more than enough money to cancel her obligation to de Grieux. But when he offers her the money she needs, she interprets his chivalrous gesture as a second purchase. She gives herself to him in hatred, and throws the sum in his face as previously she had proposed to throw it in the face of de Grieux. Polina cannot use Alexey to escape the trap that has been laid for her: in her eyes he has simply become another purchaser. Her autonomy as a person has been irreversibly alienated on the market.

Alexey's own case is even stranger than Polina's. He has no debts, desires nothing that can be bought with money, and feels contempt for those who work and save. He has no conception of working for a living himself, and says: that 'I don't look upon myself as something subordinate to capital and necessary to it.'[29] Until she comes to him, Polina is the sole object of his desires. Afterwards, he can think only of gambling. Love and gambling are identical in principle for him, victory in one promising victory in the other. In both domains he is convinced that self-conquest is the key to success. He relates to the gambling table as he wishes he could relate to a cold and indifferent beloved. To expose one's hand is to lose. Only a coldness surpassing that of the spinning ball can conquer the roulette wheel, or the beautiful Polina.

Alexey's essential masochism is revealed in his treatment of Polina. At the beginning of the story, when she is cold and distant, he says to her: 'I lose all self-respect in your presence, and I don't care.'[30] After she yields, his love for her wanes while gambling obsesses him completely. Puzzled, he comments: 'from the very moment when I reached the gambling tables the previous evening and began winning a pile of money, my love had retreated, so to speak, into the background'.[31] Polina's defeat in the struggle of the doubles removes her as an obstacle from Alexey's path and by the same token also removes her as an object of desire:

> All that is required for Polina to lose her prestige in the eyes of the *outchitel* is that she reveal her vulnerability. The empress becomes the slave and vice versa. This is why the *outchitel*, who was waiting for the 'right moment', decides to gamble.[32]

The roulette wheel offers a less yielding obstacle than even the most sadistic of lovers. 'Mimetic desire begins by transforming models into obstacles; it ends up by transforming obstacles into models.'[33]

This analysis shows the extent to which economic and erotic relations are precisely *not* identical in the novel itself, but only in the minds of certain of the characters. In fact the novel displays four variants on an underlying structure of conflicts between economic and erotic agents. They are distinguished as buyer and seller on the one side, sadist and masochist on the other, as follows. The relationship of Mlle Blanche and the General represents a seller attached to a masochist. The relationship of de Grieux and Polina represents a buyer attached to a sadist. The relationship of Alexey and Polina combines these two forms in an impossible hybrid: the masochistic Alexey is rejected as such by the sadist, Polina, who cannot accept the reversal in their relations of dominance implied by Alexey's sudden offer of money. Polina can be won neither by love nor by purchase. Alexey's relation to the roulette wheel, finally, represents the general form of the whole enterprise of extracting erotic power from economic relations and vice versa.

Why should the mixing of economic and erotic orders of desire produce such radical disorder? The answer lies in the obscure origins of the one system of exchange in the other, as is made clear in Aglietta and Orléan's analysis of the Marxian theory of monetary exchange in terms of Girard's mimetic theory of desire. The authors note the puzzling complexity of Marx's explanation of barter, which is usually seen as a self-explanatory exchange for mutual benefit. They argue that Marx's theory becomes comprehensible if exchange is seen as arising from an original relation of doubles. On these terms, the bizarre events of Dostoevsky's story may be explained as boundary problems in the transition between the two forms of relationship.

Barter, according to Marx, is the elementary form of value. Marx treats this form as a dialectical contradiction, because in it each bartered good must serve as both a particular use value offered for trade and as a measure of the value of the good for which it is exchanged. The contradiction seems purely formal until the relation of the barterers is interpreted as a relation of doubles. Then it becomes apparent that the split between use value and exchange value, and the fact that they can be expressed only in a relation between two distinct commodities, reflects an underlying social tension. This tension, by the way, is quite real and haunts all primitive societies, obliging them to ritualize exchange in elaborate ways that are often insufficient to prevent outbreaks of violence.

Considered as a relation of doubles, barter is complicated by the fact that each commodity can enter the exchange process only in so far as it is perceived as a use value by an eventual buyer. This perception in turn depends on that buyer taking the owner for a model/rival who designates an object as desirable and erects an obstacle to its possession in the form of a price. But the buyer can meet that price and overcome that obstacle only through himself serving as model/rival for the seller, designating for him another commodity in his (the buyer's) possession as a use value and erecting once again an obstacle in the form of a price. The roles of buyer and seller, which seem complementary in purely economic terms, in fact embrace incompatible positions of desire. To play both roles, the individuals must be at the same time both model and imitator for each other. But this is precisely the double bind of double mediation in Girard's theory of mimetic desire.

As a measure of value money resolves the contradiction, or at least permits it to be played out in a relatively pacific form. If the value of each good can be expressed in terms of a third object, money, publicly instituted as a measure, then the goods involved in the exchange need not each serve as the measure of the other. The interactions of the doubles is now indirect, socially mediated; hence they need not establish privately the intrinsic value of the commodities they exchange:

> The existence of a nominal currency enables each private subject to define himself in relation to society as a whole, represented as a monetary space, by naming a price in terms of a definite number of monetary units. In practical terms, this means that his desire for Being achieves expression in an asking price for the totality of his possessions, through which he seeks recognition from others.[34]

The difference between barter and sale reflects the difference between passion and monetary exchange. Erotic doubles are engaged in a relationship which is formally homologous with the relationship of barter described above. Each offers the other a unique value that can be measured only by the other's choice. The contradiction in the relationship is also the same: a happy resolution would require that each serve simultaneously as model and disciple, as master and slave. But the attempt to resolve this contradiction through the mediation of money will not work in the erotic sphere as it does in the economy. Chaos results from the interposition of a public medium of exchange between the doubles and what they offer each other in love.

Where a price is set, distance is created and, in the economic domain, a way is opened to relaxing the conflict of the doubles. But such a gesture is incomprehensible or offensive to a lover completely engaged in the struggle of doubles. Where the one offers passion for passion, self for self, the other brings in the entire society as potential bidders in a public auction of the soul. The passionate party to the relationship cannot but interpret this as a sadistic gesture, and so the passage from erotic to economic exchange is blocked.

The General responds to such a gesture masochistically: he is unable to haggle over price, and so the 'sale' of Mlle Blanche turns into something quite different because of the inability of the buyer to impose the market discipline that correlates logically with the setting of price by a seller. Polina is a sadistic character, and her response to the offer of money is hatred and rage. She interprets the attempt to monetize her relationship with de Grieux as an expression of his unconquerable pride, a victorious strategem in a struggle for domination. What appears from one viewpoint as a transaction appears from the other as an offence.

Alexey's relationship to gambling has a similar contradictory character. Like the narrator of 'The Zahir'. Alexey is involved with money not as a medium of exchange, but as a sacred object. He does not perceive money as an intermediary between himself and goods, but rather as an idol and a sign. He seeks not to be rich but to be blessed by fortune, and especially to be seen as such:

> No, it was not money that I wanted. All that I wanted was that the next day . . . they might be all talking about me, repeating my story, wondering at me, admiring me, praising me, and doing homage to my new success.[35]

Economically considered, gambling is a business, a simulacrum of capitalist investment. But gambling is precisely not a business for gamblers: it is an erotic relationship to money, the ultimate reification of the challenge of the doubles.

The Gambler is no doubt a novella rather than a novel because the logic of gambling does not lend itself to extensive treatment. The typical novelistic hero is engaged in action on a larger scale, an economic or personal struggle entwined with erotic passions revealing a broad social canvas. Yet Dostoevsky's short novel is emblematic of these wider perspectives and encapsulates the struggle of individual and society in a particularly transparent form.

To understand fully this emblematic character of the text it is necessary to return to the considerations from which we began: the relation of novelistic form to capitalist society. Lucien Goldmann, it will be recalled, suggested that they are structurally homologous. It is this homology which, for Goldmann, explains Lukács' theory of the novel as a degraded search for authentic values in a degraded world.

In an interesting article on *The Theory of the Novel*, Ferenc Feher argues that Goldmann's thesis of a homology between novelistic form and market structure is most persuasive in pointing to the 'fortuitous' character of modern individuality both in literature and society. Capitalism destroys the organic communities that preceded it and the social differences on which they were based. Social status is no longer a destiny prior to individual experience but rather emerges from the encounters of free individuals, who circulate in society according to the laws of chance. In the novel, as in life, the individual has the task of converting these accidental circumstances into a destiny through the labour of building an identity. Feher writes that individuality is 'ambivalent' under capitalism, where it

> can mean two entirely different things: . . . that individuals realize themselves or fail to do so through the accidents of competition and struggle; but also . . . that an individual's place in a given order or class . . . is no longer a personal quality of his, but the result of his own activities.[36]

Chance is thus at the core of the modern experience of individuality.

What is typically missing in Marxist accounts such as Feher's is the connection between these changes in the social background of the novel, which make possible the literary representation of individual biography and the passionate erotic struggles which accompany the characters' social struggles like a fatal complication of existence. This connection can be made in terms of the parallel structure of fortuitous individuality and the Girardian mimetic crisis. The Girardian concept of modernity is also a passage towards social dedifferentiation, the destruction of social differences and the consequent descent of the mediator, which opens the field not only to ambition but also to the conflict of the doubles.

The Gambler thematizes these problems of fortuitous individuality directly and immediately. The absence of predetermined identity in which fortuitous individuality consists is simply the other side of chance as the reigning deity of social life. The hero rejects the arduous labour of self-creation; or rather he sees in the action of chance itself the imaginary sign of self-creation. He relates to chance as though it were not the opportunity but the means of self-affirmation. To maintain this confusion, he must treat chance as an adversary rather than an environment in which he moves. But for the hero all adversaries are erotic partners, and vice versa. The hero relates to an economic activity, gambling, as though it were an erotic relation of doubles.

The series of confusions hangs together. Success at gambling, like success at love, signifies the absolute value of self, singled out by its idol from all the others. At the same time success at gambling, like economic success, signifies the moral worth of a character which has known how to conquer itself and fortune.

The hero's struggle with chance is a kind of magical reflection, a way of establishing the quality of the inner void left by the absence of social differences. Like the lover engaged in a struggle for domination with his beloved, Alexey finds that his identity as master or slave becomes visible to him via the detour of roulette. By instilling personality into the reified obstacles to personal fulfilment, the hero hopes to meet those obstacles head-on and defeat them. But this personalization of reification leads to the loss of personality of the self, its gradual voiding of all inner substance. The hero is finally destroyed as a man by the very means through which he had hoped to prove his conquering nature. For Marx this is 'the contradiction', characteristic of capitalism, 'between the personification of objects and the representation of persons by things'.[37]

Although Goldmann suggested that Girard's theory could explain the degradation of the problematic hero's search for authentic values, he never worked out the connection. The analyses presented above offer several approaches to concretizing Goldmann's suggestion. The 'problematic' hero is the individual who confounds the erotic and economic domains, interpreting the socially mediated relations of the market as a personal struggle of doubles. The hero is the centre of the narration because, in a conformist business culture, only the representation of the explosive idolatry of the doubles can offer a living subject matter for literary representation. The dead world of the market forms the environment in which the hero struggles to prove himself. But he goes at it in a profoundly confused way, not in terms of the laws of the world – laws of conventional behaviour and economic gain – but rather in terms of the logic of erotic desire. The clash generates the novelistic universe, which embraces not only the realistic representation of society but also the hero's degraded aspiration for the absolute.

Voyage to the End of the Sciences of Man

JEAN-MARIE DOMENACH

(Translated by Mark R. Anspach)

René Girard has brought about an authentic reversal of categories by taking Christianity as the basis for his anthropology. Perhaps it is paradoxically modernity which, by pushing back religion, has created the space necessary for this scientific renewal of self-understanding and allowed us to become conscious of what we are experiencing. However, if Girard restitutes the unity between our culture and our religion, if he places the Christian West back in the centre of the world, it is not at all through a triumphant operation of restoration; it is rather through a *revision*, in conformity with the best tradition of a West which never ceases reworking its myths and thereby finds itself alone able to give meaning. Self-destruction engenders self-affirmation; Girard appears at the outer limit of Lévi-Strauss's nihilism. Thus from a well-trod digging site the archaeologist of the eleventh hour unearths the decisive tablet.

The sense is found in a direction that seems to demand taking leave of the senses: God's Covenant with a people, then His entering the human race in body and spirit, and finally, most implausibly yet, the death of His Son on the cross of slaves. It is to this madness, then, that reason, having completed its ravages, resorts in order to ground its saving hypothesis, the one that will give us at once meaning and hope, the one that will reunite intellect and love, the one that permits us to be, in a single motion, scientists and believers. Here we have a magnificent and unforeseen gift – too good, perhaps, to be accepted without caution and misgivings. Not because I yield in the slightest to that atmosphere of masochism in our culture which Girard is quite right to denounce, but because I wonder about the validity of this recourse to the inexplicable in order to explain everything. Have we actually reached the end of modernity, or its ultimate ploy in this return of religion from where we least expected it: out of the hollow opened beneath the foundations of the City by the death of God? 'The necessity of the kingdom of God becomes scientific' – I like this formula if only for the furore it is bound to provoke among scientists. But the effect it produces on believers is less clear. Can the believer hold for a scientific necessity that which is an object of faith and a requirement of conversion? Reason and faith, apparently reunited, are, I believe, uneasy bedfellows. Faith wonders what is left for it to do when everything it was seeking turns out to have been there within its grasp all along. An analogous problem has confronted Marxism: what should be done to make what is necessary come to pass?

To be sure, it is possible – the Fathers of the Church admitted it – to know the God of Jesus Christ through a rational operation: the absurdity of a world with no God leads to God, and one can conceive of reason's working in this way with faith. But with René Girard, it is a question of much more than that. First because he derives from Christianity a precise anthropological hypothesis, not just the consolidation of faith through a reflection on human existence; next because he claims that this hypothesis is itself revelatory of the revelation, unveiling the meaning of divine intervention itself. An audacious enterprise and one which in other times – in other cultures – would have been judged sacrilegious; I see in it rather a sign of the vitality of a culture which never hesitates to destroy its own acquisitions. But in so doing it must accept that other dissents be expressed, for the risk of such discoveries is that they be erected into a *Truth* which then refuses everything from which it arose: the casting of doubt, dialogue, the unbounded pursuit of research. In this itinerary philosophy must contribute without letting itself be intimidated. 'Girard is not a philosopher. For a philosopher to answer him can only lead to an impasse.'[1] As if philosophy were a speciality that need concern itself only with products elaborated by philosophers!

Equally unsupportable is modernity's claim to escape philosophy through science. That outflanking manoeuvre which Marx believed he had carried off against philosophy is now being tried out by Girard against theology, which is lying low, and against philosophy which, having given up more than half the battle to the sciences of man, also hardly dares venture out in the open. Now, a 'hypothesis' of universal ambition is a matter for philosophical as much as for scientific debate, and this sort of anthropological immunity which Girard's theory claims for itself, or which others claim for it, has got to end, if only for its own good, in order to stop an ominous crystallization into an ecclesiastical system. At the same time, the irritation Girard displays regarding Popperian epistemology[2] testifies to a disturbing ambivalence between a scientific and a philosophical position. In fact he occupies both positions, but without accepting the burdens that accompany either.

The first question needing discussion is to my mind that of origins. In the beginning there is *mimesis*. Girard is visibly ill at ease in the Garden of Eden,[3] even if Adam, Eve and the serpent offer him a perfect mimetic triangulation. But where does this act symbolizing refusal to follow the Good fit into his hypothesis? The problem posed so acutely for contemporary reflection by the preference willingly given to Evil has no place in an interpretation that makes *mimesis* a constraining mechanism. Why does this *mimesis* stay in the sacrificial path until the Passion offers it the chance to readjust its trajectory? Is it a matter of blindness due to sin? But what then is the nature of this sin, its nature that would predate and be more fundamental than *mimesis*?

It is remarkable that in his superb commentaries on scenes from the Old and New Testaments, Girard gives all the action to the mimetic mechanism and none to the liberty of the actors, which he occasionally mentions but never stresses.[4] This is doubtless because no freedom can exist without a certain consciousness, and this consciousness takes form only through a long historical process which, reaching its end, unveils that 'superior intelligence' which turns out to have been stored, we know not how, in the silos of humanity; for here, as with Lévi-Strauss, the problem of foundations is posed: who set up this mimetic mechanism, who stocked up these resources of consciousness which will progressively be liberated? To this problem Hayek will respond by sketching a sort of cultural evolutionism. For Girard it seems to be a matter not of a process of selection but of a slow labour of emergence of the spirit, for which we are indebted to the Paraclete.

Just how far does this mimetic nature resist the *metanoia*? It is its refractoriness, its opacity, which in Girard's view calls for divine intervention; but it survives the Incarnation, the Passion and the Resurrection since, even after Christ's reversal and dissolution of sacrifice, it is *mimesis* which, by orientating itself towards the evangelical love that abolishes hostility and violence, will lead to the reconciliation of humanity.

In this perspective the initiating and determining factor is indeed human nature and, in this nature, the active principle of *mimesis*. To this the believer will be able to object that such a history is dominated by man, not God – and by a man who has not received his liberty from God. It would be possible to sketch out an ultrastructuralist interpretation of Girard in so far as he goes much further than Lévi-Strauss by integrating God into the system's functioning – this interpretation is a caricature, I admit, but it touches on a difficulty already brought out by André Dumas in relation to sacrifice in the Old Testament:

> What is important for the sacrifice is not so much to be offered, which would open the door to perverse demonstrations of ever greater self-punishment, as to be accepted, which effectively opens the way to purification where once remorse and rancour dominated. [. . .] Substitutive sacrifice is the active symbol of a reconciliation proposed, and acceptable.[5]

Self-sacrifice and substitutive sacrifice thus bring into play both the sacrificer's freedom and that of the God to whom the sacrifice is offered . . . It seems to me that Dumas has raised here objections that deserve better than an allusive and disdainful response. They bear, in fact, on a vision of the relation between man and God – a God relegated to the role of spectator to history:

> God [in Girard's hypothesis] has totally transmitted His divine being to human practice. There seems therefore not to be any divine exteriority, either meaningful or decisive, outside of the new ethic men adopt following Christ.

This dissociation is doubtless tied to the univocal nature of an explanation which submits the individual to a mechanism whose crushing weight brings with it in turn the idealism of the goal and of the techniques assigned to temporal salvation. The great difficulty one encounters in conceiving of an ethics and a politics in the Girardian perspective stems, I think, from being torn between a constraining nature and a remote God – a gulf which can be filled by intellect but not by action. The gnostic aspect of Girard's thought, so convincing and at times so intoxicating, thus comes at the price of the impossibility of any historical thought or practice, whether personal or collective, in the middle of such a distance.

Now, in 'entrusting ourselves to ourselves' (Bérulle), God gives us the ability to resist the most powerful determinisms. This ability is fragile, of course, and rarely employed, but it opens a moral horizon I cannot discern in an interpretation where Oedipus, to be sure, claims pride of place but Antigone is absent. Besides, how is one to imagine, before the sacrificial crisis[6] is upon us and understood, that the actor could intervene in a mechanism which at once sustains him and grinds him down, but whose gears he does not yet see?

The sacrificial crisis, if it opens the possibility of a personal conversion, forecloses the founding of a new community. Just as for Lacan there is no love act outside God, for Girard there is no political act outside God. He does not say this explicitly but it is certainly the inevitable conclusion of his demonstration, for he allows no human alternative to the dissolution of the foundational sacred.[7] Whence the dilemma: either the community shall perish or it shall convert.

For there to be a way out of this dilemma one would have to admit that the sacred is not primordial, that religion is not an 'instituting necessity'. Marcel Gauchet, who holds this point of view, would find himself in fair agreement with one whole portion of the Girardian interpretation: for him the religions of transcendence, by setting divinity at a distance from humanity, permit the latter to become aware of its powers and to emancipate itself. It is 'savage' religions, the religions of sacrifice, which fetter liberty. But for Gauchet the state in its turn established a new type of power, one capable of doing without religion, of self-instituting . . . 'The more the gods grow great, the more men become their own masters.'[8] Without being able to carry this debate any further I will merely note that it is impossible to reconcile, as some attempt to do, Girard's philosophy with that of Castoriadis, for whom democratic politics is a continual invention, the creation of a new 'social' by a liberated imagination.

Staying with the issue of sacrifice, I will limit myself to recalling the heroes who founded or revived states; their example shows that it is not always necessary to sacrifice in order to conciliate. The hero can assemble instead of excluding, like Augustus, like Henry IV . . . A golden legend runs through history in parallel to a macabre legend. It exalts noble actions while the other, as Girard shows so well, wipes out the traces of political crimes. The awareness of the fragility of institutions does not give rise only to ritual sacrifices; it gives rise to oblations as well. The blood indispensable to the social mortar is not always the enemy's; it can also be our own.

Reread in this light Bernanos's *Dialogue des carmélites*; listen to this sentence spoken by the Mother Superior: 'It is not the Rule that keeps us, my daughter, it is we who keep the Rule . . .' This lets one believe that a consent given to what draws its sole reality from the oblatory sacrifice by the few can be substituted for the scapegoat ritual. Terrestrial figure of the Communion of the Saints, point of juncture between the earthly City and the City of God. In 1940

Gilbert Dru, who would later be shot by the Nazis, wrote to me: 'There are but the lives of near-saints that can weigh in the scales.'

One can see in such examples an index of that progress of the evangelical spirit which abolishes the victimage mechanism. But before Christ, Socrates got ahead of the Law that was going to sacrifice him, sacrificing himself for it. Why should this lineage of oblatory founders and guardians be forgotten in favour of the scapegoat sacrificers alone? Is there then to be no sacrifice but of victims presumed guilty – and not also, in imitation of Jesus Christ, as the Fathers of the Church thought, a sacrifice of self, stripped of cunning and illusion, just as there are desires whose object has not been designated for them by a third party?

In truth, the more I am carried away by the extraordinary fecundity of the Girardian hypothesis, the more its imperialism stirs up resistances in me. I react most strongly against the idea, seductive as it may be to the intellectual, that our science introduces us to a knowledge so dazzling that, like an atomic flash, it burns eternally what it has touched. 'At the end of time, you will understand everything': this Gospel formula that Girard quotes does seem to mean – although he does not say so clearly – that we have entered the terminal phase. Certainly I prefer this apocalyptic glare to the entropic twilight with which Lévi-Strauss brings his research to a close,[9] but I persist in thinking that a parable cannot be entirely explicated and reduced by a gnosis and that the history of humanity is not a gigantic charade to which the solution will be delivered in one stroke. The apocalypse is in the logic of structuralism: that is where an explanation that leaves out nothing necessarily leads. But it does not go without saying that this conclusion should coincide with the conclusion of violent history.

I will be so bold as to put it this way: do we not have here something like a violence done to history itself, in order to usher in the reign of non-violent love? This history is marked not only by advances in decoding but by moral acts, by spiritual, intellectual and æsthetic inventiveness. Moreover, the power of sacrificial leaders, such as it has shown itself in contemporary anti-Semitism, leaves reason to fear that the correlative rise of Violence and Love cannot be taken care of by an awakened consciousness of a scientific, rational, anthropological character. It should push us to invent and to practise a culture, institutional forms and ways of life that maximize the possibilities open to autonomies.

Modernity encourages us to fit history into univocal theories and, in consequence, to assume with a greater or lesser modesty the status of those who know as against those who do not. Because equality has in theory won, this superiority hardly ever manifests itself any more through synchrony, but only through diachrony: the division between learned and ignorant is succeeded by the division between we who know and the ancients who knew nothing, or very little. To be sure we have, with Michel Foucault, taken the measure of the closure of epistemological fields, but we act as if it held only for bygone eras, and not equally for our own. This attitude is the opposite of that of the Renaissance humanists who, for their part, questioned with reverence the classical ages. But how can we be sure of understanding what Pascal did not understand? Of seeing what Hölderlin did not see? I do not reproach Girard with pushing his research beyond what has been found; how otherwise could there be any researchers? I reproach him precisely with abolishing this possibility after him. Berthelot's famous declaration 'There is nothing left to discover' is even less admissible in the sciences of man than in those of nature because it amounts to halting a history whose dialectical motor is the representation the society creates of itself through the sciences of man.

In a sense, René Girard's endeavour amounts to a decisive rupture with positivism, whose path he reverses and which he interprets as an infamous ruse to obscure, by piling up knowledge, the light of truth. This pernicious half-knowledge is, as Pascal believed, the worst adversary of the science of being; it shelters, behind a mask of atheistic daring and scientific objectivity, the sentimental dodge of dull religions, the perverse determination not to draw the consequences of what one knows (thus the half-knowledge of persecution, turned around by persecuting states into ideological accusations). It would therefore be inaccurate and injust to charge Girard with any kind of scientism that might serve as a substitute or prop for religion.

However, if Girard does a good job of showing knowledge to have become our false god, is it sufficient and is it not perilous to respond to this idolatry on the very ground where it has established itself: that of the sciences, and, precisely, of the human sciences? Is it conceivable, for a Christian, that the true understanding of God's design for the world should derive from that knowledge, necessarily incomplete, that modern society has developed of itself and its past? In the very idea that this knowledge could be complete (and that is indeed what René Girard seems to be telling us) and could set itself up as the revealer of the revelation, is there not something frightening – I will even say sacrilegious? I do not, to be sure, interpret the expulsion from Eden as a prohibition laid on anthropology. The *libido sciendi* is the West's grandeur, but it is also at the heart of its violence, of its imperialism. The substitution of anthropology for theology strikes me more as a sign of our overweening pride and of our disordered contemporary condition than as the means to a decisive advance in our knowledge of God.

It is significant from this point of view that Girard's opening move is the execution of Romanticism, singled out as the repository of what is illusory and fallacious. I would be more inclined to hold, with Milan Kundera, that it is the titanic Western effort since the seventeenth century rationally to reduce everything to unity that pushed the 'irrational' forces of feeling to seek refuge in the novel, Multiplicity's protest against Oneness – and that is where Girard would one day hunt out the hidden mechanism of *mimesis*, thereby reappropriating for the sole explanation what had been erected against it. But should we not also question the past for what we do not understand in it, and not only ask it to supply ammunition for our theses? If there are things hidden since the foundation of the world which modernity has illuminated, are there not other things, previously visible, which modernity has hidden?

The more I return to the work of René Girard, the more his 'hypothesis', as he calls it, appears to me as the heroic apogee of modern rationality: a voyage to the end of the sciences of man which, having reached the edge of the abyss of nihilism, do an amazing about-face that leads them back in a blazing journey to the very domain they believed they had left for ever: that of the word of God. If I voice an objection, is it to avoid succumbing to the seductiveness of an audacity that would return Christ on the cross to the centre of the world? It seems to me it is out of the fear of meeting up again with some demons I thought I had exorcized: the claim to close off history in a global explanation, the myth of a social transparency finally realized, the dream of a City that the Spirit would penetrate and dedicate to the Good. In short, a desire to know that does not know its limits and claims suddenly to illuminate all history, past, present, and yet to come, like a pyrotechnics expert igniting a Catherine wheel. The tragic, in my view, will continue its dialogue with certitude. For there will subsist until the end a share of night that is not the reverse side of day, but the place for the propagation of light.

The Christianity of René Girard and the Nature of Religion

LUCIEN SCUBLA

(Translated by Mark R. Anspach)

Having shown sacrifice to be the cornerstone of all religious systems,[1] René Girard has undertaken to construct, on this basis, a new apologia for Christian religion.[2] For, of all religions Christianity is in his eyes the only one to reveal the violent foundations of every human society and, most importantly, the only one to point to a remedy – the only one to lift men out of the sacrificial order by uniting them directly around the God of love instead of reconciling them belatedly over the grave of the surrogate victim.

This interpretation of Christianity has encountered many reservations, and indeed we shall see that a strictly 'non-sacrificial' reading of the New Testament runs into major difficulties.

The complexity of the subject would call for lengthy development, for Girard's thesis is a tissue of empirical assertions, epistemological postulates and theological inferences that raise problems of different orders. But by the force of circumstance, we will limit ourselves here to examining some particularly contentious points.

As a preliminary, since our arguments are in danger of being too succinct, we wish to forestall a misunderstanding. If we believe it expedient to voice unvarnished objections to certain aspects of Girard's work, our intent is certainly not to cast discredit on the whole of his output; it is on the contrary to return to the original core of the theory and to continue building on the solid foundations our author himself set.

While the final pages of *Violence and the Sacred* seemed to promise that an anthropology which had at last come of age would turn its new-found strength to the conquest of Christianity, we know what happened next. Arguing that men could not have discovered on their own the violent origins of their civilization, Girard undertook to show the necessity of attributing the knowledge, on which he himself had laboured mightily, of 'things hidden since the foundation of the world', not to a science sprung full-blown from an autonomous reason but to Christian revelation which had in his view made possible the advent of such a science.[3]

But for the anthropological and epistemological import of evangelical revelation really to be such, Christianity would have to represent the only, or at least the first and in any case the most radical refusal of sacrifice and exposure of the violent foundations of human institutions.

However, it is easy to show that the devaluation of sacrifice is neither the distinctive attribute of Christianity nor the major theme of Christ's teaching; and that the gospels cannot lay exclusive claim to the revelation of the violent foundations of human society.

Indeed, at least six centuries before Jesus, the Orphic tradition[4] condemned with vigour all forms of blood sacrifice and already reproached men with having founded their polis on murder, not only in the myth of the dismemberment of Dionysus by the Titans[5] but also in the story of the death of Orpheus, peacemaking hero and bard of non-violence,[6] savagely lynched for having denounced the pernicious character of sacrificial rites.[7] On the other hand Christ does not seem, in the gospels, to have pushed the devaluation of sacrifice further than the Old Testament prophets of whom He (with justification) presents Himself as the continuator, and it is difficult to see His death as less sacrificial than that of Dionysus and especially that of Orpheus, which manifestly lacks a redemptive character.

> Jesus [Girard writes] is the last and greatest of the prophets, the one who sums up and transcends them all . . . With Him comes a displacement at once minuscule and gigantic which appears as a direct extension of the Old Testament but which also constitutes a formidable rupture. It is the complete elimination for the first time of the sacrificial, it is the end of divine violence, it is the truth of all that came before finally made plain.[8]

But what exactly should we make of this?

By itself, the first part of this text displays clearly the venturesome character of the Girardian interpretation: compelled to recognize that the teaching of Christ is 'a direct extension of the Old Testament' even while it can establish the transcendence of the evangelical message only by the 'formidable rupture' which it is supposed to mark in the history of humanity. For if the Jewish prophets had already taken part in the 'revelation' one is hardly justified in refusing this distinction to the Orphics, to the Greek tragedians, and to a number of pagan philosophers, and that runs the risk of ruining the whole apologetic project.

But, for lack of space, we will leave these comparisons as they stand and look at whether Christianity really has the remarkable properties our author attributes to it.

I '. . . the complete elimination for the first time of the sacrificial . . .'

'The Gospels', we read in *Des Choses cachées*, 'never speak of *sacrifices* except to cast them aside and refuse them all validity.'[9]

In reality, the gospels always speak of sacrifice in a very measured tone. In the passage from Matthew[10] where Girard tends to see an abolition of sacrifice, 'a setting apart of the sacrificial' and even 'a revelation of its function',[11] Jesus asks of men only that they reconcile themselves with their brothers *before* presenting their offering on the altar, but far from suggesting that the offering would then be superfluous, He continues to prescribe it to them as if it were needed to seal and consolidate their union. When He heals a leper,[12] He tells him to go and present himself at the Temple to perform the sacrifices that the Law requires.[13] When He Himself celebrates Passover,[14] He commemorates the people of Israel's departure from Egypt by immolating the traditional lamb, like any pious Jew of His time. Finally, the words of Jesus are in perfect accord with His conduct. When He teaches His disciples that 'to love his neighbour as himself, is more than all whole burnt offerings and sacrifices',[15] He is not expelling the sacrificial rites into outer darkness: He confines Himself to subordinating them to love, in the direct tradition of the prophets whose precepts He repeats word for word.[16]

Looking at things carefully, one realizes it is not so much sacrifice that Christianity tends the most to devalue as relationships based on marriage and kinship. For while it is impossible to find in the speeches of Jesus any pronouncements that are flatly anti-sacrificial, there are countless gospel passages in which He expressly urges His disciples, with an energy and harshness that have embarrassed numerous commentators, to relegate family relationships to a secondary position and to neglect, if not to defy outright, customary duties in this domain.[17] And while there is a continuity from the Old to the New Testament as regards the attitude to adopt towards sacrifice, Judaism and Christianity are in total opposition on the subject of kinship relations. Judaism is a religion which puts the accent on the father, Christianity is a religion which puts the accent on the son; the former tends to emphasize the vertical relation that unites man with his ancestors, the latter to stress the horizontal relation that unites man with his 'brothers'.[18]

Even if the devaluation of natural kinship to the benefit of spiritual kinship is not an exclusively Christian trait, it is unmistakably a leading characteristic of Christianity. It is what sets it at odds with the Jewish world and with the traditional Graeco-Roman one; it is also what will impede the penetration of Christianity in China, despite the great skill and patient efforts of the Jesuits;[19] it is, finally, what will make the Christian religion one of the principal sources of modern individualism.[20]

So we see that things are clear. If there is indeed a 'formidable rupture' between the Old and the New Testament, it concerns kinship and not sacrifice. And it is because He was fighting the traditional forms of filial piety,[21] and not because He was desacralizing the tomb of the surrogate victim,[22] that Christ was able to give the impression of shaking the foundations of the social order when He opposed the cult of the dead and turned men away from their burying places. What is more, if by 'complete elimination of the sacrificial' is meant its radical condemnation, it is not here that Christianity might find the sign of its singularity; for in its era it is not Jesus but the Essenes who unreservedly proscribe the immolation of animal victims, as before them had the Orphics and the Pythagoreans with whom they have for this reason often been compared.[23]

But of course we will be told it is not a question of that. For the objection will be made that the impetuousness with which these various sects reject sacrifice shows how far they are still imprisoned by sacrificial logic, while *a contrario* the very fact of not violently excluding sacrifice demonstrates that the Gospel is utterly outside this logic. In other words, Orphism and its avatars would be *anti-sacrificial* movements, whereas Christianity would be the first, and perhaps the only, *non-sacrificial* religion of humanity. And it is for just this reason that the sects force their adherents into a rigid corset of alimentary taboos,[24] while Jesus teaches His disciples that it is not what goes into man but what comes out that is able to defile him.[25] Christ would therefore be alone in eliminating sacrifice, by substituting morality for ritualism and charity for prohibitions, whereas the sects would only substitute new rites for old rites, new taboos for old taboos, never actually breaking out of the sacrificial system. Indeed, Christianity would be the only religion to reveal not so much the pernicious character of sacrifice *per se* as the violent foundations of all human institutions of which blood sacrifice is an integral part; it would be the only one fully to expose to the light of day the victimage mechanism and the 'scandalous' nature[26] of the mimetic desire from which it proceeds.

II '. . . the truth of all that came before finally made plain . . .'

Such would be the essence of Christianity: it is by revealing the founding murder, and above all the victimage mechanism which is fundamental to it, that Jesus permits men for the first time definitively to leave the sacrificial order.

'There is no essential passage of the Gospels', Girard writes, 'which does not contain the revelation of the founding victim or which is not itself this revelation, beginning with the text of the Passion.'[27]

However, on carefully rereading the texts 'without adding anything or cutting anything out',[28] what do we find? That Jesus denounces the murder of the prophets and more generally all murders from that of Abel, which inaugurates the violent history of humanity, down to that of Zacharias, which is supposed to close it:[29] true enough; but that on this occasion He reveals to men the founding character of the murder: certainly not. Not that the victimage mechanism is absent from the gospels – it is, on the contrary, omnipresent; but its nature and effects are never explained, and its 'use' is never condemned.

Quite the opposite. Jesus often calls on the sacrificial metaphor with a disarming spontaneity, as if He too turns readily to a logic of exclusion: 'And if thy right eye [scandalize] thee, pluck it out, and cast it from thee: for it is profitable for thee that one of thy members should perish, and not that thy whole body should be cast into hell.'[30]

Just before giving His disciples this severe injunction, Christ made reference to the covetous gaze man casts on his neighbour's wife, that is to say the very thing that Girard calls the 'mimesis of appropriation'. He thus employs the victimage mechanism in order to turn it against itself, since instead of seeking the origin of evil outside man He goes back to the internal origin of human unhappiness: to envy, the source of the 'scandal'. But the fact remains that this celebrated text 'plays' a strange game with sacrificial logic. It neither reveals nor destroys the expulsion mechanism: it diverts it from its habitual use and puts it to better ends; as if it were less important for men to know the mechanism than to know how to 'trick' it.

This impression, based solely on Chapter 5 of Matthew, is confirmed by a reading of Chapter 18. The Evangelist has Jesus pronounce once again the words we have quoted, but in another context. Christ has just counselled His disciples to become like children and to be sure not to 'scandalize' them. Then, without our being able right away to grasp clearly why,[31] He recounts for His disciples the allegory of the 'stray sheep', which is constructed on a model that for once we can with justice call radically non-sacrificial.[32] And since the reference to hell fire or Gehenna evokes human sacrifice and even, more precisely, the sacrifice of children,[33] all the elements necessary for a 'revelation' in the Girardian sense of the term are thus united. All the more so as Jesus adds in conclusion: 'Even so it is not the will of your Father which is in heaven, that one of these little ones should perish.'[34] But, oddly enough, the revelation does not take place. One finds in particular no allusion in this text to collective murder.

However, the theme of collective violence figures in many another passage, and notably in the pages preceding the story of the Passion: the parable of the murderous husbandmen,[35] the parable of the wedding of the king's son,[36] the malediction of the scribes and the Pharisees.[37] Are we to believe that the Evangelist has clumsily scattered themes which Jesus, for His part, had closely associated? Or on the contrary that he is proceeding with a revelation step by step, or rather a secret initiation that follows a learned gradation culminating in the story of the Passion?

The mere fact that one may hesitate between these divergent interpretations is enough to shake Girard's thesis.

But that is not all – let us reread the celebrated curses hurled against the Pharisees:

> Ye serpents, ye generation of vipers, how can ye escape the damnation of hell? Wherefore, behold, I send unto you prophets, and wise men, and scribes: and some of them ye shall kill and crucify; and some of them shall ye scourge in your synagogues, and persecute them from city to city: That upon you may come all the righteous blood shed upon the earth, from the blood of righteous Abel unto the blood of Zacharias son of Barachias, whom ye slew between the temple and the altar. Verily I say unto you, All these things shall come upon this generation.[38]

Such are the words Matthew attributes to Jesus. And Luke spells out the rest:

> That the blood of all the prophets, which was shed from the foundation of the world, may be required of this generation; From the blood of Abel unto the blood of Zacharias, which perished between the altar and the temple: verily I say unto you, It shall be required of this generation.[39]

All the crimes of humanity concentrated in a single generation – all the vices of society concentrated in a single social class, Marx will say – with the salvation of humanity hinging on that condition: how can one fail to recognize here the selfsame illusion that is the product of the victimage mechanism and the cause of its efficacy? All Girard's talent is needed to persuade us for a few moments – but only a few moments – that Jesus, far from setting up the scribes and the Pharisees as scapegoats, is actually revealing to them the founding murder.[40] Even if we know that it is Christ who is going to die and not the scribes and Pharisees, we cannot hide from ourselves the fact that the words here imputed to Jesus are strangely consonant with persecution texts of our acquaintance.

III '. . . the end of divine violence . . .'

But let us not belabour this point. Suppose Christ is describing here the viewpoint of the persecutors, as His mission requires, without Himself adopting this viewpoint. Grant that the 'damnation of hell' is here only another name for the violent mechanism that is going to end up turning automatically against the persecutors. Can one say, for all that, that violence in the gospels is a purely human affair? That the New Testament bids a firm farewell to the old theology of divine wrath and does not impute the least act of violence to God Himself?

This is the cardinal point, the one that must in the last instance determine the sacrificial or non-sacrificial character of a text. Neither the victim's consent – contrary to what Girard had at first believed[41] – nor even the victim's innocence[42] can guarantee that a text does not belong to the sacrificial corpus; only the absolute innocence of God in a situation of violent unanimity can furnish the proof.

Now, asserts Girard, 'the idea of divine violence has no place in evangelical inspiration'.[43]

In evangelical inspiration, perhaps not; but in the evangelical text, it certainly has.

Consider, first of all, the parable of the murderous husbandmen, the three versions of which Girard compares rapidly.[44] In Mark and in Luke, it is Jesus Himself who maintains that the lord of the vineyard – that is to say God – will destroy the faithless husbandmen and put others in their place. But in Matthew it is Jesus' audience that attributes to God a desire for reprisals, or at least that responds in such a way to Jesus' question:

> When the lord therefore of the vineyard cometh, what will he do unto those husbandmen? They say unto him, He will miserably destroy those wicked men, and will let out his vineyard unto other husbandmen, which shall render him the fruits in their seasons.[45]

We readily concede to Girard that it is proper to compare the three accounts of this parable, and we would well like to suppose along with him that 'the text of Matthew is to be preferred'. It is still necessary, in order to test this hypothesis, to place the parable of the husbandmen in the entirety of its original context, which means comparing it to all other parables in the vicinity that manifestly treat the same subject. Now oddly enough, while Girard does not fail to point out a brief passage of the parable of the talents[46] that corroborates his interpretation of the parable of the husbandmen, he is silent on the parable of the wedding of the king's son,[47] which is not compatible with his interpretation even though it is closely tied to the parable of the husbandmen which it immediately follows. The two texts have the same structure, but this time, in the view of Jesus Himself, it is the king – that is to say God – who in His wrath sends forth His armies to kill the murderers and to burn their city.[48] And just for good measure, the king next banishes into outer darkness the unfortunate guest who is not wearing a wedding garment.[49]

Thus everything transpires as if in the view of Jesus Himself, and not only that of His disciples, the kingdom of heaven and the happiness of the chosen could be established only upon the exclusion of the reprobates and the unhappiness of the outcasts. All the parables agree on this point, including the parable of the talents which ends on the same violent note as the parable of the wedding.

In *Le Bouc émissaire* René Girard seems to concede this himself. '*Paraballo*', he remarks, 'means to toss something as fodder to the crowd to appease its appetite for violence.'[50] Therefore the parable would be a metaphorical discourse, still bearing the stamp of violence because destined for those who are violent. And Jesus could speak to us in parables without prejudice for the revelation, since in such a case He never fails to warn us Himself that he is speaking to us in parables. Very well. But, aside from the fact that Jesus did not express Himself in Greek,[51] what becomes here of the idea of a wholly transparent revelation, of a text to which it would suffice to abandon oneself without searching for hidden dimensions?[52] Is it not, on the contrary, throwing the door open to any and all interpretations?

However that may be, let us move on now to the death of Judas. It is true that the theme of Judas does not occupy a place in the account of the Passion sufficient to make the latter a simple variant of those folk tales in which the hero, at first the victim of a traitor, ends up triumphing over him, while the traitor receives a just punishment.[53] Girard is probably right on this score, but is it, for all that, an episode of no importance? And is not the author of *Des Choses cachées* hoping to prove too much when he maintains that the punishment of the traitor is missing from the gospels?[54] It is accurate to state that in the gospels, in the strict sense of the term, the fate of Judas is not properly speaking punishment, but rather suicide:[55] another proof, says René Girard, 'that men are never condemned by God: they condemn themselves by their own conduct'.[56] Let us admit that the text of Matthew may accommodate such a simple interpretation. It is astonishing all the same, as Thomas Stern emphasizes,[57] that our author breathes not a word of the fashion in which Peter reports Judas' death in the very beginning of the Acts of the Apostles:

> Now this man purchased a field with the reward of iniquity; and falling headlong, he burst asunder in the midst, and all his bowels gushed out. And it was known unto all the dwellers at Jerusalem; insomuch as that field is called in their proper tongue, Aceldama, that is to say, The field of blood.[58]

Here again the writer does not speak precisely of a divine punishment, but the meaning of the passage is hardly in doubt. Ought we to lay this 'violent mythology' to the sole account of the apostles, who would thereby have already fallen back into the sacrificial rut in which historical Christianity is going to settle? But where then will we find authentic Christianity?

To finish with this subject, let us proceed to the story of the Passion. For lack of space we will limit ourselves to bringing out two essential points, which are closely connected and which Girard in his commentary curiously omits: the relationship of the death of Jesus to the Jewish celebration of Passover, and the institution of the eucharistic ritual which the Synoptic gospels seem to present as a transformation of the Paschal rite. Doubtless John sets himself apart from the Synoptic account: he does not have Jesus pronounce the sacramental words in the course of the Last Supper. On the other hand, though, he develops at length the theme of Christ as the 'bread of life' whose 'flesh and blood' men must consume.[59] What is more, one finds in John the theme of the 'Lamb of God',[60] which evokes the sacrifice of Isaac as well as the Paschal rite: the lamb whose blood permits men to make white their robes when they prepare to appear before the throne of God.[61] As for Paul, we know that he openly assimilates Christ to the Passover lamb: 'Christ our Passover is sacrificed'.[62] But since the theme of the Passover lamb has perhaps lost its evocative power for the majority of our contemporaries, we advise the reader to reread Chapter 12 of Exodus to be able to evaluate these associations.

Is the rite of the Eucharist nothing, then, but a banal 'totemic meal', as Frazer, Freud and company would have it? No, we will be told, for there are at least two important differences between them. In the foundation narratives of sacrifices in the classic mode, the communal meal follows quite naturally the immolation of the victim; whereas in the story of the Passion the meal takes place before the death of Jesus. Furthermore, the eucharistic rite lays the accent on memory and not on repetition – it is less a question of reproducing the Last Supper than of taking the occasion to recall the life and the death of Christ: 'Do this in memory of me'; while in sacrifice in Girard's sense, it is important to repeat the original murder instead of remembering it.

It is true that all the disciples commune together with Jesus before He is put to death, but the presence of Judas at the Last Supper is in itself enough to rule out our seeing in that meal a peaceful ritual that would be completely foreign to sacrificial logic. Also, if that communal meal is indissociable from the Passion; if the death of Christ is to be related to the Jewish Passover, as the Synoptics suggest and as Paul declares explicitly; if Christ is indeed the lamb of God who takes away – who *takes away* and not who *reveals* – the sin of the world, as John says;[63] then the crucifixion is a sacrifice, doubtless a sacrifice *sui generis* as the Epistle to the Hebrews affirms, but a sacrifice all the same.[64] 'The doctrine of the efficacy of the cross', Girard asserts, 'has nothing to do with sacrifice.'[65] However, sacrifice is first and above all the requirement of a human or animal victim to obtain a benefit from a divinity who by this very fact runs the risk of being considered 'violent'. Now the salvation of humanity assuredly requires, for a Christian, the death of Jesus on the cross and the reactualization (not the repetition)[66] in the eucharistic ritual of what must therefore be called, whether we like it or not, a sacrifice. To maintain the opposite is to set oneself up in contradiction not only with the Epistle to the Hebrews but with the spirit and the letter of the New Testament in its entirety.

The truth is that if Girard wished to carry the logic of his thesis through to the end, instead of confining himself to ignoring the eucharistic rite, he ought to follow those commentators who believe they have found in John the justification for replacing it with the rite of the washing of the feet: a rite indeed devoid of any sacrificial character and rigorously symmetrical, where everything takes place between men who are equal and interdependent.[67] But apart from the difficulties which this interpretation of John raises,[68] it is clear that it would take us out of the traditional Christianity to which Girard remains attached, if not out of religion itself.

Let us sum up. Supposing the historical Jesus had wanted to challenge the old notion of divine wrath, to abolish sacrifice and to reveal the victimage mechanism, it is probably not demonstrable and is in any event not what Girard wanted to demonstrate. On the other hand, it is scarcely possible to doubt that our author has no basis for attributing to the Christ of the gospels the designs he does; for even if we have not demonstrated this, we believe we have shown the demonstration to be possible.

Interesting as it may be, therefore, the Girardian interpretation is not compatible with the text as a whole: he too often demands more of it than is there while totally neglecting certain of its most fundamental aspects. It is false to say that the victimage mechanism is revealed for the first time in Scripture and that it suffices to read the Judæo-Christian text to be able to read all other texts afterwards. In reality it is not the New Testament that allows us to understand primitive religion; it is Girardian anthropology that enriches our understanding of Christianity.

The Christianity of Girard is therefore not that of the gospels. But is it at least fully compatible with our author's religious anthropology? The question might seem paradoxical, but we are going to see that it is worth while to ask it.

Whereas in *Violence and the Sacred* he showed the positive effects of religious rites and beliefs, in *Des Choses cachées* Girard seems to outline a Christianity stripped of all sacredness and of all ritual. In theory only the violent sacred and violent rites are excluded, but the economy of the Girardian system makes it exceedingly hard to conceive of alternatives that would not in their turn be touched by violence.

Our author affirms the transcendence of God and rejects humanist interpretations of religion, but nothing truly indicates that the 'revelation' would require God to intervene in history, so that Christ could be mistaken for a sage come to teach men that they have always been alone with their violence and that they must hasten towards reconciliation one with the other to avoid all being destroyed one by the other.

By devaluing traditional religion in the name of true piety Girard revives in his manner, despite his denials, the traditional gesture of the philosophers who, from the dawn of Greek philosophy, have condemned 'superstition' in the name of 'reason'. To be sure, if Christianity is the true religion it doubtless has to distinguish itself from all other religions; but if it no longer has anything in common with other religions, is it still a religion?

In effect, liberated from its sacrificial matrix and indifferent to all ritual, Girardian Christianity bears a great resemblance to the 'Christianity' of Spinoza,[69] but it runs the risk of floating in the void, whereas the latter is solidly anchored in a robust theological-political system. For if the Dutch philosopher refuses, in principle, any form of 'outward worship' (while observing for his part too, be it noted, that ceremonies and rites reinforce the power of society[70]), he well knows that only a few men may attain bliss by the royal road of intellectual love for God, and that the greatest number will have to resign themselves to obtaining salvation by the ordinary route of obedience to rites or to political authorities.[71] Whereas men in Girard's vision, apparently deprived of any ritual or institutional aid, are left with no choice but all to follow Jesus Christ together or all to plunge together into the final Apocalypse.

The comparison with Epicurus is still more interesting for, apart from the fact that the philosopher of the Garden obviously owes nothing to the Bible,[72] the non-violent God of *Des Choses cachées* bears a greater resemblance to the Epicurean divinities, outside the whirl of worldly events, than to Spinoza's God, where human violence still manifests its sovereign power. For Girard, as for Epicurus, religion reduces itself to ethics and up to a certain point to the same ethics: for is renouncing 'unnatural and unnecessary desires' anything other than evading mimetic desire and all occasions for 'scandal'? It is true that Epicurean wisdom does not coincide, for all that, with Christian charity, but here again the comparison turns to the advantage of philosophy. For supposing Girardian anthropology to be valid, if men do not live in hiding, if they do not disperse themselves in small circles of friends, if everyone does not retreat into his garden, how will they avoid the worst, once they are deprived of the sacrificial mechanisms suited to checking their violence? It is true that such a return to the 'state of nature' is perfectly illusory,[73] but it is the only solution compatible with the postulates of Girardian anthropology, whereas the road that by our author's account Christ would offer is not in accord with these same postulates.

'The Kingdom', he declares, 'is perfect reciprocity, nothing more, nothing less. As long as men settle scores with each other, there is not good reciprocity; there is no good reciprocity except at the price of a total renunciation of violence.'[74]

Very well. But if all social contract theories must be rejected as naïve,[75] if the pretensions of humanism must be challenged, if the illusion of autonomy must be guarded against, it is hard to see how a good reciprocity could emerge, develop and extend itself to the whole human race, starting out from the terrifying face-off to which the people of an entirely desacralized world would be reduced. Unless they benefit from some divine grace, they will inevitably descend anew into violence. Now of such grace our author breathes not a word, for his Christianity, as Pierre Manent observes, is rigorously 'Pelagian' in the sense that once the revelation is accomplished, 'everything takes place between men'.[76]

But if everything takes place between men, their reconciliation is at once necessary and impossible. In effect, if the victimage mechanism is not only the source but also the foundation of all institutions of human society past and present, and if the misrecognition of this mechanism is the *sine qua non* of its efficacy, the Christian 'revelation' limits itself to stripping man of his ritual protections to yield him up naked to his own violence. How, then, can we not adopt the point of view that Girard imputes to the persecutors of Jesus;[77] how can we not join Machiavelli in denouncing the unintended consequences of a Christianity whose nonviolent purposes are in danger of setting the whole world ablaze at any moment?[78]

No doubt about it: if Christ came digging up the graves and exhuming the cadavers around which men have long since made their peace, and if this 'revelation' sufficed to destabilize every society, He would be abruptly destroying the work of civilization, which has little by little replaced the earliest bloody rites with more and more peaceable rituals and has slowly eroded human violence, to the point of making it appear more and more odious wherever it still retains a remnant of primitive vigour.

It is therefore permissible to believe that Jesus, far from reopening men's wounds, came to dress their injuries, to calm their memory and to teach them oblivion and forgiveness. And it is equally permissible to believe that the 'revelation' is not enough in itself to shake the walls of the human community to the point of provoking their fall; otherwise, unless it had suddenly changed its way of existence, the human race should have disappeared long ago.

But it is only now, we will be told, that humanity runs the risk of disappearing, for if the violent unanimity against Christ was able to postpone the disaster one last time, it is now that the revelation, having long been underground, emerges into daylight and approaches its goal.

Doubtless the worst is not impossible, but this is true in our opinion for another reason: what threatens to do man in is not the discovery of the violent origins of his rites, but rather the baleful illusion that he could and even should 'free himself' of all ritual.

Let us go back, in fact, to the results established in *Violence and the Sacred*. What Girard showed in this work was the violent *origin* of the earliest cultural forms, and first of all of religious ceremonies, but not the latter's intrinsically violent *nature*. As a consequence, from the fact that religion is at the source of all institutions and the victimage mechanism at the source of all rites, we cannot conclude that this mechanism is the unique foundation – apart from Christianity – of all societies past and present. Both logic and observation make us loath to go along with this.

Logic first: for the victimage mechanism, which converts reciprocal violence into unanimous violence, could well be at the origin of all rites and all institutions without, however, being the complete cause of them. Or, to put things a little more technically, it could be the 'efficient cause' of the first social structures and of the emergence of the cultural order without being, for all that, their 'formal cause'.[79]

Observation equally: for, looking at things closely, it would seem that religious rites were progressively transformed into other religious rites – or into political or judicial rites – that were further and further removed from their sacrificial origin and more and more autonomous. This is manifestly true of money, whose ritual origins have long been clearly established;[80] it is also true of monarchy, as demonstrated by the convergent and complementary analyses of Frazer, Hocart and Girard;[81] and one could easily show that democracy itself works on procedures that could with justice be qualified as ritual but no longer as sacrificial.[82]

More generally – and without reducing human history to a unilinear and determinist process – one notices a global tendency towards a lesser violence, as much in sacrificial rites as in the parasacrificial or extra-sacrificial institutions born of them. One observes neither the rupture that Christianity should have provoked nor the uninterrupted rise of violence implied by the thesis of an ever-falling (whether gradually or sharply) degree of a supposed protective 'misrecognition' (*méconnaissance*). Whether before or after the birth of Christ, we see an approximately regular diminution of violence, at least in the Western world, from the Orphics and Heraclitus who denounce sacrifice as an abominable stain, down to the recent abandonment of the death penalty, perceived as a kind of legal crime.[83]

As Kant might have said, therefore, ritual has not only civilized men, it has moralized them.[84] For it busies itself not only with deferring violence and with hiding it more and more successfully,[85] or even with containing it more and more effectively; it also succeeds in rendering it detestable. That, as we must reiterate, is why accusing ritual, revealing its bloody origins and exposing the real or symbolic violence it would like to dissimulate, amounts in reality to stirring the last embers of an ancient violence now covered by a thick layer of cinders, and it would be suicidal if it could be effective. But, thank God, it cannot: ritual is generally more powerful than its detractors and more shrewd than its demystifiers.

Indeed, it is not knowledge that destroys the victimage mechanism, it is the series of rites born of this mechanism that, as they free themselves from it, take us out from under its hold at the same time as they make possible our knowledge of it. Girard himself seems to acknowledge this:

> Violence in primitive societies is never conceived as we conceive of it ourselves. For us, violence possesses a conceptual autonomy, a specificity of which primitive societies lack the idea . . . What permits us to abstract the act of violence intellectually, to see in it an isolated crime, is the effectiveness of judicial institutions that transcend all the antagonists.[86]

The fact is all the more remarkable in that judicial institutions derive from a transformation of religious rituals anterior and exterior to the Christian 'revelation'; but Girard does not appear to see what profit could be drawn from this observation.

Whatever may be made of this particular point, it is at the very least doubtful that the efficacy of a rite should be in direct proportion to the 'misrecognition' of its nature and, *a fortiori*, of its origin. Even in the case of the victimage mechanism strictly construed, everything seems to indicate that one can at once know it and succumb to it. Scapegoat phenomena continue to be triggered spontaneously after the Christian 'revelation', apparently with a frequency and efficacy neither greater nor lesser than before it. That is why one can, like Machiavelli in Chapter 7 of *The Prince*, teach men the way to operate the mechanism, giving them, as it were, authentic 'how to' instructions.

As far as rites go, one would almost be tempted to reverse the Girardian postulate: far from destroying ritual, the 'revelation' of its origin could even contribute, under certain circumstances, to reinforcing it. Indeed, in the course of initiation ceremonies, the adults show the young people the masks of divinities with which they had terrorized them when they were younger. Now, as a commentator of Hopi customs notes,

> This ceremony of demystification and this recantation inflicted on the belief in the Katchina are going to be the institutional foundation of the new belief in the Katchina that constitutes the essential part of Hopi religion . . . Now, they tell the children, you know that the *real* Katchina no longer come dancing as *before* in the pueblos. They no longer come but in invisible fashion, and they inhabit the masks on dance days in mystical fashion.[87]

'A Hopi Voltaire', the same commentator adds, 'would say that since he was fooled once, he wouldn't be fooled again. But the Hopi distinguish, in order to contrast them, the mystification with which one fools children from the mystical truth into which one initiates them.'[88]

And it is of course the Voltairean attitude which would be naïve, and a supposed 'radical demystification' which would be the height of mystification. 'You know now', the pedagogues say, 'how human beings make babies.' A paltry revelation: for humans do not know, have never known, and perhaps never will know how babies are made in them. That is why there is more truth in the Platonic myths of the *Banquet* than in all the treatises of sex education.

And so it goes probably for all ritual. In vain might Girard object that all the Hopi, whether children or adults, equally misrecognize the nature of their rites. For in a certain sense there is always misrecognition, or more exactly partial recognition, and as Pascal has shown, it is the so-called exhaustive knowledge of the 'half-clever' that is misrecognition's most extreme form.

In fact we may note, 'last but not least',* the likelihood that God Himself could not reveal to men the ultimate nature of things, for men would not understand this revelation. Such is in any case, it seems to us, the fundamental postulate of all religious thought. The idea finds support in the Spinozist sage himself, who can, to be sure, accede to complete knowledge of two attributes of the divine Substance, but of two attributes only, when altogether there are an infinite number. As if, even by the admission of the greatest rationalists, man could not escape some form of 'misrecognition'.

In sum, then, what *Violence and the Sacred* shows is not how men bestowed humanity on themselves, but by what mechanisms they arrived at their humanity – mechanisms which they set in motion without, however, creating them. And, as a consequence, the 'revelation' could hardly ask men to undo what they did not do and could not have done. What religious thought does teach man is rather the danger to which he would expose himself if he thought he could emancipate himself from every form of exteriority. Whence the prudence of Epicurus who, it seems, suspected ritual of being wiser than human reason. For far from avoiding religious observances, he took part in all public ceremonies.[89] Indeed, he did much more: in the very interior of the Garden, if he stopped short of instituting a sort of private worship, he at least preserved and elaborated the custom of celebrating with ritual banquets the birth and death of friends and relations.[90] As if no society could subsist without rites.

Supposing, then, that Jesus had attempted to abolish ritual, his disciples could but reinvent it. For, as Alfred Loisy wrote:

> Religions are historically neither theories, nor sentiments, nor mystical aspirations, but traditions of social life guaranteed by the consecration of ritual. A spirit animates these institutions; but it is the institutions which give consistency to the spirit and keep up its action in the world. It is often said that the religion of the prophets was materialized, narrowed and lowered in the form of the Law. Strictly speaking, there never exists a religion of prophets – no more than there was a religion of Jesus – but an immense effort to raise the devotion of Israel towards an ideal more

* Translator's note: in English in the original.

> and more perfect as regards religious belief, moral conscience and social justice. In so far as this effort tended to disengage itself from any institution, it was lost and could but lose itself in the void. In so far as it was able to embody itself in institutions, it lived and acted. Jeremiah represents the pure spirit of prophetic Yahwism. It is the written Law, which he disdained, that saved that part of his generous dream that the times could use.[91]

And what holds true for Jeremiah holds true also, as Loisy says, for Jesus. To be sure, the first Christian communities might have lived without rite or myth, because they believed themselves to be at the end of time. But having perceived their mistake, they had no choice but to disappear or to elaborate what was going to become historical Christianity. The relapse into the sacrificial was not only inevitable, it was indispensable, and to it Christianity owes its survival. Without it the figure of Jesus would be more enigmatic still than that of Orpheus, supposing – and even this is not certain – that scraps of a 'Christian literature', as disparate and scattered as the 'Orphic literature', preserved for us the sole memory of his name.

But, we will be told, what seems thus to obscure or to delay the revelation is the very thing that realizes it. It is only in appearance that sacrifice survives and eludes the effects of revelation, for the mechanism is definitively compromised, mortally injured, sapped from within. In reality, the past two thousand years have seen the slow but irresistible accomplishment of a labour which the biblical text made possible and which in turn illuminates the biblical text and renders it more and more transparent, at the same time as it keeps men henceforth from attempting in vain to flee their own violence in sacrificial rites. Girard's writings would be only the final moment, or at least one of the last effects of this long movement – the fulfilment and the self-awareness of the revelation, the revelation that the revelation is now completed or that it is coming to a conclusion.

This hypothesis is not lacking in appeal, and doubtless there is some truth to it. But it is difficult to believe, like the first disciples of Jesus, that we are at the end of time, when the odds are that we are the victims of the same illusion as our predecessors. To be sure, it is possible that we find ourselves at the end of a world: for the survival of a Christianity stripped of all ritual, in accord with the curious wish of certain Christians, is at the very least doubtful. To 'return to the time of the first communities' is to return to the age when Christianity was not yet a religion and when, for this reason, it could have disappeared without leaving the slightest trace. But the decline of Christianity does not necessarily mean the end of religion, and Christians' abandonment of their rites is not perforce the augury of an entirely deritualized world.

In conclusion, apart from the fact that it reads too much into the text, the interpretation of Christianity that Girard proposes presents two major drawbacks.

In the first place, it is difficult to reconcile with the most solid parts of his fundamental anthropology. For, let us repeat, it is probably not knowledge which destroys the victimage mechanism; it is rather ritual itself which, in proportion as it distances itself from its origins, renders little by little its oldest forms obsolete and makes it easier and easier to know the mechanism which gave rise to it.

In the second place, it fits in poorly with Girard's concern to rehabilitate religious thought. For the religious way of thinking is a humble one that cannot accommodate either the desire to be liberated of all ritual, or the pretension of tracing man's humanity back to an ultimate basis in the victimage mechanism. Just as universal gravitation could not, as Newton realized, express the final essence of things, no more could sacrificial logic, which we may permit ourselves to compare with it, contain the secret of humanity.

But we will not pretend any longer to believe that René Girard is unaware of all this. All those who have had the opportunity to converse with him have been able to appreciate his extreme modesty and know that he never fails to point out the partial and lacunary character of his research and his results. 'There is reason to believe', he writes at the end of *Des Choses cachées*, 'that very important aspects elude us which will one day be brought to light.'[92] That is very likely; but is it not more appropriate, in that case, to number the victimage mechanism among the ranks of the revisable hypotheses of science rather than of the revealed truths of theology?

Towards a Poetics of the Scapegoat

MASAO YAMAGUCHI

(Translated by James Valentine)

The word 'scapegoat' has recently been attracting the attention of more and more people. It is well known that this word derives from the Old Testament, and René Girard has devoted two books to this topic: *Les Choses cachées depuis la fondation du monde* (1978) and *Le Bouc émissaire* (1982). I too have approached this subject in my article 'La Structure mythico-théâtrale de la royauté au Japon traditionnel'.[1] I have been able to show that this phenomenon of the scapegoat constitutes a mechanism which assures culture of its basic vitality. Indeed, this phenomenon opens up a profound perspective that is not limited to the realm of superficial morals: it concerns not only the superficial level of emotion but also the deeper level of human experience and of imagination. It breathes vitality into cultural domains as varied as individual mentality, politics, morals, the history of ideas and aesthetics. That is why taking up discussion of the scapegoat again is in effect seeking the sources of the dynamics of culture.

I The Genealogy of the Theory of the Scapegoat

The theory of the scapegoat has its origins before the present century. However, ethnology, which along with religious studies is particularly concerned with this subject, has for a long time shown no interest in it.

It was James Frazer who introduced the problem of the scapegoat into ethnology.[2] Frazer, however, has fallen into neglect because of his method of naïve comparison. Nevertheless, if we now examine his work from a certain distance, we can recognize in it the starting point of today's symbolic anthropology. Frazer's main thesis is that of *regicide*: in a system of divine royalty the universe, identified with the body of the king, is renewed by his ritual murder. Even though Frazer has been neglected by ethnologists, they are generally in agreement with this theory.

But Frazer was not interested solely in regicide. For him the king was a metaphor, and he searched in folklore for an image capable of replacing the ill and aged king. He gave as examples animals which are hunted by villagers during the harvest festival; or the young man who, beaten in competition, becomes the object of jesting; or again the pseudo-king of the carnival, who behaves in a debauched manner and is chased away at the end of the festival. Frazer studied carnival in relation to the scapegoat. Today there is much reference in ethnology to carnival as a typical example of a reversal ritual. However, few people remember that Frazer's subject was precisely that of reversal rituals. His work on the scapegoat was followed up by the Hungarian psychoanalyst Geza Roheim. Roheim investigated the process of construction of the scapegoat, drawing on folklore data from East European countries. Frazer's double interest in the scapegoat and the carnival was then linked to semiotics by Michael Bakhtine.[3] Bakhtine shows that carnival was the most dynamic route of the popular imagination. He also emphasizes that at the centre of carnival culture are coronation games and crownings of pseudo-kings.

Bakhtine's concept of the carnival imagination has exerted a deep influence on numerous thinkers. However, as we have already noted, this theory of carnival was preceded by Frazer's in his *Golden Bough*. If what Frazer says on the subject of regicide is transposed to the level of metaphor, we can understand how young villagers can replace the king during the carnival.

The king, considered as the incarnation of cosmic order, is believed to ensure the order of time and space on earth. But, the human mind seems incapable of maintaining for ever a fixed state of affairs, however well arranged. The continuation of such a state of things entails the stagnation of the world. Due to an assumed constancy of mind, this phenomenon is not seen as a mere mental impression but is thought instead to be the consequence of the diminution of the energy which maintains the external physical world. This diminution of cosmic energy is made manifest in increasing disease, agricultural sterility, crime and disasters of all kinds. Although such events intervene in human life only in an uncertain and unpredictable manner, people always look for a reason that will enable them to explain these phenomena. The system of divine royalty implies that it is the diminution of the power of the guarantor of order which is responsible for the breaking down of order. One therefore looks to the king himself, or else to someone who has harmful powers, for the cause of the introduction of chaos into the world.

As Mircea Eliade has shown,[4] most societies have a cyclical conception of time. In such societies time is thought to run out after a certain period during which negative energy accumulates. It is thus believed that contact with the primordial state by means of violence (as Girard has shown) enables the recovery of the original radiance.

In order periodically to renew its energy, a society must thus create the carnival event, for example at the time of the annual harvest festival, and expel someone who is burdened with the evil and pollution of the preceding year. The facts provided by Frazer explain eloquently the behaviour of the human mind in such situations.

What has been said on the subject of the conception of time in archaic societies still applies today. For example, at the time of an election the chaos of an uncertain future is introduced into the atmosphere of excitement that surrounds the election, and engenders within the society a feeling of regeneration. Change is sought because it puts an end to homogeneous time, which brings inertia to society and leaves it in anomie. But the presence of scapegoat phenomena in the politics of industrial society suggests that what is involved is the temporal structure of human experience.

If we look within contemporary ethnology for some examples of the use of facts about the carnival, they are first to be found in the work of Lévi-Strauss, in his discussion of the concept of '*clivage cosmique*'. In Mythologiques, 1 *Le Cru et le Cuit*[5] Lévi-Strauss presents a European custom (from Lithuania) in which the villagers bring to the central square of the village the furniture which was broken during the year, and with great commotion burn it all up. It is a ritual in which chaos is introduced, and time is made to die and be reborn. The cyclical and seasonal ritual of the scapegoat contributes to the punctuation of time by causing the negative image of society to appear. In numerous societies, in which homogeneous time is thought to be the cause of inertia, the appearance of the negative elements which have accumulated during the course of the year is felt to be necessary in order to dispel them thereafter. The problem of sorcery can be explained by means of the same type of logic, as Michel de Certeau has shown in *La Possession de Loudun*[6] and in *l'Absence de l'Histoire*.[7]

The American literary critic, Kenneth Burke, has shown that a theory like Frazer's concerning seasonal rituals is valid not only in the realm of ritual, but also in everyday life. He emphasizes the fact that royalty serves as an ideal and model for life. In a hierarchical order people tend to hate those who occupy the upper echelons of the political hierarchy, but to displace their resentment on to those beneath them. This partial and limited solution results in a discontent which has no outlet in the system of behaviour and communication of everyday life. If no means is available to resolve this discontent, it is manifested in dangerous forms such as violence or total anomie. Society tries to resolve this fundamental dilemma, pertaining to societies organized hierarchically, by diverting the negative energy towards the top of the hierarchy. The cathartic effect is thus obtained by the destruction of the symbol of the person at the top. The myth and ritual of regicide were the ancient form of this problem's resolution.

But royalty also found the way to divert symbolic hostility towards those who are right at the bottom of the social hierarchy – criminals, foreigners, the handicapped, etc. Thus society produces scapegoats in two ways. On the one hand the people resolve their dilemma by means of the symbolic renunciation of the king; on the other royalty looks for victims who are right at the bottom of the social hierarchy.

Burke has shown, in *Attitudes Towards History*,[8] that the Jews are laden with the double image of the scapegoat, at the same time intellectual superiors and excluded from society. It is this ambiguous image that Hitler and the Nazis exploited in such an effective and terrible manner. In this way Burke elucidated the hierarchical structure of signs in the political world, which today cultural semiotics tries to grasp, by reinterpreting the theory of the scapegoat on the level of symbolism.

Alexandre Mitcherlich, in his book *Le Chagrin perdu*,[9] has developed the theory of the scapegoat in the area of social psychology. He presents it as the ideal image of negativity in a society. To stigmatize someone as a scapegoat implies the impossibility of their adaptation. It is even forbidden to adapt. The Jews and the Blacks must stay as they are. The ideal image of negativity is imposed upon them quite aggressively. In effect the ghetto gives birth to the distorted victim. For the victims there remains only the possibility of an aggressive response as a means of improving their situation. But these aggressive responses are perceived in turn as racial characteristics, thus reinforcing the ideal image of negativity and increasing the anxiety of the rest of the population.

The image of the negative is in one sense the reverse of the positive and is used, when a problem arises, to identify the element conceived as threatening the individual or collective identity. According to Mitcherlich, the Nazis exploited the 'aggressive potential' of the Jews in imposing on them the ideal image of negativity. It is perhaps one of the ironies of the history of ideas in the twentieth century that contemporary history proved the validity of the theory of the scapegoat while ethnologists neglected Frazer.

Nazi Germany made the Jews into scapegoats; Stalin's Russia constructed a diabolical image of the Trotskyists in order to divert the attention of the masses from the political and economic failures of the government and to effect Stalinist autocracy. This means that these two regimes brought out into broad daylight the logic of 'exclusion', which in everyday life operates hidden in the depths of consciousness. In taking it out of the context of cyclical time, they transformed what had been carried out in the name of the festival or seasonal ritual into a means of political and everyday terrorism.

But at the time no theory appeared, in political science or sociology, which was capable of explaining these unfolding events. As already noted, it was in the area of psychoanalysis and social psychology that a theory began to be developed that could take account of the most important phenomenon of history.

II The Function of 'Exclusion' in Paradigm Change in Science

The academic world is not exempt from the effect of scapegoating, particularly in a period of paradigm transition. Human beings are less rational than they like to believe. They make decisions more on the basis of hidden fear than on rational grounds. We are all afraid of being rejected by the community formed around a collective decision, and of being left behind, as can be seen in the realm of fashion. It is natural to take the side of the scapegoat-makers rather than that of the scapegoat itself. So too the history of any science will show that the prevailing academic theory suddenly passes into the background, seeming to lose its power of attraction. It is this phenomenon that Thomas Kuhn analyses in *The Structure of Scientific Revolutions*.[10]

Scientists themselves thus lean towards the fashionable side. They are afraid of being identified with what is believed to be coming obsolescent and willingly participate in the effort to reject the outdated theory. But why, beyond a certain threshold, do researchers get involved so readily in this process of paradigm change? Perhaps it is because of the finite character of the models human beings construct about themselves or society. These models are not free of the limitations of the age, and the problem arises of accounting for the appearance, at the limits of a model, of phenomena which do not conform to it. A new theory, one should remember, is conceived in relation to the inexplicable aspects of phenomena. With the passage of time, the relations which existed between the phenomena excluded by a model become more and more evident; thus a new conception is developed, which is finally formulated into a model that is distinct from preceding ones. Such a process can be seen at work in, for example, the transition from the romantic to the positivist conception of history, the transition from existentialism to structuralism in philosophy, and in linguistics the transition from structuralism to Chomsky's generative grammar.

A phenomenon like this, which is at the basis of the theory of the scapegoat, can be found again in ethnology, and this is what happened to Frazer. For thirty years functionalism, based on realist positivism and on field experience in connection with colonial administration, became the paradigm in ethnology. It buried the comparative method, dubbed the theory of regicide absurd, and criticized 'armchair anthropology'. During this period it was fatal to one's career to be called a Frazerian. Certain subjects had to be avoided, such as divine royalty because it was reminiscent of the theory of regicide. Until Lévi-Strauss, myth itself was a topic that tended to be shunned. Ethnology's theory of culture was constructed from subjects concerning human behaviour and susceptible to rational explanation: law, economics, family, kinship. All these areas are characterized by manifest regularities which enable the theory to attain a certain predictive capacity. The intellectual framework of this theory was the mechanical projection of Western society's own self-portrait: an optimistic self-portrait supposedly stripped of illusions. It is an irony of fate that Frazer, who developed the theory of the scapegoat, became one himself.

One might add that René Girard also (along with Mircea Eliade) is among those thinkers ethnology tries to ignore. Thus, despite the immense interest of his works, he is rarely cited by ethnologists. It is even more surprising that certain books, such as *Purity and Danger* by Mary Douglas,[11] which touch on rather similar problems, are frequently cited by American ethnologists.

But if functionalist theory puts forward a method of decoding the superficial observable part of social reality, it has not the means of reaching the deeper level, hidden from this reality. In this way it became a theoretical scapegoat when the structuralist theory of Lévi-Strauss appeared. Still, as Girard noted in *Le Bouc émissaire*, scientific thought itself is simply an institution that produces various forms of understanding the world.

III The Provocative Aspect of the Scapegoat

Philip Slater has taken up Frazer's idea of the scapegoat in relation to the theory of small groups. In *Microcosms: Structural, Psychological and Religious Evolution in Groups*,[12] he studies the mechanism by which the members of a small group increase the power (mana) of the leader in order to be able thereafter to destroy and annul it and to strengthen their identity by sharing the power amongst themselves. The process is parallel to that seen in regicide. Slater further notes that the way in which criminals are executed in our society is rather reminiscent of the custom of regicide.

Amongst the many studies in psychology that approach the problem of aggression, the psycho-ethnological analyses of Anthony Storr[13] are especially noteworthy. He is interested precisely in the question of the scapegoat.

Storr does not consider aggression only in its negative aspect. He shows, for example, the positive value of a pecking order as amongst chickens: its function of creating stability within society on the basis of the principle of the opposition superior/inferior. Yet Storr does not restrict himself to the study of the internal relations of society. He shows that the potential conflict within a group is resolved when the aggression is directed outwards, and that the most interesting effect produced by an external threat is the disappearance of the internal divisions which existed in peacetime.

At the same time, too great an identification of the members of a group with each other can be a cause of scission. Individuals who are strong enough to differentiate the external from the internal aspect of their identity are protected from totally identifying with their fellows by bringing into play with others only the most external part of themselves. They can thus preserve their identity while happily joining in the social game. But a total identification with others involves a very strong interdependence between individuals, and because differences are insufficiently observed the stability of the group is threatened, thus giving rise to aggression.

The aggression of the majority of the group towards those who are not in conformity with it is proof not of its strength but of its weakness. But this punitive aggression which has its source in the majority shows only one aspect of reality: aggression can also be seen where the minority asserts its identity. What Girard calls the mimetic character of violence can be recognized here.

Nevertheless, minorities and the weak are not always considered to be so powerless. Storr suggests that intolerance may explain the contradictory fact that minorities are conceived as potentially strong, whilst in reality they are weak. That is true to a certain extent; but minorities – albeit weak in social terms – have on the symbolic level, without knowing it themselves, a potentially very great power of provocation. As Storr himself notes, scapegoats express themselves through weakness as well as through strength. The victors and the vanquished are united by a bond of mutual hatred which far exceeds the level of the struggle for domination that can be observed in other animal societies.

Thus the power of the weak is, for the dominant, the image of negativity supported by the power of provocation. This power is probably none other than what Rudolf Otto[14] called 'numen'.

IV Entropy and the Scapegoat

It is now necessary to consider the source of this provocative power of the scapegoat. In a word, it comes from the entropy arising from the scapegoat and threatening the vital energy that maintains the order of the world and the group.

Although the word entropy has its origins in the physical sciences, nothing prevents its acquiring a relevant metaphorical use in the cultural and social sciences. As we have already noted, in every society there tend to appear, after a certain time, inexplicable and undesirable elements, and the sum of these elements is conceived as a change in the society. In many cases these elements are independent of all external influence and are really simply the negative aspects the institution or the theoretical conception had to eliminate in order to establish itself.

Theories to explain society can be classified into two extreme categories: unidimensional (monosemic) conceptions and multidimensional (plurisemic) conceptions. Unidimensional theories imply expressions which have only one possible definition, while multidimensional theories imply expressions encompassing as many heterogeneous elements as possible, for example esoteric language. It is this multidimensional pole that animates culture. At the hidden level, culture depends on what it excludes. This is what explains the ambiguous position of provocative elements, of the scapegoat.

The example of the Jukun of Nigeria clearly shows this provocative aspect. The important elements of this culture are expressed through oppositions: masculine/feminine, right/left, etc. Women, who are classified in the second of these categories, are objects of exclusion in ritual and religious symbolism. Belief in sorcery justifies the exclusion of women, who are defined by myth as potential sorcerers. Women who are sorcerers are thus situated at the opposite ideological extreme from the king, who represents the masculine principle and is at the top of the hierarchy. However, although women are excluded as systematically polluted beings, it is in the hut of women's seclusion during their menstrual period (which is thought to be the source of great impurity) that the ritual of kingly regeneration is carried out. The king is regenerated by absorbing the feminine entropy, which he transforms into energy thanks to the ritual process. Thus all accentuation of gender amongst the Jukun is a latent expression of fear of the 'uncontrollable' power of women.[15]

In the last decade the problem of gender has become a very popular subject in ethnology. It was first approached from the feminist point of view, with research later turning to the symbolic level. Shirley Ortner in particular has situated the problem in the nature/culture opposition. In relation to the dichotomy proposed by Lévi-Strauss, Ortner notes an antagonism between nature and culture in various societies. Culture corresponds to internal order, nature to external chaos. Discrimination against women often arises from their being considered closer to nature. As much on the biological and psychological level as through their capacity for shamanism, women assume characteristics that are not prescribed in the cultural norms formulated by men. Yet because their place is within society, women are considered even more strange. Ortner calls this position of women 'mediation', and argues that this ambiguous situation is the cause of the discrimination to which they are subjected. Although this approach to the problem of gender is conceived within a structuralist framework it shows a tendency towards cultural semiotics, whose starting point is precisely the endeavour to understand a culture from its complementary aspects such as nature/culture, inside/outside, order/chaos, information/entropy. In the realm of semiotics this position of women, which Ortner defines as mediation, could be termed 'abominable'.[16]

According to Kristeva,[17] culture consists of two functions: a symbolic function, which ensures logical order, and a semiotic function, which goes beyond the order imposed by symbolism. (Des Chinoises, Paris, 1974) Anything which does not fit within the realm established by symbolism, for example Jews or women, is destined to become an object of discrimination. Cultural identity is thus based on the exclusion of semiotic excess in the guise of Jews or women. It is interesting to note that these are provocative beings, laden with semiotic excess, who are the object of discrimination because of the difference they express.

Excess is the first symptom that a difference is appearing. The identity of a community is ensured by the existence within it of heterogeneous elements and by the feeling that the interest of the community is not always shared by these elements.

As we have just emphasized, there is an intimate relationship of complicity between a community and its scapegoats. The community's continued existence requires scapegoats; while the scapegoat, whether consciously or not, continues to provoke the community through semiotic excess. Leaving aside the moral problem, the scapegoat's most brilliant moment is at the time when this provocative nature culminates in execution by the community. That is why theatre people are so often persecuted in society. Herein lies the way towards the poetics of the scapegoat.

V Digital Thought and the Principle of Exclusion

Despite the criticisms that have been raised against the structuralist method, what seems to hold true in it is the basic idea that at a fundamental level human thought presupposes antithesis. The existence of societies in which these oppositions are formulated in a form that is easy to observe has come to light thanks to the ethnological studies of the last thirty years. In such societies the essential aspects of the universe are explained in terms of oppositions like heaven/earth, fire/water, high/low, east/west, right/left, masculine/feminine, givers of women/takers of women. The first element of each pair (e.g., heaven, fire, high, east, etc.) is considered superior, and in these societies based on binary oppositions there is a risk of discrimination.

Thus amongst the Lio of central Flores, an island in eastern

Indonesia where I carried out my second field work, dualism is found along with a tendency to discrimination. However, since the metaphysical image of the mother as an explanatory model of the society is projected on to the principal ritual and the house of its enactment, the tendency to discrimination is absorbed. Elsewhere, as we have already seen in relation to the Jukun of Nigeria, the social organization of the majority of African societies is based on the opposition of masculine and feminine and on the monopoly held by men in ritual and in political organization. Associated with such a tendency, dualism seems to produce scapegoats who are women, as amongst the Jukun.

Thanks to the upheaval following the advent of the computer age, there is now more widespread acceptance of the contrast between the two modes of logical construction, digital and analogue. The digital model is a means of constructing a system using series of ones and zeros. Thanks to the development of electronic techniques, systems of processes using the digital model have become complex constructions. Nevertheless digital thought has both the advantage and the inconvenience of being reduced to an artificial distinction, because the system is based on the human choice of the figure 1 versus 0.

Hitoshi Watanabe, in his book *Digital Thought and Analogue Thought*,[18] has claimed that originally human beings, surrounded by physical nature, had the tendency to use analogue thought almost exclusively. Then language is developed as human behaviour that consists of differentiating the analogue model by means of the digital model: i.e. naming certain things, distinguishing the named things from other things, and ignoring the distinctions between the things that are not named. Only that which is named can provide information and be the object of communication.

Many societies in which a dualist classification is found, as amongst the Jukun, are based on the distinction between the right hand and the left. According to Watanabe, a mode of thought permitting a distinction between right and left is already a digital mode: the image of the body is established by presupposing an asymmetry between right and left. Thus he sees the human body as the starting point of digital thought. However, according to Watanabe digital thought can proceed in two ways: the digital mode in the limited sense which develops towards logical thought and abstracts, conceptualizes and quantifies things; and the digital mode in thought more widely, which makes a distinction = discrimination on the basis of human emotion.

In digital thought with 1/0 (one and zero) the 0 is defined as an opposition or an absent element. This arrangement appears to be objective, but in fact it already implies a mechanism of exclusion by virtue of the introduction of the distinction.

Thus, although we are inclined to ignore this fact, logic or human thought has a mechanism in common with the mode of thought that creates the scapegoat. Unfortunately, in everyday life digital thought reproduces exclusion at the level of emotion. Our conception of time develops solely through the production of negative images rather than through their rejection.

It is possible that on this point Lio society provides an ideal solution. This society can be defined as operating an ingenious synthesis between digital and analogue thought. The concepts of 'head' and 'tail' are used as basic metaphors. Here already there exists a digital mode. This metaphorical opposition is expressed in such antitheses as head/foot (for humans), interior of the house/entrance of the house, entrance of the village/exit of the village, heaven/earth, mountain/sea, giver of women/taker of women, etc. The main point of communication in this society consists in connecting or separating these two poles symbolically through festival or ritual. Amongst the Lio the house is identified as the womb and the seven chief priests carry out the ritual of returning to the mother's womb, represented by the ritual house. Here analogue thought prohibits any possibility of opposition to the cosmic harmony of original time.

Dichotomy for the Lio does not involve as radical a discrimination as that found in African societies like the Jukun. All opposition is encompassed by the image of the mother, expressed in the form of the ritual house where the reconciliation of the two poles is annually realized. How, then, is frustration or fear expressed? Through expelling from the village the seven chief priests, identified as rats, who have been the source of evil in the preceding year. This is none other than the ritual of the scapegoat. Thus instead of expressing aggression through attacking people of a lower level, according to the digital mode of logic, this society practises the logic of inclusion or the ritual of inversion, making a kind of short-circuit between centre and periphery. Here the themes of the scapegoat and the carnival are united in an ideal form.

Therefore it is perhaps by seeking to make, through art, a synthesis between digital and analogue thought that we today can reach a more satisfactory solution to the problem of the scapegoat.

VI Towards a Poetics of Culture

In a book entitled *Culture and Ambiguity*,[19] I have tried to show that the conception of order in culture is counterbalanced by the image of the periphery. We have just proposed here that the principle of exclusion is a phenomenon essential for culture to maintain its identity. We have also seen that the genesis of symbols is inevitably associated with a logic of exclusion in culture. Although the elements to exclude in the conceptual apparatus of culture are dismissed on the surface of human or social consciousness as if imbued with entropy, they shake the foundations of the order that constitutes the central part of culture and make possible their reintegration in a new system at a higher level of synthesis. We have examined above how a culture reproduces 'negativity' through the mechanism of absorption (= synthesis) and of exclusion. It goes without saying that this 'negativity' is equivalent to the 'minus' signs of culture. These are sometimes the words, images or categories in an artistic text. This negativity is perhaps what René Girard suggests as a means of transcending static structuralism:

> To transcend the limits of structuralism, emphasis must be placed on doubtful meanings, those that mean both too much and not enough: twins, for example, illnesses, all forms of contagion and contamination, inexplicable reversals of meaning, growths and outgrowths, decay and distortion, the monstrous, the fantastic in all its forms.

In this paper I have presented an analysis of the part of culture that is provocative and as a consequence is always victimized as a scapegoat. Yet it is this part that gives rise to the dynamic image of culture: the fool, the mythical deceiver, the clown. The poetics of the scapegoat would thus be the same as the poetics of culture, which includes all studies which have as their object the dynamic aspects of culture.

Founding Violence and Divine Referent

HENRI ATLAN

(Translated by Mark R. Anspach)

Without previous planning on my part, it turns out that this essay takes up, by a different through route, two of the fundamental ideas presented by M. Yamaguchi in 'Towards a Poetics of the Scapegoat'. The first is that of the sign effect of the scapegoat. The second idea is the relationship between this sign effect and a certain form of intelligence and presence in the world: that of the ruse, the clown, the trickster. M. Detienne and J.-P. Vernant have analysed well the aspect which this form of intelligence, the 'metis',[1] assumed in Greek culture, which corresponds fairly closely to what the Jews call in the kabbalist literature the wisdom of the left side.[2] I am going to return to these two ideas, then, in relation to the work of René Girard, but in a relation which is in a sense negative. Let me explain: I would like to try to show that one can – and in my view that one must – cast doubt on two theses in René Girard's work which are always presented as if they were self-evident. These theses play a fundamental role in the Girardian problematic as a whole. They appear to flow ineluctably from the primary anthropological hypothesis. I believe that nothing of the sort is true and that while maintaining the anthropological hypothesis intact, it is possible to propose alternatives to these two ideas that are coherent with the Girardian premises, thereby demonstrating the non-necessity of these theses.

The exercise I am going to perform before you – and it is probably open to criticism – consists therefore in cutting apart, in separating, in distinguishing two aspects of Girard's work. There is in the first place an anthropological aspect which I accept totally. I consider the surrogate victim mechanism to be fundamental as a means of explaining the differentiation of societies. And in the second place there is a Christian aspect which Girard always presents as following necessarily from the anthropological. The anthropological thesis then appears as the pedestal and base of a Christian vision of civilization and of civilizations, where the Revelation of Jesus plays an essential role. My goal is not to discuss the soundness or unsoundness of this vision of the world, but simply to show that the second part does not necessarily follow from the first.

Two ideas govern this apparently necessary logical progression. Again they are generally conceived as going without saying, but it is enough, I think, to analyse them in order to accomplish the division I propose.

The role of misrecognition (*méconnaissance*) in the victimage mechanism is the first of these ideas. According to Girard the mechanism for the resolution of the crisis can work only if its functioning remains unknown to those who effect it. As soon as the actors understand the mechanism and know how it works, it collapses and fails to reconcile the community. This proposition, fundamental as it is in Girard's theory, is never analysed or posed as a problem and, obviously, never proved. It is presented as self-evident. This attitude strikes me as the consequence of a common idea which originated with the work of Freud and according to which it suffices to become conscious of – to disclose – a hidden phenomenon in order for it to disappear. Now this idea is, even where Freud is concerned, uncertain to say the least.

The second idea that seems to go without saying is that of the God of love. I think it is tied to the first, the idea of misrecognition, or at least it appears as intimately linked to it functionally. For if the internal logical needs of the theory lead us to conceive of a divine revelation, this revelation can only be that of the God of love. The God of love opposes violence, and through the intermediary of the revelation of Jesus, He brings men the means of combating violence, of suppressing it even. Astonishingly, the theory at the same time asserts that all human societies are founded both on mimetic violence and on the rescue or recovery from it through the victimage mechanism.

Let us begin with the first idea, misrecognition. It is something which often came up in the course of our discussions with René Girard; Jean-Pierre Dupuy and I even wrote an article on it.[3] There are several ways of challenging this idea. One of them consists of asking oneself what is, logically, most fundamental in the victimage mechanism, conceived as a mechanism of social differentiation. The answer is a truism: it is a matter of the passage from an undifferentiated state to a differentiated state. To obtain a differentiated state, one must obviously start out from an undifferentiated (or less differentiated) state and see how it becomes differentiated. When one reflects on the ideas of undifferentiation and differentiation, one perceives that repetition or redundancy is a particular case of undifferentiation. Manifestly, imitation is an operator of repetition or redundancy. Imitation furnishes peculiar and fundamental examples of undifferentiation. One of the interesting points in Girard's theory is that it shows us how, out of these undifferentiated states, differentiated states may arise.

The passage from one to the other raises some basic and very difficult problems. It so happens that this difficulty – how to understand the accomplishment of the transition from an undifferentiated to a differentiated state – is also one of the central questions in contemporary biology. On one hand, every process of biological maturation is a differentiation; on the other, the question of the evolution of living beings comes down to nothing else. How, starting out from simple, primitive forms of life, did more complex, more differentiated forms appear?

Now Girard's answer, at least in its logical form, is comparable to the answer biological theory brings to the same problem, in so far as both assign an important part to randomness or chance. Starting out from an undifferentiated state made repetitive through the labour of mimesis, very slight perturbations in the way in which these repetitions take place lead to a process of differences and of differentiations. *A posteriori* this differentiated state appears to be charged with meanings, in so far as it corresponds to a functional state. In the case of a society, the individuals on the interior of this functional organization cannot conceive of it otherwise than with its meaning. Inversely, an external observer who saw the process unfold and who knows how the transition was effected recognizes that it is only the result of a perturbation, of a small impact that directed towards a given form a movement that was originally disordered and undifferentiated.

Girard analyses this mechanism in more precise fashion, and insists on the role of violence. It intervenes in the two moments of the mechanism: at the stage of undifferentiation and at the stage of differentiation. At the stage of undifferentiation there is the violence of all against all, and mimesis is the source of an absolutely generalized violence. At the stage of differentiation there is the violence of the expulsion of the victim, and this time mimesis makes the violence of all converge against one. It is there, in the determination of who will be expelled, that randomness intervenes in the fillip of chance that orientates the system towards one social form rather than another. And it is at this level, Girard asserts, that the mechanism cannot function unless the actors misrecognize it – unless they do not know that the victim they are expelling, the foundation of the social order that is theirs, has been designated at random. More precisely, they have to believe that the victim is authentically guilty or responsible for the crisis, and that his designation has a sense to it. They must subscribe to something which is of the order of myth – the origin of meaning – for the mechanism to work. As soon as one informs the actors that the victim could have been anybody else, that he was designated at random but that a victim was necessary for the mechanism to function, the latter will, Girard holds, collapse. It is this proposition, so central to Girard's argument, that I wish to challenge.

To do so it suffices to appeal to the logic of the passage from the undifferentiated to the differentiated, of the passage from the repetitive to the complex by way of random perturbations. This passage cannot take place – or, more precisely, it cannot be observed – unless the observer positions himself on two separate levels of observation: on one hand the system itself within which the phenomenon occurs; on the other the encompassing level constituted by the observation from without.

When the process of creation of difference out of undifferentiation is analysed with the help of information theory, as I have proposed doing in biology, one witnesses an inversion of the effects of noise depending on the level considered.[4] At the first level one observes the destruction of information by noise; at a more encompassing level, which is that of the system as a whole, the observer this time perceives that the same noise-producing random perturbations give rise to a reorganization accompanied by a new mode of functioning, a new organization. The observer is then obliged to recognize on the interior of the system itself a transformation of what appeared to him before as noise, randomness, into what now appears to him, *a posteriori*, as something on the order of a new functional meaning. It is therefore only in so far as the observer can move from one level to the other – from that of the sub-system where the perturbations occur to that of the global system – that randomness can be transformed into increased diversity, destructive ambiguity into the autonomy producing ambiguity.

In biology we can go no further. We cannot, if you will, put ourselves in the molecules' place to try to experience the way in which they transform random perturbations into sources of new meaning. More precisely, in the rare cases where we can, so to speak, put ourselves in the molecules' place all the formalism of information theory becomes superfluous. It is no longer necessary to talk in terms of undifferentiation and differentiation, simply of chemical kinetics.

If we now transpose this purely formal and logical schema to the problem of social differentiation, we suddenly find ourselves in a radically different situation.

Indeed, the parts, the components of a social organization, are human individuals, which is to say ourselves. And we can either place ourselves outside the system to play the role of the external observer, or place ourselves inside where the transition from one level to the other takes place, where randomness is transformed into new meaning. If we place ourselves outside we will be in the position of an objective observer and will view the transition from undifferentiation to differentiation under the impact of random perturbations in the manner I have just described. But here it suffices to make a little jump; it suffices to cross over the circle that separates the observer from the system observed, in order to find ourselves on the inside and to watch the new meanings appear. This time there is no longer any question of talking about random perturbations because, from the inside, we see the mechanisms by which the random perturbations are experienced as endowed with meanings.

Now all that has just been said about the possibility offered to us of being in two places at once, on the outside and on the inside of the system, means that we can consider the same phenomenon either as the result of random perturbations or as a process of creation of meaning. That does not, however, mean that we are schizophrenic. It does not mean that both interpretations are wrong. Nor does it mean that only one of the two aspects exists, whether this be the random character of the perturbations or their charge of meaning. Quite simply, two different positions of observation allow us to perceive two aspects of the same phenomenon.

I think this is something which is very clear in the minds of the members of societies where rites were – or still are – experienced as reproducing and representing the surrogate victim mechanism. The best example that I might give is that of the scapegoat rite itself,[5] as it was experienced and ritualized in the Jewish tradition. Once a year, a goat was taken to the temple and sacrificed after the high priest had laid all Israel's offences upon it. I say was, because today the sacrifice is no longer performed. But there still exists a very important rite which in a sense replaces it; this consists quite simply in reading the story of the sacrifice. Here it is a matter of an 'internalized' form of sacrifice. To be sure, one could discuss indefinitely the question of which form is preferable, the internalized and symbolic form or the concrete realization. Whatever the case, the attitude with which we are dealing here is profoundly different from the one suggested by Girard, which consists of saying that we must get rid of all sacrificial institutions, since it is impossible to do otherwise once we have become aware of the origin of sacrifice.

In fact, for those who continue to carry out this rite, a central aspect of the ritual is precisely the drawing of lots to select the goat which will be sacrificed. The random drawing actually takes place between two goats, one sacrificed to God and the other to the devil. This is something rather astonishing for the Jewish tradition, a monotheistic tradition *par excellence*. It happens that for once everything takes place as if one were suddenly practising a sacrificial cult of devil worship. It follows that the goat sacrificed to God is no longer the one which expiates the offences of Israel. It is the goat sacrificed to the devil which bears these offences. Between these two goats, originally identical, the high priest casts lots to discover which one will be sacrificed to God and which to the devil. Thus the random drawing is absolutely fundamental to the ritual, yet it does not contradict its significance because everyone knows that it is thanks to this ritual that Israel is going to continue to live, thanks to it that there will be, as Mr Yamaguchi put it, 'rejection of evil', that all the evil that has accumulated within the community over the course of the year will be expelled.

I am going to proceed now to the second of the ideas which I said were treated as self-evident in Girard's work. This second idea is tied to the first which I have just outlined: that misrecognition is necessary for the operation of the victimage mechanism. Girard's reasoning is, I believe, as follows: since all societies can exist only thanks to the victimage mechanism and, more precisely, thanks to the misrecognition of it, its revelation can only be of divine origin. And this divine revelation allows the mechanism to disappear. In so far as this mechanism is accompanied by violence at every level – as much at the level of differentiation as at that of undifferentiation – everything takes place as if the primary objective of the divine revelation were to do away with all violence. And this implies, as a seemingly evident consequence, that the divine revelation can only be the revelation of the God of love.

At the risk of appearing excessively provocative, I am going to try to defend the idea that there exists an alternative to this recourse to the divine referent – an alternative which, in my view, does not destroy the theory at all but in fact reinforces it. This alternative is the recourse not to the God of love, but to the God of violence.

Perhaps you will recognize in this something like a reversal of Simone Weil's accusations against the God of Israel, God of war and hence a cruel God. It is obvious that I do not subscribe to Simone Weil's accusations. I intend, on the contrary, to attempt to show that what seemed shocking to her, and could but be shocking seen through her Christian eyes despite her Jewish origins, appears in a very different light if one adopts the point of view internal to Jewish tradition. It is then apparent that the same objective is pursued here as in the Christian tradition – the disappearance (destruction?) of violence – but by an opposite tactic, a sacrificial tactic. This tactic of cunning and of the diversion of evil culminates in the displacement, by the rabbinical literature, of the notion of a god of war from real wars to what the Midrash calls 'the war of the Torah'[6]: i.e. from actual physical violence to the violence of the discourse of textual interpretation and the uninterrupted search for truth.

This is in fact a reversal of the second part of René Girard's reasoning. From the moment one grants that the surrogate victim mechanism is what founds all human societies, the struggle against the violence that accompanies this mechanism can no longer be carried on by attempting to eliminate all sacrificial institutions, simply because that is impossible. Since no society can exist without this mechanism, the struggle against violence must be accomplished by trying to bend the mechanism and to trick it, using a technique rather similar to that of judo, which consists in employing the adversary's own force to bring him down. It is in exactly these terms that the Jewish tradition describes the rites of the Day of Atonement, the day when the rite of the scapegoat is performed. And it is obviously the reason for the devil's presence in this rite. The idea is to make him participate in the rite in order to destroy him.

To be able to understand this, one must see that in the Jewish tradition sacrifice is always experienced within an economy of forgiveness that contradicts the literal interpretation of the *lex talionis*: an eye for an eye, a tooth for a tooth. The *lex talionis* in a sense exposes the mechanism of the founding violence, the system of an infinite violence made up of retaliation, destruction and counter-destruction. Forgiveness will seek a way to put an end to this mechanism. To this end, the mechanism of violence will be diverted and replaced; its process will be displaced through an effort to fool the adversary, but not to eradicate it, because one knows that to be impossible.

This displacement will initially take the form of a transformation of human sacrifice into animal sacrifice. It is remarkable that for Girard there is no difference between human sacrifice and animal sacrifice, in the sense that he has a global conception of the sacrificial. Men are either on the interior or on the exterior of the sacrificial. From this view-point the passage from human to animal sacrifice can assume no other significance than that of a step forward on the road leading to the disappearance of sacrifice. But this transition constitutes in reality a trick played on the sacrificial, given that we know it cannot be left behind.

The second form of displacement rests on a transformation of the *lex talionis*. The literal interpretation 'an eye for an eye' is abandoned in favour of an interpretation in terms of economic compensation.

In point of fact, in the empirical Jewish law the *lex talionis* was never applied literally; *a fortiori* it never is today. It rests concretely on a principle of material compensation, on the fact of repaying in money the damage created by trying to evaluate the exchange value of such and such a damage.

It is important also to realize that this displacement of the retaliation, its diversion from its primary objective, is conceived as being indispensable in order that repentance and forgiveness be possible. Possible, that is, in a world that is real, not illusory; in a world that can exist only thanks to the victim who founded it. The pure and simple elimination of sacrifice would lead to an illusory forgiveness. For the forgiveness not to be illusory, it must be accomplished within the framework of this world founded on violence. The only way to obtain this result is to displace and deceive the mechanism of the founding violence.

One finds in the Jewish tradition numerous examples of this approach to the problem of violence and atonement. The story of Jonah is a completely characteristic instance; that is why the text of this story is recited on the Day of Atonement, Yom Kippur. Many people wonder what relationship there is between the Day of Atonement and the story of Jonah. The relationship is actually rather obvious: at the end of the Book of Jonah the inhabitants of Nineveh are in fact forgiven because they have repented. But what is interesting in all this is the position of Jonah himself.

Jonah is afraid to announce the punishment of Nineveh; that is why his first act is to flee. Why is he afraid to announce this punishment? Because he knows that if the inhabitants of Nineveh repent and if they are in fact forgiven, then there will have to be a scapegoat. Somebody will have to pay, because Jonah knows there can be no forgiveness without a displacement of the sacrifice. He also knows that he is the one who will pay. The victim will be chosen at random and, as if by chance, the lot will fall on him. Why? Because it was he who announced the destruction of Nineveh.

There is an event at the beginning of the story of Jonah that prefigures what will take place at the end. Jonah flees his prophetic vocation, he embarks on a ship, and soon the ship is caught in a storm. The worried sailors ask themselves what could be the reason for the storm, and they cast lots. The lot obviously falls on Jonah, and it is then discovered that because he disobeyed his God, Jonah is the cause of the storm. Later, Jonah will be obliged in spite of himself to do what he did not want to do: to announce the destruction of Nineveh. The inhabitants repent and are forgiven the evil they had done. At this moment a 'great unhappiness' assaults Jonah.[7] He turns towards God and says to Him in so many words: 'I knew that it would be like this, I knew that you would forgive and that the evil would fall on me; that is what I wanted to avoid and that is why I fled. And now take my life, for I prefer to die.'

One finds the same economy of forgiveness and violence, the same relationship between the two, in the Talmudic legend of the shrinking of the moon. But this legend is interesting for another reason: it ends with an explanation of the ritual sacrifice that was performed with each new moon, at the beginning of each month. Here is the legend:[8] The biblical account of Genesis says that in the beginning God created two great lights and the stars; a little later it is said that God created the greater and the lesser lights. The Talmudic commentary expresses surprise at this: is there not a contradiction here? First we are told of two great lights, then of a greater and a lesser. The answer, the Talmudic commentary continues, is very simple: at first the moon was the equal of the sun, then a peculiar phenomenon took place: the shrinking of the moon. Why? Because the moon, seeing itself to be the equal of the sun, complained to the Creator, saying, 'It is not possible to have two kings under the same crown.' God answered, 'You are right, get smaller.' 'What,' said the moon, 'just because I'm right I have to be the one to pay!'

A dialogue ensues in which God attempts unsuccessfully to console the moon. He begins by saying, 'You will shine not only at night, but also in the daytime.' And the moon answers, 'Some privilege, in the daytime I will be as bright as a candle at high noon.' Then God continues, 'You will be used for the calendar, thanks to you the children of Israel will be able to count the months and the holidays.' And the moon replies, 'Yes, but the sun will play a role here too, for the children of Israel will be obliged to take account of the seasons in establishing the calendar.' God then finds a third form of consolation in the fact that being little carries with it a certain grandeur, rather along the lines of 'small is beautiful'. All the great righteous men of Israel were called little: one is told of little David, little Samuel, etc. At this the moon makes no reply, but the text adds that God can see it is not satisfied. So God says, 'That is why at every new moon [at the start of each month] the children of Israel will perform an expiatory sacrifice.'

Now the biblical text which records the commandment for this expiatory sacrifice of the new moon uses a rather peculiar grammatical form[9] which can be interpreted as meaning that what must be expiated by this sacrifice is an offence on the part of God. It is a question of a sin offering for God which can be interpreted as a sacrifice destined to expiate an offence committed by God. In this context the offence can only be the shrinking of the moon, which was, however, indispensable to getting history started by introducing a differentiation.

At issue here is a form of contradiction between an ethical demand, a demand for justice – why should the moon have to become smaller than the sun? – and a foundational demand, a historical demand: history can be set in motion only by an asymmetry pregnant with violence and suffering. Differentiation is necessarily violent.

Now this alternative to the God of love as the divine referent is encountered once more in a quite unusual rite that some Jews continue to practise very faithfully even today, every day on a regular basis. The rite consists in wearing little boxes. These boxes are ritual objects of black leather, called 'phylacteries' in English. One box is put on the forehead and the other on the left arm, and they are both held in place with the help of leather thongs. These boxes play a fundamental role inasmuch as they are conceived of as signs of the God of Israel although the God of Israel is posited as unattainable, invisible and inconceivable, as the One Whose name cannot be spoken. Through these boxes, paradoxically, God is suddenly made visible – or at least His name is, in a very concrete fashion. To be sure, several other rites exist which serve as signs, such as circumcision, the Sabbath, holidays, etc.; but these signs, including circumcision, remain in the last analysis more abstract, whereas here what represents the God of Israel is boxes, something one can touch. There is a kind of paradox here, because we are simultaneously dealing with an abstraction, a total dematerialization of the God of Israel, and a rematerialization under the most concrete and most immediate form possible.

This rite is quite simply the application of the biblical commandment which says, 'And it shall be for a sign unto thee upon thine hand, and for a memorial between thine eyes, that the Lord's law may be [fluent] in thy mouth: for with a strong hand hath the Lord brought thee out of Egypt.'[10] There are two aspects to this sign. On the one hand it is a question of rendering the law fluent in the mouth of the one who recites it; on the other it is a question of remembering the flight from Egypt. More precisely, it is a question of remembering the founding violence of the Hebrew people: with a 'strong hand the Lord brought thee out', He killed the first-born of the Egyptians. And this murder of the first-born was a condition *sine qua non* for the creation of the Hebrew people. That is what shall 'be for a sign unto thee' between the eyes and upon the hand.

Now in a sense what is involved here is not only a sign but truly the divine referent itself. This is indicated by the fact that the sign should serve to make the Law 'fluent in thy mouth'. The reference here is to a difficulty of a linguistic order concerning the subject of the law. The primary object of the revelation is not so much the being of God (the whole problem is that its nature remains essentially unknown to us) as the Law. The primary object of the revelation addressed to Moses is the content of the Law.

But in the text of this Law, there is in fact a subject who speaks. The subject of these sentences in Hebrew is designated by different names. These names differ profoundly among themselves, and the uniform translation of them as 'the Lord' is completely inadequate. Each time the names designate a particular referent, and what they have in common is, precisely, inexpressible. It can be neither said nor thought. But if we can neither say it nor think it, how can the Law be fluent 'in [our] mouth'? How can we speak a text, recite a text of which we cannot conceive the subject?

The problem here is that of the designation of the name. For a name to have a meaning it must either be a proper name, so that one may say, it is X, and point at X with one's finger; or X must be an idea which through a series of associations refers ultimately to a concrete experience. From the moment a name no longer designates either someone or something to which one can point, or an idea, it becomes impossible to talk. That is why there is a difficulty as to the way in which the text of the Law should be used. How can the text of the Law be fluent in my mouth if the subject of the Law can be neither conceived nor designated?

That is how it comes to be designated by these boxes, which serve as a concrete referent at which one can point one's finger. But what then do these boxes have about them that is so extraordinary that they can thus serve as concrete signs of the divine referent? The self-referential aspect of this ritual should be mentioned here. These boxes made of hide, of leather, are painted black, and the black is important because it is the most neutral sign possible. But inside these boxes there is something else still: there are four rolls of parchment on which certain passages from the Bible have been transcribed. Which passages? Among others, precisely the one which reads 'it shall be for a sign unto thee', etc. Thus this sign is but the sign of a sign. But that is only the most obvious aspect of the ritual; there is another that is more hidden. This passage is itself inserted within another, also transcribed on the parchments, which recalls the destruction of the Egyptian first-born as the founding event of the Hebrew people and institutes the rite of the redemption of the first-born, the rite of the sacrifice of first-born animals and of the redemption of first-born humans.

There was in fact among the Hebrews an obligation to sacrifice the first-born of their domestic animals. By first-born is understood the infant that is at once male and the first to leave the womb of the female. It should be taken to be sacrificed. The same goes for humans, each time a first-born boy leaves a woman's womb. But as far as people are concerned, it was no longer a question of sacrifice but of redemption. The first-born had to be replaced, redeemed in the course of a ceremony in which the father redeems from the priest his son, who belongs to the priest because he is the first-born. Now this redemption and these sacrifices of the first-born are presented in these passages as being at once a reminder of and a compensation for the murder of the first-born Egyptians.

This rite also takes us back to a more fundamental origin: to the more foundational violence related in the story of the first murder, that of Abel by Cain, and illustrated by the mark of Cain. If Cain survives his crime, it is evidently because of its foundational character. It was necessary that Abel not be avenged, that Cain not be killed right away. That is why Cain was branded and protected by 'a mark . . . lest any finding him should kill him'.[11]

The foundational character of this first murder refers back to the relationship of undifferentiation that exists between the mother and her first-born. Traditionally, Cain's name is connected with his mother Eve, and more precisely to the manner in which she gave birth to him. At the moment when Eve gave birth to Cain, she realized that it was the first time a man was born of a woman, since Adam was not born of a woman but of the earth. So Eve is identified with the totality as the 'mother of all living',[12] and so in a sense she still encompasses Cain even though he is already born. Eve gives birth to Cain and says, 'I have got [Caniti] a man with the Lord.'[13] This sentence can evidently be understood in two ways. It could mean: I have got a man by lying with the Lord, since the Lord impregnated me. Or it could mean: I have got a man, and in the same instant I have got the Lord, in that I have acquired one of the essential attributes of God, the only one up until now who could make a man. Here Eve becomes, if I may say so, actively involved in the process of creation.

Now this way in which Eve experiences her childbirth can be conceived of as the primary factor determining Cain for murder. This determination is affirmed in other verses, where it is said that 'sin lieth at the door',[14] and in a number of exegeses in the Midrash. It is the undifferentiation between the mother and the masculine first-born, who leaves her womb without yet being sufficiently detached and who continues to live in an undifferentiated mode, which condemns Cain to murder as an act of separation, of cutting off, as the only means of existing as a being differentiated from the other.

All this culminates in a vision of a God of violence, but a just God. Or of a God who, if He is unjust on the level of ethics, is just on the level of the founding effect. This is illustrated by another legend[15] which refers this time to the flight from Egypt properly speaking, that is to the extermination of Pharaoh's army in the Red Sea that follows the massacre of the first-born Egyptians. It is taken up by the Zohar[16] and transposed to the Yom Kippur rite of the scapegoat discussed above: the latter is handed over to Satan, the exterminating angel, when he comes accusing Israel, demanding a reckoning for its sins. This is a new ruse which uses evil against evil; while Satan is busy feeding on the evil produced by the sins, the evil is turned against him; he can no longer be the accuser; 'the accuser becomes the defender' and forgiveness for the sins becomes possible. The legend takes place at the moment when the Hebrews, pursued by the Egyptians, find themselves on the shore of the Red Sea and when God is getting ready to separate the waters, letting the Hebrews pass and engulfing the Egyptians. At this moment an angel speaks up, and we understand that it is the angel of evil but also the angel of justice, because it stands before God accusing Him in the name of a rigorous Justice. It says to God:

> Why are you going to save the Hebrews now? By what right? They have no more reason to be saved than the Egyptians. You said to Pharaoh, 'Let the children of Israel go or else I will kill the first-born Egyptians.' He didn't let the children of Israel go and the first-born Egyptians died. They are even. On what grounds are you now going to break with justice, open the Red Sea and massacre the Egyptians again, not only the first-born this time but their fathers and brothers as well? All this to deliver a people that is no more deserving than any other.

There follows a long list of the sins of Israel. 'And if the Egyptians commit all these abominations, the children of Israel commit them also', the angel adds; 'neither of these two peoples is more deserving than the other.' God then answers the angel, saying, 'Have you seen my servant Job and how righteous he is?' 'Not at all', the angel replies. 'Job isn't righteous, he simply has never experienced misfortune.' 'Well then,' God says, 'go ahead and try to tempt him and you will see for yourself what happens.'

In other words, the legend directly ties the flight from Egypt to the beginning of the Book of Job, where it is said[17] that Satan participated in a meeting of angels 'about' (or, in the Zohar's version, 'against') God. When, without its being clear why, God draws his attention to the merits of Job, he answers that it is not for nothing that Job is an upright man; he has everything he wants, etc. And that is when God apparently rises to the challenge that He Himself provoked of putting Job to the test, and delivers him to Satan. Everything takes place as if there were a gap to be filled in the text, an unanswered question about the context of this meeting of angels, a question typical of those raised by the Midrashic exegesis[18] regarding what is left unsaid in the Book of Job. An answer to this question is provided by the legend in the Midrash, which consists of saying: this meeting took place at the moment of the flight from Egypt, at the moment when Satan was pleading the cause of the

Egyptians, with good reason in a sense, in the name of justice. And at that moment it is God who deceives Satan and hands Job over to him.

There is, however, a double scandal here. In order to bring the children of Israel out of Egypt, which is already an injustice owing to the new massacre of Egyptians involved in this departure, God commits a new injustice. He seizes on a poor unlucky soul who never did anyone any harm, considered to be upright by God Himself, and delivers him up to Satan, who is going to overwhelm him with misfortunes. The legend concludes by saying that what God did resembles the action of a shepherd who wants his flock to cross a difficult ford when suddenly a wolf appears. He takes one of the rams, the strongest of the flock (the scapegoat or Job, depending on the context) and delivers it up to the wolf. While the wolf is busy tackling the ram, the shepherd helps his flock across the ford.[19]

That is how these texts describe the birth of the Hebrew people. And they imply an image of God, precisely the one hidden inside the phylactery boxes: an image that is evidently the opposite of that of the God of love. It is the image of a God of violence, or *more precisely the image of a God who takes upon Himself the founding violence*.

Now it strikes me that in so far as one is going to refer to God in the struggle against violence – *which is not indispensable* – it is perhaps more economical – more effective and less dangerous – to refer to the God of violence rather than the God of love. For if the world of men implies violence, if one is indeed convinced of the ineluctable character of the mechanism of differentiation starting out from an undifferentiated state, involving violence both at the level of mimesis and at that of the surrogate victim, the only chance we have to succeed one day in eliminating violence in a theological context (which, again, is not indispensable) lies in considering it legitimate only when it comes from God. That is the only means of prohibiting all recourse to violence by *ourselves*.

Indeed, by rejecting on to God the violence which He controls, we can be responsible for eliminating this violence. Men can in this way conceive of themselves as being responsible for the elimination of violence. Otherwise one falls into another theology, which one finds in Girard's writing and which leads to men's damnation, since by definition they cannot respond to God's message of love: there is too radical a gap between the demand for love and concrete reality. If, as Girard says, this demand for love can only be divine, this God has no place in the reality of the world, since this world can only be founded on violence.

To put it in another way: the idea that God is entirely love, whereas the world can function only thanks to violence, means that the search for love or the love of love is in some sense counterproductive; one must leave the world in order to find it, while violence, which can be attributed only to men or the devil, becomes the normal horizon of our experience in the world.

Inversely, the belief that violence in its founding functions – therefore in its justified aspect, transformed into the sacred – can be attributed only to an invisible and unattainable God means that men's normal horizon can be perceived, *in its normality*, only as *non*-violent. The best way to rid the world of the violent sacred is to reject it on to a transcendence. The transcendence of violence in its founding functions – in other words this function's sacredness perceived *consciously as such* (and not misrecognized) – culminates in its being expelled from the normal horizon of things. All men have to do, the only thing for which they are responsible, is to combat it despite its founding functions and even while recognizing its sacred character. This violence that is necessary, and in some sense justified, can never be justified in the hands of men : it is the violence of Nature, of a transcendent God. Even if it exercises its power through men, the very fact that they understand it means they cannot possibly turn this justification to their advantage from the viewpoint of moral law. The God with whom we are dealing here is not a God to be imitated but, on the contrary, one who must be opposed ('God decides, the righteous nullifies'[20]).

Given the context of our discussion of imitation and differentiation, it is interesting to call attention to the opposition that exists here between two possible attitudes towards the divine: on one side, imitation of a God of love with the danger of violence inherent in all fusion or mimesis – the danger, therefore, of a practice of violence based on a discourse of love; on the other, differentiation from a God of violence who, in addition, orders us to love. The danger this time is of being trapped by the ruse itself. For one does not imitate in performing the rite, one plays and acts through trickery with the danger of being tripped up by paradox, of not being able to overcome the apparent contradiction and being cast into the desiccation of rupture and separation.

In the face of the abysses these theologies open before us it is understandable that 'humanist', 'secular' quests for a 'natural' non-violence are not without their appeal, despite or because of their naïveté. If it is impossible to imitate a God of love because we are human, and if it is too difficult to oppose a God of violence while at the same time serving Him, it is as well to combat violence without thinking too hard about it and without resorting to God! This can sometimes be no less effective.

In the guise of a conclusion, I am going to tell you one last story. You know that Moses was punished, that he was forbidden to enter the land of Israel. The story goes that at the moment when Moses first caught sight of the Promised Land, God told him he would not be able to enter because he had killed an Egyptian, and this was the punishment for the murder he had committed. Moses, indignant, then said to God: 'How's this? You're punishing me for having killed a man when you yourself have massacred thousands!' And God replied: 'Yes, but I'm entitled to, because I bring them back to life.'

From Mythical Bees to Medieval Anti-Semitism

CESÁREO BANDERA

If we but slightly manipulate a mythical text and give it a historical setting, by changing its circumstances and modernizing the style, we are likely to end up with a narrative that will be clearly recognized as a text of persecution of the type found in Guillaume de Machaut's *Jugement du Roy de Navarre* dealing with the plague and the Jews. This is what René Girard does with the Oedipus myth in *Le Bouc émissaire*.

He does it in order to show that mythology is nothing but a persecution text in disguise, *the* representational system *par excellence* of a murderous, persecuting humanity that does not recognize the fundamentally arbitrary character of its own violence.

His point is also that such a mythical disguise is wearing very thin. And one of the reasons why it is wearing so thin is the fact that we can now see the structural homology between mythical texts and historical texts of persecution.

His little 'maquillage' (doctoring), 'changement de décor' (cosmetic changes), to the Oedipus myth is illustrative, and it does make a point. But he must rely on 'la bonne volonté du lecteur' (the goodwill of the reader) automatically to situate his narration 'quelque part dans le monde chrétien entre le XIIe et le XIXe siècle'. (somewhere in the Christian world between the twelfth century and the nineteenth century). Nobody could possibly believe, for example, that his 'décor' looks medieval at all. Thus there is a danger that the very strength of his argument may be undermined at this particular juncture in the eyes of those unwilling to provide that minimum of goodwill necessary for his little experiment to be fully effective.

In this regard it would be ideal if he could show that his narration of the Oedipus myth is not really his but a translation, let us say, or a paraphrase of an authentic medieval text. Furthermore, imagine if he could also show that the author of such a medieval text were actually inspired in his description of the contemporary event by his reading of the old Oedipus myth! Surely we could then say that the myth itself had become historically a text of persecution.

I wish I could provide Girard with such an ideal text. Lacking this, however, in what follows I will analyse a text which, though not the ideal one, may in my judgement be as good an approximation as we are likely to get. Perhaps while doing this we shall also learn something about the special character of at least one common type of medieval persecution text. For, as we shall see, this type of text can be a rather complex intellectual exercise.

The text in question was written by an illustrious member of the Church in thirteenth-century Belgium: Thomas of Cantimpré, Doctor of Theology and suffragan bishop. In the words of his seventeenth-century editor, Georgius Colvenerius, 'Venerabilis Thomas de Cantimprato fuit vir urbanae eloquentiae et militaris prosapiae, natus de villa Liewis S. Petri, iuxta Bruxellam in Brabantia [i.e. Belgium].'[1] The Renaissance humanist Justus Lipsius said he was a disciple of Albertus Magnus; according to others, he was a condisciple of Thomas Aquinas.

He wrote a book entitled *Bonum Universale de Apibus*, 'In which the universal norm [*ratio*] for organizing a good and Christian life is taken from the marvellous republic of bees, elaborated with great artifice, a varied and delectable work, with miracles and memorable examples from his own time inserted everywhere.'[2]

The book is to some extent an amplification of Saint Ambrosius' allegorical treatment of bees in the *Hexaemeron*. He either quotes or paraphrases Saint Ambrosius and then proceeds to amplify, explain, and illustrate.

One of his illustrative miracles or examples must be of interest to us. It occurs in Book II, Chapter XXIX, where the theme is 'De virtute castitatis' ('About the virtue of chastity'), while he is elaborating on the natural 'fact' that 'the purity of a virgin body is common to all bees.'

This belief about the virginal chastity of bees was indeed widespread and very old. 'According to Pindar, the prophetess at Delphi was called the "Delphic Bee". . . The reason for the name was that bees were supposed to be chaste.'[3] The temple of Vesta (with its vestal virgins) was in the shape of a beehive. There is therefore nothing specifically medieval about this belief. What is specifically medieval is the conviction that this 'fact', like any other natural fact, is ordained by God as a figuration or prefiguration of something, the meaning of which is made explicit through the Christian Revelation.

It is through this revelation that the secrets of nature become significant.

Needless to say, the natural virginity of bees can only be a *figura* of the virginity of Mary, Mother of God. And it is repeatedly used throughout the Middle Ages as an argument against 'impious Jews' who cannot believe that a virgin can be a mother. If nature offers examples (vultures are also supposed to give birth 'without contact with a male') of generation without mating, so the argument runs, you cannot deny that it is naturally possible.

Thomas says:

> Bees do not mix among themselves to lie with each other, nor do they yield to libidinous desire, and yet they produce the greatest of offspring. In a literal sense [*secundum litteram*] one can see the greatest marvel here, and one of nature's most profound secrets. Therefore, if this can be observed in insignificant animals, why do you refuse to believe, oh! Jews, that one single virgin among Christians may have given birth?[4]

It is within this context that our miracle-example is introduced, somewhat casually, with the following words: 'Now, since I have mentioned the Jews, I will tell you of a most famous miracle, which happened in the year of Our Lord 1271, in the German city by the name of Pfortzheim.'

Slightly abridged, it is as follows: An evil old woman stole a seven-year-old girl from her parents and sold her to the Jews to be sacrificed. They took her to a secret place, laid her upon several layers of clean linen, stopped her mouth, made incisions in all the joints of her arms and legs, and then, 'exerting the greatest pressure' (*maximo conamine*), they squeezed her blood out and collected it in the layers of linen. Then they threw her body, tortured and dead, in the waters that flowed near the fortress and put many stones on top. After three or four days, however, she was discovered by fishermen when they saw her hand 'erect pointing at heaven' (*per manum erectam ad celum*), and they carried her inside the fortress amid the horrified outcry of the people against so much infamy perpetrated by impious Jews. A prince happened to be in the neighbouring county. After hearing of such a scandalous crime he immediately came to the body, which sat up at once and extended a hand to the prince as if asking for her blood to be avenged, or perhaps as a sign asking for mercy. Soon after midday the body resumed its defunct position. The impious Jews were brought to see the spectacle, and immediately all her wounds began to bleed profusely in testimony of her nefarious death. At once the crowd raised its clamour to the sky and became totally of one mind (*totaliter animatur*) to ask for heaven's vengeance. Some clues led to the old woman, who was convicted, especially when one of her children, a little girl, revealed everything, because children and Jews always confess the truth. Those Jews who had put their criminal hands on the girl were also caught, put to the torture wheel and hanged with the old woman. Two of them, however, cut each other's throat. Brothers Reynerus and Aegidius of the preaching order, who were in that city three days after these events, truthfully told us what had happened.[5]

Thus Thomas. There really is no reason to believe that he made up the whole story. In all likelihood something happened in or around 1271 in the city of Pfortzheim, and some Jews were massacred. It is even possible that there were a Brother Reynerus and a Brother Aegidius, who may have been in that city some time after the events. But if this is so, we shall never know exactly what they heard, in what context and from what sources. We shall never know, either, what they actually told Thomas. For we must keep in mind that Thomas' overriding intention is not that of a chronicler but of a moralist who feels deeply that his primary duty is to make the case fit the didactic purpose at hand, to serve as an illustration.

But this is precisely where the problem with Thomas' text begins. The problem is twofold. First, after reading this particular 'example' in context, one must wonder what this may have to do with the virtue of chastity – the explicit theme of the chapter – or with the Virgin Mary, who is not even mentioned. Our surprise is reinforced by the fact that Thomas is usually very good, in the rest of his book, at fitting the example to the theme. There are all kinds of miracles in the book, performed by the Virgin Mary. A tempest is calmed by singing *Salve Regina*, a nun is freed from the devil's possession by the words *Benedictus Jesu fructus ventris tui*, a respectable matron is cured of a disease (*iliaca passione*) through the intercession of Mary, etc. Any such thing would have fitted nicely. In a book full of Marian miracles one would expect a really good one, when dealing specifically with the question of virginal chastity.

Secondly, even though the accusation of infanticide against the Jews was common throughout Europe in the Middle Ages, the manner in which this particular infanticide is carried out is rather unusual. This question of method has great importance for a medieval allegorist such as Thomas. Perhaps any manner of crime would do for the violent and indignant crowd at Pfortzheim. As long as the crime is outrageous enough, they would likely blame it on the Jews. But this is certainly not the case for interpreter Thomas writing and thinking about it in the solitude of his study. For him Jews do not *just* commit crimes, they commit them in a 'meaningful', 'Jewish' way, which must always reflect in one way or another *the* Jewish crime, the crucifixion of Christ.

There is an abundance of written texts describing the crucifixion of children at the hands of the Jews, this being the most obvious and allegorically clear method. In Spain, for example, one of the most famous 'cases' was that of the so called 'Martyrdom of the Saint Boy of La Guardia', a town near Toledo. One of the accused, the Jew Jucé Franco, was burned in Avila on 16 November 1491. The legal proceedings, handled by the Inquisition, were published by Father Fita in the *Boletín de la Real Academia de la Historia*, XI (1887). The boy – a seven-year-old again – was supposedly crucified.

Another 'case' is that of the boy of Alcalá (near Madrid), an almost exact replica of the La Guardia story:

> Eight or ten people, who pretended to be Christians, one day secretly took a seven-year-old boy to a mountain, and there they crucified him as if he were Jesus Christ. The boy, seeing himself in such a situation, asked them why they were doing that to him. They answered that it was important for him to die; then they stabbed him through the ribs with a small spear . . . and after extracting the heart from his body they buried the body; then they burned the heart and turned it to ashes. Some people accused them; they were arrested and interrogated; it was then learned that they had mixed those ashes with other substances and intended to cause the death of the king and other Spanish nobles. Because of all this they were burned after being tortured to the best of the people's ability[!]; and all their goods were confiscated for the king.[6]

In cases like these, the 'meaning' of the method used in the infanticide is perfectly obvious. But what in the case of Thomas' text? Obviously he felt that some kind of explanation was needed, because at the end of his text he attempts to provide one:

> Later I heard one of the most learned Jews of our times, converted to the faith, say that one *quasi*-prophet of theirs, just before he died, prophesied to the Jews, saying: know this for certain, in no way will you be relieved of that by which you are punished in a most shameful way, except through Christian blood. But the Jews, always blind and impious, rushed precipitately upon such words and deduced that they were to shed Christian blood every year in every province so that they would be cured with such blood.

Notice once more the equation between blindness and impiety on the one hand, and on the other the 'raping of the word' (*verbum rapientes*). Implicitly the constant, underlying theme of the book, its ultimate lesson, is how to read a text properly: above all the 'text' of nature itself, God's own text.

This 'explanation', however, while confirming the fact that for Thomas Jewish crimes are meaningful as a misreading or travesty of the Christian sacrifice – that is, as witness to the truth in spite of themselves – does not solve the problem of the particular method used in this infanticide or of its thematic connection with either chastity or virginity.

Now, Thomas is not a fiction writer, certainly not in any modern sense. He does not simply invent things; he is a commentator, a text reader in typical medieval fashion, searching for the hidden meaning of things, God's veiled messages. He adapts, transforms, elaborates. Just as I do not think that he purely imagined the events at Pfortzheim, I cannot think that he imagined the elaborate method of this infanticide. On the other hand, it is equally difficult for us to imagine that he got every detail in his text from whatever report he heard of the events at Pfortzheim. Therefore the question must be: what else did he have in mind? Whence came those details? What was he reading, in the sense of interpreting, in connection with or in the light of those events? If those details, like everything else in his text, are already an interpretation, what more is he interpreting?

Writing as he was at that moment about the non-sexual reproduction of bees, he must have been reading about the ways in which bees are generated out of something other than bees. For this was a widespread theme in Christian literature. 'Bees do not come out of bees,' says, for example, John Cassianus in his *De Incarnatione Christi*, 'they are workers, not procreators; they come out of little flowers in the grass.' Therefore – this is Cassianus' point – it is not true 'quod dissimilem sibi res quoelibet parere non possit' (that nothing can give birth to anything dissimilar to itself), for 'quid simile herbis et animantibus?' (what is the similarity between herbs and animated beings?).[7]

But there is another method of generating bees from something other than bees – a method backed by the unquestioned authority of Virgil and also mentioned by some of the greatest authorities in the Church: St Augustine and Origen, for example.[8] Briefly reconstructed from Virgil's *Georgics* IV, supplemented by other sources, the procedure is as follows: A young bull is taken to a small enclosure. A large number of young men surround the bull and pound on it with wooden sticks or rods until it collapses. They immediately stop its mouth and nostrils with clean linen and continue pounding on it while they also exert great pressure on the body, as if kneading, in order to mix flesh and bones into a pulp. It is important, however, not to spill any blood. To that end the blows must be such that they leave the hide intact. They lay the young bull, thus battered down, on fresh cassia and thyme. Then they leave, closing the door and windows and covering them with mud so that no air can come in or out. Later on they will make some openings to admit fresh air and light. After a few days a new swarm of bees will arise from the rotten flesh and blood.[9]

It does not take an eye specially trained, as Thomas' was, in the art of searching for subtle and meaningful parallels and analogies to see the surprising similarity between the group of Jews stopping the girl's mouth and pressing her body and the group of men massing on the young bull. Even the 'small enclosure' into which they take the bull, and which they later cover up carefully, has the air of 'a secret place' about it.

This similarity, however, no matter how intriguing, would still be too little. It is indeed a most curious coincidence, especially happening where it does in Thomas' text. But it can only be a first step, something to alert the reader to the possibility that a significant piece of the puzzle has been found.

Let us concentrate, then, on what I will call from now on the bull method. Its central feature is undoubtedly the special way in which the bull is killed. It is a prescribed, ritual way. Apparently any ordinary killing will not do the trick. Unless they manage *not to spill the blood*, by keeping the skin intact and stopping the mouth, and unless they also *break the bones* and press everything under the skin into a pulp, the killing of the young bull will be useless, meaningless. In other words, the way they kill the young bull must be precisely symmetrically opposite to the way in which Thomas' Jews kill the young girl at Pfortzheim: they squeeze the blood out and leave the bones intact (this detail is further emphasized by the raising of the hand and the ability of the body to sit up straight).

What a shocking, pagan, anti-Christian way of producing none other than bees, the very symbol of chastity and virginity, the *figura* of Christ's incarnation and of the Virgin Mary! The shock, of course, has nothing to do with the revulsion a modern sensitivity may experience before such a spectacle. It is an intellectual shock. It has to do with the fact that in the bull method the procedure is exactly the opposite of what happened to Christ on the cross: He was bled to death but they did not break His bones, as they did those of the two thieves who were crucified at His sides, as every Christian has always known, especially in the Middle Ages.

On the one hand, such a shocking method of producing chaste and virginal bees could only be regarded by medieval allegorists as something sacrilegious or blasphemous, the very work of the Devil. That is to say, precisely the sort of thing that 'impious' Jews would relish doing, *if only they could*. But, on the other hand, they could not. Jews could not perform a sacrilegious crime in that way.

To a superficial or distant observer it might appear as if the Jews were doing to the girl what the pagans were doing to the bull. But thoughtful Thomas is no naïve allegorical sleuth. He knows that the Jews were blind to the spirit but not to the letter of Christianity. They had to perform their crime according to the Christian letter, while at the same time hiding its meaning. Thus he makes them hide, camouflage, the clue that would give them away: the incisions in the joints through which they drained the blood. In other words, they hide the traces of the truth precisely where an alert Christian would look for them: in those joints which, of course, they could not break and through which the dead body of the girl would bleed profusely, thereby making it plain to everybody that it was the Jews who did it and turning their crime into a miraculous symbol of Christ's Passion.

Needless to say, what gives the Jews away for Thomas is precisely what gives Thomas away for us. But the important thing about this allegorical interplay between the Pfortzheim 'example' and the bull method is that the similarities are as significant as the differences; they reinforce and give meaning to each other.

The bull method was revealing precisely to the extent that it was shocking. It allowed Thomas to see the Christian sacrifice as a reversal of the pagan one. In Christ's death what had been, so to speak, upside down was turned right side up. And, quite logically, this transformation of pagan ritual into a symbol of the Christian ritual could not have been accomplished without the providential – though blind – mediation of the Jews. In his sacrificial view of Christianity, where meaning itself is produced sacrificially, Thomas' transformation of pagan meaning into Christian meaning required still another sacrifice, that of the Jews. The Jews were simply the victims the allegorical coherence of his text demanded.

The similarities and contrasts between the bull method and the Jewish method of the example are such that in order to deny a deliberate connection between the two one would have to deny that Thomas had ever read Virgil's *Georgics* or any of the other texts that describe the bull method and frequently refer back to Virgil as an authority on the matter. Such a denial, when dealing with a thirteenth-century learned churchman who, in addition, was a 'bee specialist' cannot possibly be maintained. One did not even have to be very learned to know that bees can also come out of the flesh of young bulls. For, as commentator Gazeus says, such a notion was 'common knowledge' (*vulgatum est*).[10]

On the other hand, if the connection was indeed deliberate we should not expect to find any explicit reference to any text where the bull method is described, not even Virgil's. And this is exactly the case, which with regard to Virgil would be most surprising under any other circumstances. Nothing in Thomas suggests that he knew about the bull method. This was a matter of elemental prudence, not necessarily because he thought he might be accused of having done something dishonest but most probably because since he was writing to provide instruction for the unlearned faithful in general, an explicit connection with the shocking bull method would have complicated his task or blurred the didactic value of the Pfortzheim example.

He was by no means the only one to skirt carefully around the shocking bull method when allegorizing about the chastity of bees. Saint Ambrosius himself, Thomas' acknowledged guide, did just that in spite of the fact that he knew the *Georgics* so well that many times he simply transcribes Virgil's own words into his *Hexaemeron*, as pointed out also by Gazeus: 'Hucusque Ambrosius multis phrasibus ex Virgilio mutuatis'.[11] Yet there is no mention of the bull method.

This means in effect that Thomas managed to solve, with the help of the Pfortzheim case, a difficult hermeneutic problem for Christian allegorists. In another sense, of course, he fell victim to his own solution because it is clear that such an obstacle was for him much more than just a difficult hermeneutic problem. It may, in fact, be misleading to characterize the problem as primarily intellectual. His intellectual need to solve the problem posed by the bull method was driven by something more fundamental and immediate. It was a scandal, a genuine stumbling block in the path of the allegorist. And he ran straight into it. He saw, and was blinded by what he saw. At some point it was no longer a question of simply solving an intellectual problem but of finding a living example bearing the guilt for such an outrage. As a consequence of this all his allegorical ingenuity – his subtle, even brilliant intellectual exercise – was ultimately a way to fit the guilt of the Jews into God's providential plan: a plan whereby God Himself pointed an accusing finger at the Jews, thus revealing the victim that had to be sacrificed both in the flesh, by the indignant crowd at Pfortzheim, and allegorically, in Thomas' text. In spirit at least he joined the clamouring crowd of persecutors, even though on a conscious and reflective level he was trying to impart a pious teaching.

But to come back to Girard and *Le Bouc émissaire*: it is important to realize that if Thomas was able to transform a pagan mythical text into a text of persecution, it was only because *that is precisely what he saw behind the mythical text: a scandalous, unjustified persecution of an innocent victim*. In a sense, what he saw in the pagan text is what we see in his account of the Pfortzheim case: a kind of warning signal, because to the extent that we may easily become scandalized, in turn, at what we see in his persecution of the Jews, we would simply be repeating once more his sacrificial gesture.

I say 'in a sense', because Thomas' scandalized reaction to what he saw is inseparable from his immediate assimilation of the victim to Christ. It is not because the innocence of the sacrificial victim had been discovered that it was associated with Christ, but the other way round. It was the assimilation of the victim to Christ that revealed its innocence to him.

In the final analysis, the determining factor for the immediate assimilation of the bull method to Christ's sacrifice was not the empirically particular details of the method, although these details definitely suggested to him the manner of the Pfortzheim infanticide. In Thomas' mind any sacrificial scene would have triggered the association with Christ, not in an abstract or symbolical sense but as a historical *figura* of the empirico-historical event of Christ's death. This is why he would have seen the Jews at work, regardless of the particular details of any sacrificial text he might have contemplated. The striking details of the bull method simply made his task irresistibly easier. Ironically, it was because for Thomas *all* sacrificial victims were innocent that he saw the Jews killing victims all over the place. Not because the Jews were essentially evil – a notion that would have run counter to his Christian doctrine – but because they were mistaken, they had been tricked by appearances, they did not know how to read the hidden meaning of things: that is, how to read them allegorically.

But the question now arises: did Thomas see the bull method scene as a sacrificial one only because of his characteristic Christian perspective? Perhaps an ancient non-Christian observer would have seen there only a rather peculiar manner of cattle slaughter for apicultural purposes.

Hardly. As a matter of fact, we do not have to guess at all. We have the testimony of the most perceptive pagan mind of all: Virgil's. What did Virgil see behind such a strange scene? The answer is in the Aristeus-Orpheus myth at the end of *Georgics* IV, a passage about which classicists have written extensively, but none, to my knowledge, from the perspective adopted here.[12]

After describing the bull method to generate a new swarm of bees when all of them have been lost, Virgil asks:

> Quis deus hanc, Musae, quis nobis extudit artem?
> unde nova ingressus hominum experientia cepit? (315–16)
> (What god, ye Muses, forged for us this device?
> Whence did man's strange adventuring take its rise?)[13]

The question is asked regarding, of course, 'this [particular] device' (*hanc artem*), but it is immediately rephrased in more general terms applicable, by extension, to any other 'ingressus hominum nova experientia' (first step into something new, unprecedented). In other words, what is the origin of that original step?

At the origin there is, as could be expected, a myth of origin. There is a plague, that is to say widespread disease and famine among the bees. They all die. Aristeus, the first beekeeper, feels desolate and complains bitterly to his mother Cyrene, 'that dwellest in the flood's depths'. She tells him that in order to find out what lies behind the fatal plague he must forcibly fall upon god-monster Proteus, the ever-shifting, capable of changing his form into anything, and hold him fast. If he can do this, the terrifying Proteus will be forced to reveal the truth to him. Aristeus does as he is told and finds out that behind the plague is the anger of another god, Orpheus, his rival because of Eurydice, who died bitten by a snake while fleeing from the beekeeper, thus triggering the chain of events that led to the killing of Orpheus himself at the hands of Dionysiac maenads, who tore him to pieces.

When he hears this from the monster Aristeus is even more befuddled and fearful than before, because now he knows it was no accident, but he does not know what to do about it. His mother appears again and tells him that he must offer a suppliant sacrifice to atone for the sacrifice of Orpheus and the death of Eurydice:

> But first I will tell thee in order the manner of thy supplication. Pick out four choice bulls . . . and as many heifers of unyoked neck. For these set up four altars by the stately shrines of the goddesses, and drain the sacrificial blood from their throats, but leave the bodies of the steers within the leafy grove. Anon, when the ninth Dawn displays her rising beams, thou shall send unto Orpheus funeral dues of Lethe's poppies, shall slay a black ewe and revisit the grove. Then to Eurydice, now appeased, thou shall do worship with the slaughter of a calf.

Aristeus does as instructed and on the ninth day, as he revisits the grove, he spies 'a portent, sudden and wondrous to tell': from the molten flesh of the oxen huge clouds of bees emerge and hang in clusters from the branches.

We must notice that Aristeus is as surprised to see the bees come out of the decomposed bodies of the oxen as Virgil probably was at what he thought to be a real natural phenomenon. That is, he is not trying to provide a scientific explanation for such a phenomenon, as his admired Lucretius might have done. The sense of his question is different: what were the original cultural conditions under which the phenomenon could be observed for the first time? And his answer is clear: those conditions could only be sacrificial. The young bull that the people of the Nile delta used to generate bees was a replica of the original sacrificial bull.

In fact, apart from making obvious its sacrificial character, there is very little in the Aristeus-Orpheus myth to suggest an empirical direct link with the procedural details of the bull method. The only thing Virgil is saying is that the original discovery was not a purely empirical accident but rather a by-product or side-effect of a sacrificial operation. It was discovered in the vicinity and as part of a sacrifice to an angry god. For in a mythico-sacrificial world, what but the anger of a god could be thought to be the cause of any disastrous calamity? He then goes on to explain that anger as arising from a story of rivalry and retaliation.

It is also important to notice the way in which Virgil approaches the description of the bull method and its sacrificial explanation. Such a method is never considered an expedient way to increase the number of a farmer's bees. The passage occurs while he is telling of the different remedies to be used when bees fall sick, 'because they are affected by the same ills as we are' (*quonian casus apibus quoque nostros vita tulit*). Only if the usual remedies do not work, and one is confronted all of a sudden with the fact that the entire population of bees has failed, 'then it is time' for him to reveal the bull method of the Egyptians. This procedure is not used on just any occasion, only when something terrible has happened to the bees.

In other words, the plague is always there behind the sacrificial character of the bull method. It is because the procedure is seen as sacrificial that the plague is linked to it. Or the other way round: because the plague is there, the procedure becomes sacrificial. And the same can be said about the plague and its connection with the story of rivalry and retaliation. These two things go together also; one is not thought without the other.

Thus there is a bull method because there is sacrifice, and sacrifice because there is the plague, and the plague because there is rivalry and conflict. As Virgil searches for the origin of the bull method the story of Aristeus' bees becomes the story of Aristeus himself, a human (or divine) story. And the plague among the bees clearly resonates with echoes of other mythical plagues in which the victims are human.

Let us also remember that for Virgil, even more than for any medieval scholar, the republic of bees was the symbol *par excellence* of the republic of men. Let us remember, for example, that Aeneas' father, Anchises, carried his household gods from Troy on his way to Italy, where the second Troy would be founded, on his shoulders in a small shrine shaped like a beehive. It has also been found that the hut-beehives of Italian farmers were but a small-size replica of the beehive-huts of the ancient people of Latium.[14] We have already seen that the ancient temple of Vesta, with its vestal virgins, was also in the shape of a beehive.

Besides, what does it mean to say that the bull method is ultimately a sacrificial practice? Obviously it means that what works to restore the republic of bees is exactly the same thing that works to restore the republic of men. As perceptive a reader of Virgil as Ovid concludes his reading of Virgil's account of the bull method with the significant line *mille animas una necata dedit* (*Fasti*, I, 380): the killing of one yielded a thousand lives. This is the very rationale behind the killing of any sacrificial victim. *In extremis*, when everything is at stake, one will always have to be victimized for the sake of many; or as Virgil says in the Aeneid, *unum pro multis dabitur caput*: one head will be given for the sake of many (V, 815).

At the root of the sacrificial institution, the cornerstone of the organized, productive life of the community of men, lies always the plague, that is to say, rivalry and conflict. Not just any conflict, but a generalized one involving everybody in a most violent confrontation.

In the *Aeneid*, where there is no mythical cover of 'bees', Virgil fully displays before the reader's eye what lies at the foundation of Rome's most sacred institutions, the pillars of the *pax romana*: reciprocating human violence driven in ever-widening circles to peaks of insanity – the madness, 'inane fury' (*iram inanem*) that has no issue except through the victimization of one. The poem itself becomes a deliberate sacrificial process as its focus narrows down towards the final identification of Turnus as the required victim.[15]

Thus, as both Virgil and Thomas look at the same text describing the spectacle of a group of men ritually killing a young bull, Virgil, the pagan mythographer, sees in it the image of the very origin of human society: human society literally emerging from the dead body of the sacrificial victim. Thomas, the Christian allegorist, sees there the outrageous persecution of an innocent victim, a sacrilegious misreading of God's own sacrifice. But whether it is seen as a sacrificial perversion of the only true sacrifice or as another particularized instance of the original founding sacrifice, both agree that they are dealing with a state of sacrificial violence. The difference is not so much in what they see as in what it means to each of them.

For Virgil, as opposed to Thomas, the question of who is the sacrificial victim and whether or not the victim is guilty or innocent is ultimately irrelevant. There is rivalry and jealousy, there is the 'plague' because there is retaliation, and the only way out is through sacrifice. Sacrifice is precisely the only mechanism that will work when nothing else does. Virgil knows the frightening truth that lies behind the civilized spectacle of carefully regulated ritual sacrifice. But all he can do, all he actually does, is bow his head in sombre pessimism, because there is no other way. It is either the head of the victim or utter annihilation, no human civilization at all.

This comparison between Virgil and Thomas should teach us something about the relationship between mythical texts and historical texts of persecution, within the context provided by *Le Bouc émissaire*. First of all, by looking at the evidence provided by Virgil's reading of the mythical text, it may be somewhat misleading to call a mythical text a 'text of persecution in disguise', not because we cannot see it in this light – we certainly can – but because they, pre-

Christian pagans, could not, even if they could see all the structural elements that Girard has convincingly shown us. In other words, the question is: can there be such a thing as a 'text of persecution' before Christianity?

Virgil is fully aware that from a rational or objective point of view, the choice of the victim is purely arbitrary. It is not reason but mad violence that blindly 'chooses' its victim. Yet there is not the slightest indication that he regarded this situation as an unjustified persecution. How could it be unjustified if it was at the very root of human society? He was aware of all the fundamental facts hidden underneath the surface of the ritual process, including the fact that they were and ought to be hidden. But he had no awareness of any weakening at the root of the sacrificial mechanism.

Secondly – to the extent that we may consider Thomas' text representative of at least one very common type of medieval persecution text – the characterization of such texts as debilitated or worn-out mythical representations, if not inaccurate, is at least insufficient because it does not reveal what appears to be their most significant feature: that of being, either implicitly or explicitly, as in the case of Thomas, a completely new way of reading the mythical text.

It is not as if an autochthonous self-weakening of the mythical representation gave rise to texts of persecution in some sort of unbroken continuity. On the contrary, such texts of persecution must be viewed as actively engaged in bringing about the collapse of the mythical text. As we have seen, Thomas' text is a lot more than the recorded echo of a lynching mob, even though he is far from immune to such echoes. The fact that it does not see its own violence does not mean that it cannot see somebody else's violence – the violence that structures the mythical text.

Virgil is a witness to the fact that even the most radical weakening of the mythical representation – in the sense of its wearing so thin, so unlike the 'granitic' texture of which Girard speaks, that it becomes transparent over the violence behind it – does not of itself give rise to a text of persecution. The transparency of Virgil's poetic myths can only strengthen the need for the mythical representation to exist. Virgil must surely have wished he had never seen what he saw as he lifted the mythico-sacrificial veil. For Virgil the sacrificial process is a producer of mythical representations, which are desperately needed to cover up the most horrible despair.

The weakening of the mythical veil does not of itself produce any enlightening or scientific revelation. The only truth the lifting of the mythical veil can reveal to Virgil is the terrible danger that must await any society daring to penetrate the forbidden truth. The perfect myth must be one capable of convincing everybody that there is nothing else behind it. The perfect myth ought to be totally self-referential, if we want to put it in modern parlance; but we must keep in mind that in discovering the vital necessity for mythical self-referentiality Virgil got none of the tingling sensations that some of our contemporaries derive from discovering the self-referential character of their own texts.

Virgil was too scared to accuse anybody. He could never have produced a text of persecution. In the final analysis, perhaps the only accusation possible for anybody under such circumstances would be that of having stepped too close to the truth, never an accusation of not knowing enough or of being mistaken.

Even the formally scientific discourse of the age is driven by this profound fear of the terrifying unknown. It is not designed to penetrate the forbidden secrets of the unknown but to escape from them, to substitute a different kind of language for the language of the sacred, not because the latter is thought to be silly or intellectually absurd but because it can no longer calm the terrors of a too-perceptive mind. Epicurus, Lucretius' master, was already quite clear about this:

> One must know, first of all, that knowledge concerning celestial phenomena, whether they are considered in connection with other phenomena or in themselves, has no other goal but the peace of the soul and a firm confidence . . . in effect, we do not need particular theories or vain opinions, but to live without trouble. (*Letter to Pythocles*, 86–7)

So was Virgil, in that famous passage of *Georgics II* (490–4), where he echoes Lucretius' language, but with a significant addition:

> felix, qui potuit rerum cognoscere causas
> atque metus omnis et inexorabile fatum
> subiecit pedibus strepitumque Acherontis avari,
> fortunatus et ille, deos qui novit agrestis,
> Panaque Silvanumque senem Nymphasque sorores.
> Happy the one who can know the scientific causes of things and thus be able to overcome all fear, and inexorable fate, and the howls of hungry Acheron. But equally fortunate is the one who knows the gods of the fields and their rituals.

If one can live a simple life protected by the mythico-ritual veil of hallowed traditions, one is just as happy as the scientist or philosopher who knows the cause of everything, and obviously for the same reason.

Scientific discourse attempts to be the perfect myth, the ultimate (or latest) cover-up, for those for whom the mythical veil has grown too thin. This is science driven not by confidence but by fear. This can explain Virgil's profound admiration for Lucretius, and also illuminate his incredible daring in laying bare the most terrifying secrets. And perhaps it may equally explain the profound meaning of the old belief that Lucretius became mad, a traditional belief of which it can be said: *se non e vero e ben trovato* (in more senses than one).

It is important, therefore, to differentiate between the underlying, structuring sacrificial mechanism and its mythical representation. The former can survive untouched by any shape or form in which the latter can be structured. The mythical word, no matter how perceptive and penetrating, has no power whatsoever over its sacrificially structuring machine. Before something like our typical text of persecution can appear on the scene of history, the underlying mechanism itself must be shaken at the core and deprived of the opportunity to justify itself through its mythical representation. The medieval text of persecution is perhaps the first representational result of a staggering sacrificial mechanism being forced to shed its old and by now useless garb, though still retaining the power to find new victims. It will still kill, but it will have to justify the killing in an unprecedented way.

At the representational level there is a fundamental incompatibility between the mythical text and the persecution text. They are both sacrificial, but they do not speak the same language. In spite of all the differences, Thomas' text already speaks our own language. This is why we can perfectly justifiably accuse him of not knowing what he was doing, of making a mistake, of turning his own argument against himself. Because, at least theoretically, he *could* have known. And we know that he could because we learned it from him, since that is precisely the basis of his accusation against the Jews. He was speaking against the Jews with the same kind of language that we can use against him. On the other hand, we simply cannot level such an accusation at Virgil. If we were to talk to him in the same manner as to Thomas, even though he was much more intelligent than Thomas, he would not know what we were talking about or would be scandalized by it.

Nevertheless, in case anybody thinks that I am trying to save Virgil from contamination from Thomas' persecuting mentality, let me hasten to add that even after all these 'corrections', Girard is still right. *For us* there is no other correct and objective way to look at the text of mythology but as a text of persecution. Once we know that there is such a thing as a text of persecution and what it is, we can no longer look in good faith at Virgil's illuminating reading of mythology as if nothing had happened, pretending that what *we* see has nothing to do with persecution. If we did that it would simply mean that we have learned absolutely nothing from the testimony of all the medieval Thomases. Or worse still, it could mean that the text of persecution has become for us as much of a stumbling block as were the Jews for Thomas, in the way of our understanding the text of mythology.

This is, perhaps, what has already happened. Our post-medieval, modern approach to the text of mythology encountered the medieval text of persecution as a stumbling block from the start. How could it be a mere historical coincidence that modern man began to discover the text of persecution while engaged in bringing about a revival, a humanistic reading of the text of mythology?

The only thing Girard forgets to mention when he talks about the new, modern and perceptive way of seeing the text of persecution for what it really was is that it was the medieval Thomases who, in their own way, took the text of mythology seriously because they saw behind it something real and historically relevant. Their modern attackers, on the other hand, were happily busy turning mythology into a beautiful poetic, but fundamentally irrelevant ornament. I believe that this modern poeticizing of mythology into irrelevance is only the other side of our modern, scandalized way of rejecting the medieval text of persecution – a text based, for good and for bad, on a serious reading of the mythical text.

Our modern view of the text of mythology has long been caught in this sacrificial interplay between blindness and insight. And it is by exposing and analysing the sacrificial character of such an interplay that the text of mythology and the text of persecution can throw light on each other. Thomas and Virgil must be read side by side.

I think this is ultimately what Girard is doing. If we wanted to place him, at his best, in reference to Thomas and Virgil, I would suggest that he stands equidistant from both: like Virgil plus Christianity, like Thomas minus the *skandalon*.

The Founding Murder in the Philosophy of Nietzsche

RENÉ GIRARD

(Translated by Mark R. Anspach)

As our meeting draws to a close, I feel myself swayed by contradictory emotions – joy, melancholy, gratitude, anxiety. I think of the marvellous hospitality of Edith Heurgon and Cerisy-la-Salle and of the tireless work of Paul Dumouchel and Jean-Pierre Dupuy. I think of all the friendships to which the seas and continents proved no obstacle. I think also of our imminent separation.

I think finally of 'the responsibility incumbent upon me'. In less pompous terms, I am afraid of disappointing you. With the desire to fulfil your expectations comes a specific anxiety, the one whose mimetic nature is only confirmed by overly explicit denials: the anxiety of facing the other. Not so long ago, when writing was still sacred, the writer took refuge in the claim that he wrote only for himself. These days, he works coldly at self-advertisement. But often this is another mask, or rather it is the same one which he has put back on his face after turning it inside-out like a glove. A meeting like this does not favour any of these charades. That in itself is no small merit.

I stand revealed by these days of debate as a man of a few ideas, so simple in their principle that perhaps they amount to no more than a single idea. It would in that case qualify as an '*idée fixe*'. The suggestion has been made, and I see no reason to quarrel with it. I am struck by the relevance of the *idée fixe*, but I intend to participate myself in defining it.

It seems appropriate to call the surrogate victim mechanism an *idée fixe* in that it is what fixes all ideas. For its own part, however, it owes its power of fixation to the fact that it exists only in the form of the sacred; in other words, that it is not an idea at all. Without this absence of idea there would be no coherent 'system of representations', no stable structure. Everything would be cast adrift in the turbulence of the sacrificial crisis.

To underline the absence of conscious choice in the selection of scapegoats, I therefore speak of a 'mechanism'. But that means being immediately taken for a 'mechanist'. A snare lurks behind every word. So, what is wrong with *idée fixe*?

Is the motor of all symbolicity to be sought in the surrogate victim *effect*? That is the intuition I am pursuing. If it is false, then I am wrong, but I cannot pursue it without aiming for universal results. My personal psychology may play a role here – that is possible – but the 'imperialism' is inherent in the nature of the research. I cannot renounce it without renouncing my entire enterprise.

To look for the fixed point is to look for the underlying basis of all collective representation; the project is rooted in the hubris of our culture, but it appears to me as henceforth ineluctable. The conjuncture as a whole dictates it to us. This project is akin to much recent research, but it culminates in conclusions that are diametrically opposed. Its realism and its systematic recourse to religious texts push me towards religious conclusions that displease many people. Certain oppositions are inevitable, but they can remain friendly. Others arise from misunderstanding.

To reproach me with reducing all cultural diversity to a few themes blown out of proportion is to misapprehend the nature of my research, which is not thematic. I do not dream of rearranging and ranking the contents of the positivist encyclopaedia. My *idée fixe* lies beyond all deconstruction, in a point of origin that is assuredly hypothetical but very nearly verifiable if the genetic, structural and destructuring analyses that spread outwards from it are truly able to sweep up the phenomena of the religious, ethnological, literary and philosophical encyclopaedia.

Misunderstandings necessarily proliferate because unlike what takes place in Lacanian theory, where the symbolic is carefully detached from the vicissitudes of the real, of the imaginary as they say, here the thematic spin-offs lend themselves to confusion. They dissimulate the essential dimension of the research, which is at once genetic and structural.

The arbitrary victim is not only a *hidden* structuring principle, it is also the ritual theme which everybody sees immediately; it is above all an essential part of the biblical revelation. In our day, finally, it is that same revelation tarnished by the mimetic usage made of it; it is the journalistic gimmick with which you are familiar. The mimetic reading easily slips into the facileness of the gimmick without losing absolutely all its relevance. That indeed is what discredits it in the eyes of the sensitive. I regret the misunderstandings and I do my best to dispel them, but that best is very inadequate if I am to judge by the results. Sometimes I envy Lacanians their way of tossing all real conflicts into the netherworld of the *imaginary*, nobly cloaking themselves afterwards in their inaccessible *symbolic* . . . Unfortunately this kind of victory is bought by falling back into the 'romantic' illusion, and the game is not worth a candle.

Our endeavour is, I think, as foreign to tawdry esotericism as it is to cynical or naïve exploitations of the scapegoat gimmick. From a distance, however, all these things resemble each other and catastrophic approximations abound.

To the system-builders we appear too literary; to literary types, too systematic and repetitive. And we are without doubt all that, for we are interested in the relation of all the great texts to the operation of violence and the sacred.

It is well known that critics 'project' their own pet ideas on to the texts they claim to be criticizing. They exhibit their 'discoveries' triumphantly and rhapsodize over their relevance without ever suspecting that they have retrieved unaltered the very thing they fed the machine in the first place to ensure its functioning.

I understand all too well, then, the wariness that the 'surrogate system' inspires. Confronted with the breadth and perfection of what I call its power of *ratissage*, of sweeping up everything around it, I sometimes cannot help wondering about it myself . . . I am sure you divine my meaning . . . Send any masterpiece you like my way, literary, cultural or religious, and it will be quite a miracle if I do not come back to you, a month or a year later, with my mimetic desire, my sacrificial crisis and above all – give the Devil his due – that bloody atrocity with which I am infatuated, the primordial, founding act of violence: the collective murder of the deity.

Forgive me this spell of melancholy. All around me, everything is 'renewing' itself and I, too, dream of renewing myself. But I never succeed. Where might one find *something else* to talk about? What text might grant access to *something else*?

An idea comes to me: Nietzsche. I must have recourse to Nietzsche. People have been talking about him constantly for a hundred years and nobody ever detects in his work the slightest collective violence, the faintest trace of a founding murder. Maybe he will cure me of my monomania. This is one philosopher who always has fashion on his side. Between 1930 and 1950 he had a few bad moments, but, thanks to our valiant critics, he always extricates himself admirably. Here he is among us once again, all freshened up and reinvigorated. Yesterday's sombre thinker has been replaced by a merry '68-style dissident; this is the playful, insouciant and frisky Nietzsche whom neither Lou Salomé nor Cosima would recognize.

That is what I need. Without further ado, I turn to a text that should be just what the doctor ordered for my case of religious obsession, aphorism 125 of *The Gay Science*. This is the capital text, it seems, on the subject of the definitive demise of all religion.

I shall begin at the beginning:

> Haven't you heard about the Madman who, having lit a lantern under the noonday sun, ran to the marketplace and cried incessantly, 'I seek God, I seek God!' As many of those who do not believe in God were standing around just then, he provoked much laughter. Why, have we lost him? said one. Did he lose his way like a child? said another. Or is he hiding? Is he afraid of us? Has he gone on a voyage? or emigrated? Thus they shouted and laughed.

This crowd is already modern because it is atheist. But it does not recognize its atheism in the Madman's message and that is why, from the start, it makes fun of him. The orator is 'mad' only from the view point of the crowd. Foreseeing the misunderstanding, he does his best, curiously, to aggravate it. He provokes his listeners with his strange symbolism of the lantern lit under the noonday sun. By polarizing the many against him the Madman hopes to arouse the curiosity of the rare individuals liable to comprehend him: those who find themselves exposed, like him, to the hostility of mediocre minds.

On one side there is the atheism of the crowd, vulgar atheism, and on the other the presumed atheism of the Madman. The author himself sets the rules for the game of interpretation. He suggests we reject the vulgar atheism and embrace another, more distinguished brand which must be carefully defined.

That is how all the interpreters understand this exordium. Unfortunately, they go searching for their distinguished brand of atheism everywhere in the works of Nietzsche save in the aphorism itself. It would be better at least to begin with the latter and to switch to other texts only as a last resort. The explicators conscientiously read the first lines, those I have just read you myself, but the next thing you know they are off in a cloud of dust, never to be seen by the aphorism again. Take a look, for example, at *Holzwege*, the celebrated essay by Heidegger. In principle its focus is aphorism 125. In reality the philosopher talks of everything but that.

This is a bad example, and I reject it. I have always been told that the conscientious critic deciphers his text word by word, and that is the example I am going to follow. Let me resume reading at the point where I left off:

> The Madman burst into their midst and pierced them with his gaze. 'Wither is God!' he cried. 'I shall tell you. We have killed Him – you and I! All of us are His murderers.'

Alas, alas . . . There it is, the trap: the collective murder! Exactly what I was dreading. And I have no one to blame but myself. If only I had done what everyone else does. My accursed presumptuousness has sunk me. I wanted to distinguish myself, to escape the other critics' routine, and straight away I fell back into my own. Luckily, I warned you. That is my only consolation. Your expressions tell me that your surprise is not total.

You have to admire the sly obstinacy of the *idée fixe*. Nobody ever pulled the collective murder out of this text before. I grab hold of it and, in less time than it takes a psychoanalyst to say 'Oedipus complex', there it is, like the head of John the Baptist on its silver platter. It is no longer a success, it is a fatality. If I tried to extract from the aphorism the thousand and one amazing things our colleagues extract from it, I would fail miserably. The collective murder follows me like my shadow.

Perhaps the fault lies with the translation. When one does not find what one is looking for in a text in a foreign language, the translator, as a rule, serves as the scapegoat. Why not also when one finds what one is not looking for? Let us examine the original German: '". . . *Wir haben ihn getotet – ihr und ich! Wir alle sind seine Morder*."' The idea of underlining we have killed Him is not the translator's nor even mine; it is Nietzsche's. And it is Nietzsche who insists on the unanimity of the murder, with a heavy hand that reminds me of my own: '"We have killed Him – you and I! All of us are His murderers!"'

The translation is depressingly faithful. I feel as if I were going mad; maybe I am the Madman himself reincarnated, the one in the aphorism, of whom no one ever speaks. Things had none the less begun well. But my opening moves cannot be trusted. There is a first stage in which I often succeed in concealing what I am up to, in deluding myself if no one else, but after a few lines, infallibly, I fall back into my infernal orbit, the collective murder – my own personal eternal recurrence.

I envy those who do not share my obsession. The murder is spelled out clearly in my oddly distorted vision of the aphorism. It is totally absent from theirs. How do they manage? Their recipe is simple. Never do they quote the formulas Nietzsche uses here: '"we have killed Him"', '"all of us are His murderers"'. They carefully refrain from doing so. Something much better is at their disposal. They all go about very sweetly repeating, 'God is dead . . . God is dead . . .' without adding anything whatsoever.

It seems quite innocent, but it completely changes the meaning of the text. The formula 'God is dead' has enjoyed and will always enjoy an extraordinary success in our universe. It possesses a virtue so powerful that a thousand successors to Nietzsche – but are they really his successors? – seize on it every day and channel it towards new fields so that they may make a name for themselves among men. This tactic has long yielded spectacular results. Thanks to it, metaphysics is dead. We all kept vigil at its bedside. Next we went into mourning for philosophy as a whole. And since around 1890, once a generation, we are solemnly informed that man himself is dead. Every time, the news causes an enormous sensation. Truth is long dead, and sartorial fashion more recently deceased. I have myself said that the death of God is in the process of dying, and doubtless I am now in the process of repeating it. Nobody escapes this obituary itch.

Nietzsche entitled his aphorism 'The Madman', but one would scarcely suspect it. Intellectual opinion knows it only under its own title: 'God is dead'. If you want to hear 'God is dead, God is dead' repeated in marvellously grave tones, the slightest reference to aphorism 125 will suffice, or even to Nietzsche's work in general . . . It is the Pavlovian reflex of modernity. Nietzsche is taken to be the great prophet of the *natural* death of God.

The formula 'God is dead' figures not only in the text but in the title of a considerable number of essays. I have already mentioned the one that is most in vogue, that of Heidegger. It is entitled, of course, *Nietzsche's Phrase 'God is Dead'*. It caps an immense body of literature that maintains only the most nebulous relationship with the text on which it pretends to be commenting.

This famous 'death of God' is not, however, the invention of the commentators. It does need to figure somewhere in aphorism 125. The transfiguring power of my obsession alone will not be enough, I hope, to conjure it away. If I look for it, I will find it in the end.

Let us read what follows . . . Nothing . . . But yes; ten lines further down, there it is at last, the sentence so often repeated . . . Even here it is repeated: 'Gott ist tot! Gott bleibt tot!' God is in no danger, thank God, of reviving. This formula is the happiest day of my life. It may yet make of me a critic like any other.

Equipped with this philosophical life-buoy, I resume reading from the delectable 'God is dead . . .!'

> God is dead! God remains dead! And it is we who have killed Him. How shall we, murderers among murderers, comfort ourselves? What was holiest and most powerful of all that the world has yet possessed has bled to death under our knives. Who will wipe this blood from our hands?

This is most dismaying. The more I try to flee my obsession, the more it pursues me! Renewal, where are you? 'God is dead! God remains dead!' It was perfect . . . Why couldn't Nietzsche have left it at that?

For a hundred years the best minds turn aphorism 125 round and about in every direction and never do they come upon the horrible bogey that haunts me unceasingly. The second apparition is more sinister than the first. The blood spilling . . . the knife. . . . It is all in very bad taste. Nietzsche, decidedly, does it on purpose.

Having written 'God is dead', Nietzsche returns immediately and overpoweringly to his idea – or maybe to mine, I no longer know which. One would say that he is seeking to prevent the kind of falsification to which his aphorism has always been subjected. He can guess his readers' desire to escape the murder. Shrewd as they are, they will take advantage of the somewhat too-neutral formula 'God is dead' which the author has imprudently handed them. To forestall this danger, Nietzsche insists once again on the murder. The caricatural, *Grand Guignol* quality of the description contradicts categorically the connotations that the habitual consumers of the aphorism have always conferred on 'God is dead', its connotations that exclude collective violence.

'God is dead' is not incorrect in its context. In writing this sentence, Nietzsche says nothing that contradicts his message or in any way attenuates it. Of someone who has got himself murdered one can always say, among other things, that he is dead. There is no risk of making a mistake. The passive formula is always accurate. Whether someone dies murdered or not, the result is the same. But, death from natural causes being the most common sort, that is quite obviously what is understood when it is said simply that somebody has died without its being specified how.

In the aphorism, 'God is dead' is framed by two thunderous announcements of collective murder. Taken out of context, 'God is dead' slips quietly back into meaning the natural death of God. The murder is dropped as if by an inadvertent gesture which passes without notice. One must admire the efficacy of a manoeuvre which is all the more deft in being ignorant of its own cunning. A quotation from Nietzsche is provided which is in appearance accurate and complete but in reality truncated, due solely to the fact that it is emphasized separately, made into the title of the aphorism. The 'God is dead' which circulates in this world does not sum up the Madman's words, it grossly falsifies them.

For the philosophy of the Englightenment, God can only die a natural death. Once the naïve period of humanity is behind us religion ceases to be 'credible', as we say these days. Rationalist optimism is supposed to be long dead, fallen victim in principle to the epidemic triggered by the death of God. In reality, it survives in the very idea of a God who dies of senile exhaustion. This first idea supposes a second: modern atheism is more *reasonable* than its predecessor, religion. For beings who have attained the 'maturity' on which we pride ourselves, such atheism alone is truly 'credible'. Other beliefs are purely medieval, not to say antediluvian.

The 'death of God' manoeuvre evacuates the Nietzschean idea to return on tiptoe to the easy idea, the banal idea, the *vulgar* idea. Nietzsche is careful not to cross his t's. Part of him fully enjoys being the misunderstood madman. The aphorism lays a kind of trap for us which everyone identifies but falls into all the same: the trap of vulgar atheism.

The real difference between the crowd's atheism and the Madman's thinking is none other than the difference between death and murder.

Through the intermediary of the formula 'God is dead', all those who start out by making fun of the Madman end up co-opting the aphorism and cutting it down to the size of their own thinking. They claim to distance themselves from vulgar atheism but they reinstall it serenely in the very text which repudiates it, with a mighty helping hand from the incantatory formula 'God is dead . . . God is dead'.

If the interpreters quote only the first lines of the aphorism that is because, in the rest, there is no longer any question of anything but collective murder. At the first appearance of the latter everyone runs away, like the disciples at the time of the Passion. And the same reasons which render this rout universal render it invisible to those who participate in it. Insist on the murder and you will immediately be taken for a 'madman'. It happens to me all the time . . .

You see . . . my obsession has triumphed. I have renounced resisting it. You can expect to see the rest of the aphorism blend itself into the rest of my system. You are familiar with all that, and I will spare you my commentary. The theory has its own ideas, and I will let it lead the way all by itself.

What does it demand, this theory, *before* the collective murder? The sacrificial crisis, of course, the abolition of differences. All that figures in the aphorism, but *after* the initial announcement of the murder. The crisis first appears as a consequence of this murder, not as a preliminary condition. That is a small anomaly, and I beg you to excuse it. In any case it is quickly rectified. *After* the sacrificial crisis comes the second announcement, the one I have just read to you, and in relation to this one our sacrificial crisis finds itself back where it belongs, right *before* the murder.

Let me read you the passage which appears between the two announcements, the one I skipped over a moment ago in the hope of arriving at a death that would not be the result of a murder:

> But how have we done this? How were we able to drink up the sea? Who gave us the sponge to blot out the whole horizon? What did we do to unchain the earth from its sun? Where is the planet spinning to now? To what place is its movement carrying us? Far from all suns? Have we not tumbled into a continuous fall? A fall backwards, sideways, forwards, in every direction? Do high and low still exist? Are we not wandering as if across an infinite void? Do we not feel the breath of nothingness upon us? Is it not colder? Is it not night-time unceasingly and more and more night-time? Must we not light our lanterns even in the morning? Do we hear nothing yet of the noise of the gravediggers who have buried God? Do we smell nothing yet of the divine putrefaction?

We are often given *philosophical* commentaries on this text. It can be compared with Pascal. Two quite distinct infinities, the large and the small, still perpetuate the shadow of a fixed point, their point of intersection where man is situated. The spot from which we observe the real remains a kind of centre. In our aphorism, even this ghost of a centre has disappeared.

This state of affairs makes our aphorism very similar to myths, to rituals, to Greek tragedy. Everywhere, in 'primitive' texts, the collective murder is associated with the confusion of day and night, of the sky and the earth, of gods, men and animals. Monsters swarm. Everything begins with the abolition of differences, the monstrous twins, the 'evil mixture' of Shakespeare, the mixing of what should be distinguished.

It is indeed the sacrificial crisis described a thousand times, but no longer quite the old carnival masquerade, the inversion of roles and hierarchies during a brief festive period, strictly delimited. The affair appears more serious; all guideposts are gone, in time as well as in space. There is no longer either difference or deferral, no more horizon, no more fixed point anywhere to provide sense or direction. It is on the former God that the *humanization* of the real rested, and what little remains of this is in the process of rotting.

Everything is presented in the form of questions; no affirmation is possible. One is tempted to conclude that it is a version of the crisis that is 'more radical' because it is 'modern' and more modern because it is radical. But perhaps it is simply our own particular version, one we are incapable of relativizing. We cannot yet ritualize it . . . Maybe all we need is the collective murder once more . . .

We have our sacrificial crisis, we have our collective murder . . . To complete the cycle of violence and the sacred, we now need the return to the ritual order. Can one really demand that of an aphorism said to be devoted exclusively to the disappearance of religion in the modern world? It is doubtless asking too much, but you may count on the *idée fixe* to cause everything it needs to spring up around it.

The second description of the murder opens on to a passage that is the opposite of the one which followed the first description – in other words, it is exactly what we are looking for:

> How shall we, murderers among murderers, comfort ourselves? What was holiest and most powerful of all that the world has yet possessed has bled to death under our knives. Who will wipe this blood from our hands? What lustral water is there to cleanse us? What ceremonies of atonement, what sacred games shall we have to invent?

How can the lustral water, the ceremonies of atonement and the sacred games be defined, if not as ritual procedures rising out of the collective murder and so hard to distinguish from it to begin with, like the gesture of washing one's hands, that the description of the murder itself must be quoted again to be sure none of them is left out?

The murder is commemorated 'to comfort ourselves', the drama is replayed to render the memory of the event tolerable by transfiguring it. And suddenly, we have before us a new religion. The destruction of the old religion culminates in the collective murder and the collective murder, through the intermediary of the rites, produces the new religion. Ritual reproduction and religious production are one and the same:

> what sacred games shall we have to invent? Is not the greatness of this deed too great for us? Must we not become gods ourselves to appear worthy of such a deed? There never was a greater deed than this – and whoever is born after us shall belong, by virtue of this same deed, to a history superior to everything that history ever was until then!

Quite obviously, it is a question here of Zarathustra and of the superman, who are in the process of germinating in Nietzsche's thought. If the licensed Nietzscheans tell me that these themes must not be qualified as religious I will bow down low before their wisdom and take their word for it, but I am much too near-sighted, much too limited to the letter to go outside my aphorism. I want to hear nothing but the letter of the aphorism. It furnishes me with the exact word – 'gods' – at the precise moment when the theory of violence and the sacred requires it: 'Must we not become gods ourselves . . .?'

And that is not the end of it. The following passage brings us another cog in the victimage mechanism, the paradoxical *misrecognition (méconnaissance)* of the murder by the murderers themselves:

> Here the Madman fell silent and examined anew his listeners: they too were silent and watched him without understanding. Finally he hurled his lantern to the ground so that it broke and ceased shining. 'I come too early,' he said then, 'my time has not come yet. This tremendous event is still on its way, still wandering – it has not yet reached the ears of man. Lightning and thunder require time, the light of the stars requires time, deeds require time even after they are done, before they can be seen and heard. This deed is still more distant from them than the most distant stars – and yet it is they who have done it!'

The crowd knows nothing of the murder, yet it is itself the perpetrator. The commentators around the aphorism, like the crowd within the aphorism, fall back irresistibly into the attitude they seek to escape: vulgar atheism, that which consists in refusing the murder. The aphorism is therefore itself subject to the very type of misrecognition that the Madman denounces.

The natural death of God is the alibi of the murderers who deny the reality of their murder. How could we have killed the biblical God, they repeat, since He died without help from anyone, in the last stage of senility?

The only text constantly associated with 'the death of God', the only truly memorable text, is aphorism 125. Other texts exist which genuinely say what the aphorism does not say; it is nevertheless the latter which is made to say it. Nobody is interested in the texts which genuinely speak of the death of God.

There is something surprising in the predilection of our atheists for a text which aims at subverting their own vision. Neither literary nor philosophical criticism can explain this paradox which in truth they do not see, convinced as they are that they respect the aphorism in extracting from it their mealy 'death of God'.

If this strange phenomenon is to be located and understood, it must be seen that the usage made of the aphorism is ritual in the very sense of which Nietzsche has just reminded us. The rite consists in reproducing the collective murder without recognizing the event reproduced. That is exactly the type of relationship which exists between the modern intelligentsia and the aphorism, but at the level of representation rather than of action.

The murder is indispensable to ritual practice as long as it remains unrecognized. To be made sacred, the text must conceal the collective murder in the precise sense of dissimulating it. If you draw attention to it, it will be granted importance only on the plane of aesthetics or, better yet, of rhetoric. You will be told that its *language* confers on the aphorism a type of superiority which should not or cannot be defined with precision. The aesthetic quality is ineffable.

One must rid oneself of the murder, *but without eliminating it entirely*. It is therefore made into a dramatic and moving manner of speaking, the metaphor of a reality deemed utterly banal. In sum, the natural death of God alone appears real. One always comes back to that. Modernist tradition favours only those approaches destined to dissimulate the murder behind its harmless 'death of God'.

We maintain with Greek tragedy a ritual relationship analogous to this one. It passes for 'critical' but, in truth, nothing is less critical than the rite. The collective murder of Pentheus cannot be foreign to the fascination exercised by Euripides' *Bacchae*, but if you examine the matter too closely you transgress the imperative of dissimulation and your 'discourse' will not be 'acceptable'.

Aphorism 125 owes its place among us to a misunderstanding of which it is systematically the object. It fascinates for the same reasons as tragedy. It lets modern intelligence mime its own tragedy. One must burn one's fingers a little bit on the collective murder, but not too much. A century after the aphorism, the Madman's moment has not yet arrived. He will have to break his lantern one more time.

To exorcize the horrible murder, the veil of fashionable philosophies is thrown over it. The religious character of the operation is betrayed in the solemn, almost sacramental style that is unconsciously adopted as soon as reference is made to 'the death of God'. This ritual consumption is an inverted Eucharist.

The ritual process does not take only the text as its victim. It rebounds on to the person of Nietzsche himself; it is repeated in our relations with the author, in a weakened form, of course, as with all the rites of modernity. There is nothing original about it. It reproduces the classic schema of great men who serve as scapegoats in their own lifetime, the better to be converted into sacred figures after their death.

The process unfolds over two generations. The first curses the living geniuses, the second makes sacred the dead amidst unanimous indignation against the murderers. Each generation believes it redresses the injustices of the generation before without committing equivalent ones. But it will itself appear to the following generation as the pitiless persecutor of its unappreciated great men. It is the old process of the primitive sacred which perpetuates itself among us while fragmenting and 'deferring' itself more and more. This is the process which was defined for the first time in the lightning words of the famous 'Curses against the Pharisees':

> Woe unto you, scribes and Pharisees, hypocrites! because ye build the tombs of the prophets, and garnish the sepulchres of the righteous, And say, If we had been in the days of our fathers, we would not have been partakers with them in the blood of the prophets. Wherefore ye be witnesses unto yourselves, that ye are the children of them which killed the prophets. Fill ye up then the measure of your fathers.
>
> (Matthew 23:29–32)

The posthumous sanctification does not bring genuine understanding. The way in which the crowd greets the Madman's message can be read as a sketch of the twofold process of persecution and sanctification which the Nietzsche of *The Gay Science* has begun to undergo.

The opening gibes give way, after the Madman's speech, to an embarrassed but already respectful silence. The crowd still does not understand the message but it is transfixed by the strange eloquence of the messenger, it is already ripe for veneration.

Elsewhere than in the aphorism, Nietzsche reveals clearly the ritual character of his relations with the public. Not without coquetry he protests against his future canonization, but he prepares the way for it by setting out to become a living scandal. He behaves like a proper sacrificial beast. He spontaneously, or rather mimetically, commits provocations which render him fully 'sacrificeable' to begin with, and thus canonizable later. The fact that Nietzsche voluntarily co-operates with the sacrificial system for which he serves as victim does not keep him from suffering terribly. In the language of pious biographers, that is called scorning immediate success for true glory.

The requirement for transgression, preliminary to immolation, appears aberrant and unintelligible to us when we observe it in the context of human sacrifice 'in the strict sense', yet it figures in the literary rites which moderns play out themselves every time they canonize a 'damned' poet or a demented philosopher. The process remains rooted in the collective murder which it reproduces ritually in a form that is simultaneously caricatural and attenuated: 'This deed is still more distant from them than the most distant stars – and yet it is they who have done it.'

Nietzsche is an expiatory victim in the place of God. He is that madman who cannot announce the murder of God without exposing himself to the murder, at least symbolically. The aphorism closes on a collective expulsion of the Madman that reproduces, one more time, the original matrix of all religion:

> The story has it that on that same day the Madman entered different churches in which he intoned his *Requiem aeternam Deo*. Thrown out and enjoined to explain himself, he retorted incessantly, 'What good are these churches, if they are not the vaults and tombs of God?'

From the remotest prehistory, through the Egyptian or Aztec pyramids, to all the cults of the dead in antique or primitive societies, the funerary and the religious have always been indistinguishable. All the tombs are temples and all the temples are tombs.

Notice that it is a liturgical chant which the Madman intones. The attitude presented as blasphemous, as negational of religion, is none other than the fundamental religious attitude. And the Madman is the object of a properly religious expulsion. It is impossible to call up the forces which weaken or destroy religion without simultaneously calling up those which restore it. They are the same forces, as we have the occasion to observe once more.

From start to finish, aphorism 125 is identical with the 'victimage theory of religion'. The Nietzscheans will unanimously call me mad, but the letter of the text vindicates me. The letter vindicates violence and the sacred. In order never to have to take account of it the letter is sometimes neglected completely; while sometimes, inversely, it is fetishized, which amounts to the same thing.

The perspective of violence and the sacred is needed to reveal a religious anthropology which is not even latent in the aphorism but fails to appear clearly because the text has been cornered by a philosophy that negates its true content.

In a few sentences, Nietzsche defines in rigorous fashion the passage from disorder to the sacrificial order through the mediation of the collective murder and the rituals which spring from it. One cannot kill the gods, any gods, without engendering new ones.

What is the relationship of Nietzsche himself to what is said here? I will spare you references to the 'unconscious'. The thinking expressed is real, but it is not quite like the rest of Nietzsche's thinking and does not necessarily correspond to all his opinions on the subject of religion. In Nietzsche's intellectual panoply, a philosophy that satisfies the desired conditions does, in effect, exist. It sometimes happens that Nietzsche designates it as 'the most elevated philosophy', the philosophy of eternal recurrence.

By taking up the eternal recurrence in a philosophical perspective, one may tangle the problem up to one's heart's desire. One cannot resolve it, and often one does not wish to. One seeks to give the impression that fathomless depths lie hidden here, infinitely superior to the linear vision of history or to Judaeo-Christian 'simple- mindedness'.

This confusionism must be replaced by the true context of the eternal recurrence in pre-Socratic thought or in post-Vedic India: the mythic and ritual context. The philosophy of the eternal recurrence is a reflection on the identity of the forces of life and death in antique and primitive religion. Every dissolution is a new creation, and vice versa. Everything is always in the process of beginning and finishing. The belief in an absolute end and beginning is the illusion of individuals who accord too much importance to the cycle of which they are a part. One must lift oneself above current history to see the totality of cycles and to recognize linear time as illusory.

In the second half of the nineteenth century ethnologists discovered the unity of the central drama at the heart of the world's religions, the extreme frequency with which violence appears, often in collective manifestations, in the myths and rites of the whole planet. They also perceived that the most violent rites, those which they judged to be the most primitive, were the ones which were structurally closest to the Christian Passion. Everywhere the language of *sacrifice* is present. From Frazer to Marcel Mauss, without of course forgetting Freud, every thinker emphasized the symbolic analogies between primitive sacrifices and the Christian theology of sacrifice.

The influence of this ethnology combines with his knowledge of Greek mythology and pre-Socratic philosophy to enable Nietzsche to elaborate his synthetic vision of the eternal recurrence. The lyricism of the eternal recurrence should not keep us from seeing that the synthesis is faithful to antique sources and compatible with the rationalism of modern ethnology, and even the positivism which says: 'All religions resemble each other and in consequence all religions are of equal value.'

Nietzsche does not betray the traditional idea of the eternal recurrence. The aphorism demonstrates this to us. Life and death are reciprocally exchanged. The one passes eternally into the other. The idea would be as banal in Nietzsche as everywhere else if there were not something more in the aphorism, the idea of making the collective murder into the engine of the perpetual movement. Before *Totem and Taboo*, this idea appears nowhere but here, I think, in such explicit form. Nietzsche precedes Freud by nearly thirty years.

If the gods are born from the collective murder which aphorism 125 describes, they die from its absence. They die from living too long in the peaceable universe which the regularity of worship ensures for their devotees. In a universe with no mimetic and sacrificial crisis, the gods appear useless and their existence becomes problematic. But their very disappearance plunges everything into a violence and disorder from which, finally, new gods arise.

If religion once again dies a violent death in our world it will certainly be reborn in another form, it matters little which. The crisis of the modern world is but an episode in the middle of an unending process. The prodigious importance which we attach to our history is due to the narrowness of our vision.

If it is permissible to see even in the decline of the Christian God a murder rather than the sempiternal death of the rationalists, the symbolic functioning will reproduce itself. Modern irreligion constitutes only a particular variation on a drama which stays essentially the same through every repetition. The decisive break which Christian rationalists, then deists, and then atheists have thought they recognized in our own history, the history of the modern West, is but an insignificant fold in the gown of Maja. Nietzsche writes his aphorism in a timeless and parabolic style which heralds that of *Zarathustra*.

The eternal recurrence crushes all claims to absolute singularity. It relativizes our world in the midst of an infinity of worlds. It contradicts the Judaeo-Christian conception of a unique history dominated by the divine determination to ensure the salvation of humanity. There is no alpha and omega.

The weapon is so powerful that in truth it is hardly usable. It empties all oppositions of their content. It destroys all concrete polemics; it deprives cultural analysis of its piquancy. Ultimately it re-establishes between Dionysus and the Crucified an equality which most often Nietzsche abhors, even if he occasionally accepts its principle in very special moments of enthusiasm or resignation. An absolute weapon can really serve only as a means of dissuasion. Nietzsche keeps it in reserve but almost never resorts to it.

Most often, what renders all religions similar and makes them all perpetually spring one out of the other is less interesting to Nietzsche than the opposite: what differentiates them, what renders pagan religions, symbolized by Dionysus, incomparable to Judaism and above all to Christianity.

The aphorism is a remarkable but veiled exception. Neither Dionysus nor the Crucified is mentioned, for they figure here on an equal footing. Heidegger is wrong to assert that only the Christian God is referred to in the aphorism. How could this be true, since it is a question of the eternal recurrence?

In the final period, in *The Anti-Christ* and above all in the *Fragments* of 1888, Nietzsche is no longer interested in anything but the irreducible opposition of two religions. But this opposition does not contradict the universality of the collective murder, as aphorism 125 defines it. Quite the contrary. It is grafted on to the identity of the central drama in the myth of Dionysus and in the Christian Passion:

> Dionysus versus the 'Crucified': there you have the antithesis. It is *not* a difference in regard to their martyrdom – it is a difference in the meaning of it. Life itself, its eternal fruitfulness and recurrence, creates torment, destruction, the will to annihilation . . .
> In the other case, suffering – the 'Crucified as the innocent one' – counts as an objection to this life, as a formula for its condemnation. (*The Will to Power*, no. 1052)

The difference is not in the martyrdom . . . In other words, the collective murder is present in both cases. But the positivists who deduce from this identity the equivalence of all religions neglect, as always, the role of interpretation. Collective violence speaks powerfully, but it does not say the same thing to those who inflict it and to those who suffer it.

Christianity represents the viewpoint of the *innocent* victim concerning a collective murder which Dionysus and all of paganism conceive from the perspective of the persecutors.

The viewpoint of the Passion is not only the opposite of that of Dionysus, it is an engine of war against the latter and against all paganism; it is an effort to discredit the collective murder, to ruin its basis, to destroy all non-Christian religions by showing that they are founded on an arbitrary violence.

Far from taking Christianity to be just another sacrificial religion, Nietzsche reiterates several times that its great fault is to 'prevent sacrifice', to render impossible the acts of violence necessary to the smooth functioning of society. Nietzsche is very close to seeing the *mechanisms* and the *effects* of the surrogate victim, and above all to seeing that the gospels see them and, seeing them, discredit and derail them. The Gospel reveals 'things hidden since the foundation of the world', and through the intermediary of Nietzsche this revelation begins to become self-aware.

Christianity is always accused of justifying suffering, of glutting itself on it. Nietzsche sees quite well that nothing of the sort is true. It is pagan religion which 'affirms even the harshest suffering: it is sufficiently strong, robust and divinizing for that' (op. cit.). The greatness of Nietzsche is that he apprehends the truth of Christianity with incomparable force. Nietzsche's drama, and his madness, is his obstinate preference for Dionysus, his conscious choice of violence, pursued with too much intellectual rigour not to culminate in the atrocious texts of the *Twilight of the Idols* and other writings:

> The individual was taken so seriously, he was posited as such an absolute principle, that he could no longer be *sacrificed*: but the species only survives thanks to human sacrifices . . .

The conception of aphorism 125 could not have been simple. It must have been transformed during the course of its elaboration. I would readily accept the supposition that Nietzsche started out from the modern situation. He was thinking first of all of the death of the Christian God, in a banal sense analogous to that of the aphorism's exegetes.

This death changes on the way into a murder by virtue of the Christian

Passion, a true object of 'repression' that accomplishes its return. A moment ago, I pointed out an anomaly. The first death of God does not lead to the restoration of the sacred and of the ritual order, but to a decomposition of meaning so radical and irremediable that a bottomless abyss opens beneath the feet of modern man.

The aphorism gives one the impression that this abyss closes up again finally when the second announcement leads this time to the order of Zarathustra and the superman. The aphorism affirms the eternal recurrence. But it reveals its engine, the collective murder of arbitrary victims. It goes too far in its revelation. It destroys its own foundation.

The engine driving the cycles is of course the surrogate victim whose innocence, once revealed, prevents our believing in the soundness of the basis for other victims' suffering and, breaking thereby the mainspring of the eternal recurrence, leads us this time to the idea of an end without a new beginning.

This knowledge is not quite present in the aphorism, yet it is already there implicitly in the role of scapegoat which the Madman plays *because he reveals the truth of the collective murder*. The Madman is an image of himself which Nietzsche only appears to control. Like all images of himself, it transforms itself irresistibly into an *imago Christi* of unusual relevance.

Aphorism 125 proclaims the victory of the eternal recurrence over Christianity. But by the very fact that it founds the eternal recurrence on the collective murder, its true foundation which must remain hidden if it is to remain foundational, the victory is undermined, secretly subverted by the very Christianity over which it believes it has triumphed. At the first announcement of the murder, the world spins out of its orbit *because the collective murder has been revealed*.

The power of the aphorism derives from its hesitation between the solution that is adopted and the opposite solution. I perceive in it a kind of muted premonition of the 'God of the Jews, you have won' which Nietzsche strives desperately to reduce to silence in the last fragments but which resounds from them none the less like the trumpet of the Last Judgement.

The two announcements of the murder are not quite on the same plane. They do not really have the same meaning; the first is infinitely formidable because it is the Christian one; the second alone carries the reassurance of the eternal recurrence. In the last Nietzsche understands that the revelation of the innocent victim marks the definitive end of the eternal recurrence. The first announcement cancels the second. The eternal recurrence is the past which Christianity has abolished. History from now on treads the bottomless spaces of Christian knowledge.

One finds the same ambiguity at the conclusion of the *Twilight of the Gods*. One does not know if the colossal finish marks the end of a cycle only, the promise of a thousand renewals, or if it is truly the end of the world, the Christian apocalypse, the bottomless abyss of the unforgettable victim.

Notes

Introduction

1. René Girard, '*To Double Business Bound*', *Essays on Literature, Mimesis, and Anthropology* (Baltimore: Johns Hopkins University Press, 1978; London: The Athlone Press 1988 p.200).
2. On the question of the relationship between knowledge and literature in Girard's work, see Paisley Livingston, 'Girard and Literary Knowledge', *Stanford Literature Review*, vol. X, 1986: 221–36.
3. Paris: Grasset, 1961; English translation entitled *Deceit, Desire, and the Novel* (Baltimore: Johns Hopkins University Press, 1966; London: The Athlone Press, 1988).
4. First published by Plon (Paris, 1963); Reprinted in René Girard, *Critiques dans un Souterrain* Lausanne: L'Age d'Homme, 1976).
5. This criterion is typically epistemological. What is asked of a new theory is that it explains all that its predecessor explained, and simultaneously that it contradict its predecessor, that it explain the instance that falsified its predecessor. Hence a new, better theory should be able to generate its predecessor as an imperfect model of itself. Cf. A. Grunbaum, 'Can a theory answer more questions than one of its rival', *BJPS*, vol 27, 1976: 1–23.
6. Or when he does, as in his *Dostoïevski* (op. cit., Lausanne, 1976, pp. 47–52), it is to show that the difference between reality and fiction has all but disappeared, not to explain novels with the help of biographical data.
7. Though Proust is chronologically later than Dostoevsky, he is, from the viewpoint of the evolution of mimetic desire, less modern. Cf. *Mensonge romantique*, op. cit., p. 55.
8. Cf. '*To Double Business Bound*', op. cit.; *Critiques dans un Souterrain*, op. cit.
9. Of course, Cervantes is not the only author who draws the line through literature itself; both Dante and Flaubert do the same. Cf. 'The mimetic desire of Paolo and Francesca' in '*To Double Business Bound*', op. cit.; and *Mensonge romantique*, op. cit., Chapter 1.
10. George Eliot, *Silas Marner* (London: Penguin, 1976), p. 58.
11. Ibid.
12. It blinds us also, because we are accustomed to associate imitation with

conformity and harmony, with agreement. They love the same things, we say, and they are the best of friends. We forget that if they *really love the same thing*, conflict will follow.

13. Op. cit., p. 61.
14. From Silas' point of view this is the belief on which William is acting for the following reasons: Silas knows that William is the true culprit; simultaneously he still believes in William's dream. It follows that William must consider that God does not rule the earth righteously and bears witness against the innocents. George Eliot is well aware that Silas and William have, through this process, become doubles of each other; she knows that Silas has now become evil and the whole novel is the story of his recovery. In that sense, *Silas Marner* begins where *Don Quixote* ends. It is an inquiry into what happens to the 'knight-errant' once he has demystified the madness by which he lived. At this point, Cervantes kills his hero; George Eliot begins her story.
15. Until the end, that is, until the very last chapter of the second book, at which point Don Quixote dies physically but is cured spiritually.
16. This means that according to Girard, mimesis is not unconscious in Freud's sense. Freud's unconscious is a reservoir of representations and past experiences. On the contrary, mimesis acts without representations, and from present experiences. Further, Freudian psychoanalysis always explains one's conflict with others as proceeding from a conflict between the different demands of the self: ego, id, and superego. Girard's explanations move in the opposite direction. They demonstrate how conflicts within the self, resentment, hallucinations, or sexual perversions, result from conflicts with others. Girard's approach is sociological rather than psychological. In fact, he even conceives of the self as a result of interactions with others. Cf. *Mensonge romantique*, op. cit., Chapter VIII; *Des Choses cachées depuis la fondation du monde*, (Paris: Grasset, 1978), pp. 93–114, 307–415; English language translation: *Things Hidden Since the Foundation of the World*, (London: The Athlone Press, 1987; Stanford: Stanford University Press, pp. 84–89).
17. This is, of course, another reason why we tend to be blind to the imitation.
18. *Silas Marner*, op. cit., p. 172.
19. This double imitation from which desire itself arises constitutes, in fact, the most simple and most general figure of mimesis. Cf. Jean-Pierre Dupuy, 'Le Signe et l'Envie', in Paul Dumouchel and Jean-Pierre Dupuy, *L'Enfer des choses* (Paris: Seuil, 1979), especially pp. 64–76; *Des Choses cachées*, op. cit., pp. 319–22.
20. George Eliot knows that a conflict should follow from this mimetic origin of Silas' desire. She knows it so well that she feels obliged to defuse the situation and to explain why the normal consequences will not follow. Hence, a few pages later, she causes the Doctor to deliver the following speech: 'I've known a time when I might have quarrelled with him [Silas]

for it [the child] myself. It's too late now, though. If the child ran into the fire, your aunt's too fat to overtake it: she could only sit and grunt like an alarmed sow' *Silas Marner*, op. cit., p. 176.

21. It is not certain, to me at least, that Girard would maintain today the privileged relation he then established between the novel, as a cultural form of expression, and desire, as a culturally relative form of mimesis. Certain articles on Shakespeare tend to indicate otherwise. Cf. 'To Entrap the Wisest': A Reading of *The Merchant of Venice*', in *Literature and Society*, ed. E. W. Said (Baltimore: Johns Hopkins University Press, 1980, pp. 100–19); 'Hamlet's Dull Revenge', in *Stanford Literature Review*, Fall 1984: 159–200.
22. First published in French as *La Violence et le sacré*, (Paris: Grasset, 1972; English translation, Baltimore: Johns Hopkins University Press, 1977; London: The Athlone Press).
23. H. Hubert and M. Mauss, *Sacrifice: Its Nature and Function*. (London: Cohen & West, 1968).
24. Cf. Rodney Needham, 'Remarks on the Analysis of Kinship and Marriage', in *Remarks and Inventions* (London: Tavistock, 1974), pp. 38–72; Rodney Needham, 'Polythetic Classification', in *Against the Tranquility of Axioms* (Berkeley: University of California Press, 1983), pp. 36–66.
25. This idea of a principle of substitution, Needham tells us, is borrowed from W. S. Jevons, *The Principles of Science: A Treatise on Logic and Scientific Method*, 2 vols (London: Macmillan, 1874). It is another version of the principle of induction, and as such the difficulties that arise from it are not essentially linked with the existence of polythetic classes. On the problem of induction, see K. R. Popper, *Objective Knowledge* (Oxford: Clarendon Press, 1979), especially Chapters 1 and 2.
26. Needham's argument about polythetic classes is not quite as simple as is reported here. There are in fact many sources and many arguments. In *Remarks and Inventions* he develops two different arguments in parallel. One argument is in favour of a reformation of anthropological vocabulary on the basis that everyday terms, like kinship and marriage, are misleading. This argument is introduced and illustrated by references to polythetic classes: i.e. the use of the term patrilinear is misleading because we associate it with one defining feature only while in fact it refers to a polythetic class of decent systems. The other argument is more or less the one reported here, from the polythetic nature of anthropological objects to the difficulties of comparativism. A third argument is found in 'Polythetic Classification' and in Rodney Needham, *Symbolic Classification* (Santa Monica: Goodyear Publishing Company, 1979). It advances the idea that many symbolic classifications are in fact polythetic classifications. These are in fact entirely different arguments, and it is not clear that the reference to polythetic classes is in any way essential to the first argument.

27. When condition (2) is fulfilled, when no feature is common to all members of the class, the class is said to be fully polythetic. Cf. 'Polythetic Classification', op. cit., p. 44.
28. Op. cit., p. 37.
29. Ibid., p. 43.
30. It is usually considered that predictions cannot be derived from the theory of evolution. Yet the theory of evolution entails that individual species should constitute polythetic classes, and in that sense it is a prediction of the theory. Its negation is a potential falsifier of the theory. Of course, the term 'prediction' is used here in its logical and not in its chronological sense. It is irrelevant to the issue that the polythetic aspect of species was known before the theory of evolution was first proposed.
31. G. Ryle, *The Concept of Mind* (London: Hutchinson, 1949), Chapter II.
32. To a philosopher, dominance patterns have a strange Hegelian ring. They have an air of the master/slave dialectic in the *Phenomenology of Mind*. The animal who fears death submits to his more courageous rival. He becomes his slave; he will not challenge his new master. Unfortunately dominance patterns do not give rise to anything like a culture. Rather they prevent such an evolution.
33. According to Girard, it is an increased mimetism which destroyed dominance patterns among the immediate ancestors of humankind. Cf. *Des Choses cachées*, op. cit., pp. 93–114.
34. T. Hobbes, *Leviathan* (Penguin, 1968), p. 469.
35. J.-J. Rousseau, *On the Social Contract* (Indianapolis: Hackett Publishing Company, 1983), p. 23.
36. Professor H. Atlan has challenged the necessity of the blindness of the process. According to him, the agents can discover the arbitrary aspect of the mimetic convergence and the process none the less remain efficacious. Cf. Atlan's contribution to this volume.
37. Cf. René Girard, *Le Bouc émissaire*, (Paris: Grasset, 1982); English translation: *The Scapegoat* (Baltimore: Johns Hopkins University Press; London: The Athlone Press, 1986).
38. Cf. *Violence and the Sacred*, op. cit.
39. On the notion of spontaneous order see F. von Hayek, *Law, Legislation and Liberty*, vol. 1 (Chicago University Press, 1973).
40. On the relationship between the mimetic process of victimage and the invisible hand mechanism, see: J.-P. Dupuy, 'Shaking the Invisible Hand', in *Disorder and Order*, ed. Paisley Livingston, (Stanford University: Amna Libri, 1985) and Paul Dumouchel, 'L'Ambivalence de la rareté' in Paul Dumouchel and Jean-Pierre Dupuy *L'Enfer des choses*, op. cit.
41. The reason for this is simple: without a real process of victimage no reconciliation can take place; there can be no end to the crisis.
42. Cf. Nietzsche, '*The Anti-Christ*', in *The Complete Works of Friedrich Nietzsche*, vol. 16 (London: T. N. Faulis, 1911) and Max Weber, *Ancient Judaism* (Glencoe, III.: Free Press, 1960).

43. Cf. *Des Choses cachées*, op. cit., pp. 238–43.
44. Ibid., pp. 203–76.
45. Cf. *Le Bouc émissaire*, op. cit.
46. Cf. Max Weber, *The Protestant Ethic and the Spirit of Protestantism* (London: Allen & Unwin, 1976); R. G. Tawney, *Religion and the Rise of Capitalism* (London: Penguin, 1938); and more recently Marcel Gauchet, *Le Désenchantement du monde* (Paris: Gallimard, 1985); I have also argued elsewhere that the thesis is already to be found in Hobbes; see my 'The Impossible Christian Commonwealth: Hobbes' Reading of the Bible', forthcoming.
47. Op. cit.
48. For an interesting essay on this question see Jean Baechler, *The Origins of Capitalism* (Oxford: Blackwell, 1975).

Ouverture

1. P. Dumouchel and J.-P. Dupuy (eds), *Colloque de Cerisy: L'Auto-organisation de la physique au politique*. (Paris: Seuil, 1983); the symposium took place from 10 to 17 June 1981.
2. P. Livingston (ed.), *Disorder and Order*, (Stanford University: Amna Libri, 1984).
3. Postal address of the two centres: 1 rue Descartes, Paris 75005, France.
4. About the relationships between the surrogate victim hypothesis and theories of self-organization see:

(a) H. Atlan and J.-P. Dupuy, 'Mimesis and Social Morphogenesis', in G. E. Lasker (ed.), *Applied Systems and Cybernetics*, vol. III, (New York: Pergamon Press, 1981).

(b) P. Dumouchel and J.-P. Dupuy, *L'Enfer des choses* (Paris: Seuil, 1979) and P. Dumouchel, 'Mimetisme et Autonomie', in *L'Auto-organisation de la physique au politique*, op. cit.

(c) J.-P. Dupuy, *Ordres et Désordres* (Seuil, 1982); 'Epistémologie de l'économie et analyse de systèmes' in J. Lesourne (ed.), *La Notion de système dans les sciences contemporaines*, t. II (Aix-en-Provence: Librairie de l'Université, 1981); 'Paradoxes de l'erreur creatrice: prophéties auto-réalisatrices' in *L'Erreur* (Presses Universitaires de Lyon, 1982); 'De l'économie considérée comme théorie de la foule', *Stanford French Review*, Summer 1983.

(d) 'La Contingence dans les affaires humaines' (debate between René Girard and Cornelius Castoriadis) in *L'Auto-organisation de la physique au politique*, op. cit.

(e) *Cahier du CREA*, No. 1, Paris, 1982.

(f) 'Workshop Discussion', in *Disorder and Order*, op. cit.

(g) The essays of J.-P. Dupuy and H. Atlan in this volume.

5. R. Descartes, 'Méditations métaphysiques', in *œuvres* (Paris: Gallimard, [Pleiade], 1953), p. 308; my translation.
6. Which is what Pierre Bourdieu is actually doing in France.

A Gabonese Myth

Abbreviation: *B. E.*: *Le Bouc émissaire* (Paris: Grasset, 1982; English translation *The Scapegoat*, Baltimore: Johns Hopkins University Press, 1986; London: The Athlone Press).

1. Christiane Frémont, 'Trois fictions sur le problème du mal', in Michel Deguy and Jean-Pierre Dupuy (eds), *René Girard et le problème du mal* (Paris: Grasset, 1982), pp. 279–300.
2. Louis Aragon, *La Mise à mort* (Paris: Gallimard-collection Folio, 1965), pp. 104–9. I have quoted long passages spread among these six pages.
3. Lucien Scubla, 'Contribution à la théorie du sacrifice', in *René Girard et le problème du mal*, op. cit., pp. 103–67.

Bibliography

Bureau, R., 'Connais-tu la mort? Les trois nuits rituelles du *Bwiti fang*', in *Annales de l'Université d'Abidjan*, Series D (letters), vol. 6, 1973.

Bureau, R., *Péril blanc, propos d'un ethnologue sur l'Occident* (Paris: L'Harmattan, 1978), Chapters 3 and 4.

Mary, H., *La Naissance à l'envers: Essai sur le rituel du Bwiti fang au Gabon* (Paris: L'Harmattan, 1983).

The Theology of the Wrath of God

1. H. Diels, W. Kranz, *Fragmente der Vorsokratiker* (vol. 3), 7th edn (Berlin, 1954): 1A, 14B (I,5).
2. Cf. J. Pépin, *Mythe et Allégorie. Les origines grecques et les contestations judéo-chrétiennes*, 2nd edn (Paris, 1976), pp. 85–111.
3. Heraclitus, *Quaestiones Homericae*, ed. Soc. Philol. Bonn. (Bibliotheca Script. Graec. et Rom. Teubner 1400). Lipsiae, 1910, 32.
4. We find in him a similar ambivalence in relation to mimesis. He rejected the imitative works of the poets but considered his own philosophy to be educational theory, to which the following applies: 'On the two conceptual innovations of the ancient Greeks of paradigm and mimesis, example and imitation, rests the whole of Greek *paideia*.' W. Jaeger, *Paideia* (vol. 3), 3rd edn (Berlin, 1954) *et seq.* 2,339.
5. Plato, *Phaedrus*, 247a.
6. Plato, *Timaeus*, 29e (E. T. B. Jowett, Oxford, 3rd edn, 1892).
7. Pépin (see note 2), pp. 147–9.
8. Philo, *Quod deus sit immutabilis*, Nos 26–32.
9. Ibid. No. 52.
10. Ibid. No. 66 *et seq.*
11. Ibid. Nos 54–6; 61–9.
12. A. Nissen, *Gott und der Nächste im antiken Judentum* (Tübingen, 1974), p. 307. Cf. Ps. 30:6 and against this Jer. 7:20.
13. P. Kuhn, *Gottes Trauer und Klage in der rabbinischen Überlieferung* (*Talmud und Midrasch*) (Leiden, 1978), pp. 200–39.

14. Ibid., pp. 61–4.
15. M. Corbin, 'l'Idole et la Peur', *Christus* (Paris) 29 (1982): 414.
16. Ibid., 413.
17. Cf. Tertullian, *Praescrip. ad haer.* 7 (PL 2, 19).
18. Tertullian, Ad. Marc. II, 16 (PL 2, 303); cf. M. Pohlenz, *Vom Zorne Gottes. Eine Studie über den Einfluß der griechischen Philosophie auf das alte Christentum* (Göttingen, 1909), p. 21 *et seq.*
19. Maximus the Confessor, *Quaest. ad Thal.* 65 (PG 90, 765 AB).
20. Maximus, *Amb.* (PG 91, 1129 CD).
21. Ibid., (PG 91, 1132 C).
22. Maximus, *Quaest. ad Thal.* 52 (CChr. SG 7,417).
23. Ibid., 65 (PG 90,764 CD).
24. Ibid. (PG 90,745D–784A).
25. Ibid. (PG 90,756A).
26. Ibid. (PG 90,760C).
27. Maximus, *Quaest. ad Thal. 1* (CChr. SG 7,49).
28. Even Lactantius, who apart from Tertullian is almost the only person to discuss divine wrath without inhibitions and who even wrote a book on this theme, interprets it as the just punishment of sinners.
29. Pohlenz (see note 18), p. 128.
30. Maximus the Confessor, *Or. Dom.* (PG 90, 877D–880A, 901AB); *Amb.* 30 (PG 91, 1273CD); *Amb.* 32 (PG 91, 1284C–1285B).
31. Quoted in Origène, *Contre Celse* IV 51 (SC 136) (Paris, 1968), p. 315.
32. Ibid., VI 42 (SC 147) (Paris, 1969), p. 279.
33. Ibid., pp. 279–85.
34. Pépin (see note 2), p. 451.
35. Cf. Ibid., pp. 453–62.
36. Ibid., p. 462.
37. Ibid.
38. Quoted in Eusèbe de Césarée, *Histoire ecclésiastique*, VI 19, 4 (SC 41) (Paris, 1955), p. 114.
39. Ibid.
40. Pépin (see note 2), p. 466.
41. Ibid., pp. 466–74.
42. Cf. Augustine, Ep. 138, 12–15 (PL 33, 530–2, 535–7); *Contra Faustum* 22, 74–9 (PL 42, 447–53).
43. Bernard of Clairvaux, *De laude novae militiae ad milites templi*, I 3 (PL 182, 924).
44. Walter Kasper, *Der Gott Jesu Christi* (Mainz, 1982), p. 20.
45. E. Krebs, *Die Stunde der Heimsuchung. Gedanken über den großen Krieg* 2nd edn (Frieburg in Breisgau, 1915), p. 23.
46. D. Vorwerk, 'Darf der Christ hassen?', in Hammer, *Deutsche Kriegstheologie 1870–1918* (Munich, 1971), p. 292.
47. La Guerre allemande et le catholicisme, ed. A. Baudrillart (Paris, 1915), p. 21.

'I am Joseph': René Girard and the Prophetic Law

1. He is a Jew, and thus he understands what he must understand in his milieu and his culture, that the sacrifice must be stopped, that there must be a substitute . . . (Michel Serres, *Le Parasite* [Paris: Grasset, 1980], p. 219; English translation: *The Parasite* [Baltimore: Johns Hopkins University Press, 1982], p. 164).
2. Eric Gans, Pour une esthétique triangulaire', *Esprit* 429 (November 1973): 581.
3. For a bibliography of Girard's writings and the critical response, see M. Deguy and J.-P. Dupuy, *René Girard et le problème du mal* (Paris: Grasset, 1982), pp. 315–33. The book in which this bibliography appears is itself an excellent sampling of some of the critical response to Girard's work in France. For recent applications of Girard's ideas in psychoanalysis and in psychiatry, see Mikkel Borch-Jacobsen, *Le Sujet freudien* (Paris: Flammarion, 1982), and Jean-Michel Oughourlian, *Un Mime nommé desir* (Paris: Grasset, 1982). For recent readings of Girard's work in context of the Christian Bible and theology, see Raymund Schwager, *Brauchen wir einen Sündenbock?* (Munich: Kösel, 1972), and Norbert Lohfink, *Gewalt und Gewaltlosigkeit im Alten Testament* (Freiburg: Herder, 1983).
4. See P. Dumouchel and J.-P. Dupuy, *L'Enfer des choses* (Paris: Seuil, 1979), I. Prigogine and I. Stengers, *La Nouvelle Alliance* (Paris: Gallimard, 1979), and J.-P. Dupuy, *Ordres et désordres* (Paris: Seuil, 1982).
5. The proceedings from the conference at Cerisy were published by Grasset (1985). A conference on the work of René Girard, Michel Serres, and Ilya Prigogine was held at the University of Texas at Austin in 1980. Another conference on 'Disorder and Order', centred more focally around the work of Girard and the 'mimetic hypothesis', was held at Stanford University in 1981. The proceedings have been published (see P. Livingston (ed.), *Disorder/Order*, Stanford Literature Studies, 1 [Saratoga, Ca.: Anma Libri, 1984]). Finally a conference on 'auto-organization' in the human and natural sciences took place in 1981 and its proceedings appeared last summer (see P. Dumouchel and J. P. Dupuy, *L'Auto-organisation*, colloque de Cerisy [Paris: Seuil, 1983]).
6. René Girard, *Mensonge romantique et vérité romanesque* (Paris: Grasset, 1961).
7. René Girard, *La Violence et le sacré* (Paris: Grasset, 1972), English translation, *Violence and the Sacred* (Baltimore: Johns Hopkins University Press, 1977; London: The Athlone Press, 1988).
8. René Girard, *Des chose cachées depuis la fondation du monde* (Paris: Grasset, 1978), English translation, *Things Hidden since the Foundation of the World* (London: The Athlone Press, 1987; Stanford: Stanford University Press) and *Le Bouc émissaire* (Paris: Grasset, 1982), English

translation, *The Scapegoat* (Baltimore: Johns Hopkins University Press, 1986; London: The Athlone Press).

9. For further discussion of Girard's views on the Christian Gospel, see 'Discussion avec René Girard', *Esprit* 429 (November 1973): 528–63, and René Girard, 'Les Malédictions contre les pharisiens et la révélation évangélique', *Bulletin du Centre Protestant d'Etudes* (Geneva, 1975): 5–29.
10. '*Nouveau prophétisme*' is a phrase that was used, for example, a few years ago by commentators in France to characterize the work of the '*nouveaux philosophes*'.
11. On the shift away from essentialistic conceptualizations in philosophy and in literary criticism, see Emmanuel Lévinas, *Autrement qu'être, ou au-delà de l'essence* (La Haye: Martinus Nijhoff, 1974), and Paul De Man, *Blindness and Insight* (New York: Oxford University Press, 1971).
12. The theme of the '*tiers exclu*' is persistent throughout Serres's work. See, for example, his early book on communication, *Hermès ou la communication* (Paris: Minuit, 1968), p. 41, and his recent book on the foundations of Rome, *Rome, le livre des fondations* (Paris: Grasset, 1983), p. 169. It is interesting that in English we say 'excluded middle' where in French one says '*tiers exclu*'. It is as if in each linguistic context we have domesticated the notion to read either as a middle or as a third, excluding commonly their conjunction – that the '*tiers exclu*' is at once between the communicants (a middle) and outside of them (a third).
13. I know of very little that has been done on this very interesting aspect of Girardian thinking concerning the inefficacy of sacrificial structuration at the moment of the appearance of Greek humanism, Judaism, and in general, modern cultural forms.
14. On the centrality of the notion of anti-idolatry to Hebraic religion, see Yehezkel Kaufmann, *The Religion of Israel*, trans. Moshe Greenberg (New York: Schocken, 1972). On the centrality of the notion of the prophetic, see also Martin Buber, *On the Bible*, introd. Harold Bloom (New York: Schocken, 1982). For a penetrating account of the criticism of idolatry in non-Jewish writing, see John Freccero, 'The Fig Tree and the Laurel: Petrarch's Poetics', *Diacritics* 5 (1975): 34–40.
15. For a discussion of the way in which the 'secondary' or interpretative texts of Jewish tradition extend Torah, see Susan Handelman, *The Slayers of Moses* (Albany, N.Y.: SUNY Press, 1982), p. 38, and Emmanuel Lévinas, *L'Au-delà du verset* (Paris: Minuit, 1982), p. 7. The standard authority, in the English-speaking world, for discussions of Jewish spirituality and mysticism is, of course, Gershom Scholem. See, for example, his *Major Trends in Jewish Mysticism* (New York: Schocken, 1972).
16. The specific commandment against idolatry has often been taken to be the second: 'Thou shalt make unto thyself no graven images'. The first commandment has been taken, on the other hand, as the statement of Hebraic monotheism. It may be, however, that by virtue of the second

commandment we may understand the first as the law of anti-idolatry ('Thou shalt have only an external God, no internal Gods'). The reading, then, of the first as a statement of monotheism would reflect already an exclusion of the second and in general of the diachronic or prophetic context in which the first appears: the only context, in fact, in which such a list of commandments can be read as a text or narrative. For the biblical text see A. C. Feuer and N. Scherman, *Aseres Hadibros/The Ten Commandments* (Brooklyn: Mesorah, 1981). On the shift away from viewing Hebraic monotheism as opposed to polytheism and towards viewing it as opposed to paganism, see Bernard-Henri Lévy, *Le Testament de Dieu* (Paris: Grasset, 1979).

17. The importance of the work of Emmanuel Lévinas to this discussion – and in general to the notion of the exteriority of transcendence – cannot be overestimated. See, for example, his *Totalité et infini* (La Haye: Martinus Nijhoff, 1961), and *Autrement qu'être, ou au-delà de l'essence* (1974). For Lévinas' work on Judaism, see his *Difficile Liberté* (Paris: Albin Michel, 1976), *Du Sacré au saint, Cinq Nouvelles Lectures talmudiques* (Paris: Minuit, 1977), and *Quatre Lectures talmudiques* (Minuit, 1968). The work of Maurice Blanchot in this connection is also important (see his *Le Livre à venir* [Paris: Gallimard, 1959]). For an application of these ideas within a political context, see Bernard-Henri Lévy, *La Barbarie à visage humain* (Paris: Grasset, 1977). For other important accounts of Judaism, see André Neher, *L'Existence juive* (Paris: Seuil, 1962), and André Chouraqui, *Histoire de Judaisme* (Paris: Presses Universitaires de France, 1957); English translation: *A History of Judaism* (New York: Walker, 1964).

18. The phrase '*la pensée du dehors*', of course, belongs to Blanchot. But Foucault uses it as the title of a little-known but important essay on Blanchot ('La Pensée du dehors', *Critique* 229 [1966]: 523–46). For a profound meditation on the themes of exodus and the desert in Dante, see Giuseppe Mazzotta, *Dante, Poet of the Desert* (Princeton: Princeton University Press, 1979).

19. The text of Exodus is from A. Cohen, *The Soncino Chumash* (London: The Soncino Press, 1979). For other important editions of Torah and its commentaries, see J. H. Hertz, *The Pentateuch and Haftorahs* (The Soncino Press, 1978), and A. B. Isaiah and B. Sharfman, *The Pentateuch and Rashi's Commentary* (Brooklyn: S. S. & R., 1949). On Genesis alone, see also the monumental Artscroll edition of M. Zlotowitz and N. Scherman, *Bereishis/Genesis*, 6 vols (New York: Mesorah, 1977–81). This edition, if completed in the manner in which it has been projected, promises to become one of the most important source books for biblical study in English. The aim of the project is to produce the Torah in its entirety (in English and Hebrew) with representative samplings in English of Talmudic, Midrashic, and rabbinic commentary on every line. Thus far, only Genesis has been completed. In six volumes of mostly small print, it runs to two thousand pages.

20. For a similar account of the name of God, see Buber, *On the Bible*, pp. 80–92. For further commentary, see Lévinas, *L'Au-delà du verset*, pp. 143–57, and Jacques Derrida, *La Carte postale* (Paris: Flammarion, 1980), p. 179.
21. It may be just such a notion – that the Torah itself may be understood as a covenant – that has led non-Jewish historical critics of the Bible to see the 'Old Testament' as structured around the notion of covenant. See, for example, Walther Eichrodt, *Theology of the Old Testament*, 2 vols, trans. J. A. Baker (Philadelphia: Westminster Press, 1961–). For a more personal account of covenant in the 'Old Testament' and the Christian Gospel, see J. Bishop, *The Covenant: A Reading* (Springfield, Ill.: Templegate, 1982).
22. It is customary, of course, within orthodox synagogues, for women to sit segregated from the men.
23. E. A. Speiser, for example, in his prestigious edition of Genesis in the Anchor Bible series, summarizes this long and persistent tradition of biblical criticism in which scholars have divided up the text into distinctive compositional sources – a 'J' document, an 'E' document and so on – in accordance with the various words employed for the naming of divinity. My own interest – as I hope will be clear in this essay – is not to challenge this important work, but to ask a different question: namely, by what principle of coherence can these admittedly diverse and heterogeneous materials be seen as 'going together', a principle to whose unifying power the very fervour with which we pursue an interest in heterogeneity in the text may offer ample testimony? On the shift away from traditional historical concerns to a closer reading of narrative and poetic detail, the ground-breaking book, of course, is Robert Alter's *The Art of Biblical Narrative* (New York: Basic Books, 1981). It is Alter, for example, who takes Speiser to task over just such issues. Whatever the potential pitfalls of an organicist approach – namely, that it be developed at the expense of historicism – Alter's book is profoundly exciting. He allows us to envision a new biblical criticism as yet in its infancy, one which would cull the insights of both formalism and historicism (eschewing the limitations of each) into a critical position which is something like that of the Bible itself.
24. Jacob's blessing of the sons of Joseph is itself an interesting moment in context of our presentation. Instead of blessing Manassah (who is Joseph's first-born) with his right hand, and Ephraim with his left, Jacob crosses his hands and blesses Manassah with his left hand and Ephraim with his right. He does this, he tells Joseph, because Manassah's younger brother 'shall become greater than he'. Is Jacob continuing the sacrificial reading of earlier, favouring the younger son, the gesture which set the whole drama into motion (and, perhaps, recalls his own position as second-born)? Or does he reflect an anti-sacrificial position, perhaps one that he has learned from the events that have transpired, recognizing at

once that Manassah is first-born and that Ephraim must not be slighted, a view which contrasts with the rigid distinction between Cain and Abel at the other end of the Torah? Malbim suggests that Jacob placed his left hand above the right, thereby blessing Manassah with the hand that was on top and Ephraim with the right, refusing to some extent, that is, to distinguish between them. What seems clear is that the text of Jacob's blessing of the sons, like the Joseph story proper, and like Jacob's hands within that text, superimposes one view upon the other. Jacob has 'wisely directed his hands', Rashi tells us in his interpretation of this passage. I thank Holli Levitsky of the University of California, Irvine, for drawing my attention to this passage in context of the above argument.

25. Scholem, *Major Trends in Jewish Mysticism*, pp. 141–2.

Totalization and Misrecognition

1. In Marcel Mauss, *Sociologie et Anthropologie* (Paris: Presses Universitaires de France, 1973), pp. XXXVI–XXXVII. Lévi-Strauss makes reference to two books: Norbert Wiener, *Cybernetics* (New York and Paris, 1948) and C. E. Shannon and Warren Weaver, *The Mathematical Theory of Communication* (University of Illinois Press, 1949).
2. Vincent Descombes, 'L'Equivoque du symbolique', *MLN* (Baltimore: Johns Hopkins University Press), vol. 94, No. 4 (May 1979): 655–75. The journal *MLN* was at that time edited by René Girard.
3. Ibid., p. 658.
4. C. Lévi-Strauss, 'Introduction à l'œuvre de Marcel Mauss', op. cit., p. XXII.
5. Cf. P. Dumouchel and J.-P. Dupuy, *L'Enfer des choses* (Paris: Seuil, 1979); J.-P. Dupuy, 'Mimésis et morphogénèse', in *Ordres et désordres* (Seuil, 1982); J.-P. Dupuy, 'Epistémologie de l'économie et Analyse de systèmes', in J. Lesourne (ed.), *La Notion de système dans les sciences contemporaines*, vol. II, 'Epistémologie' (Aix-en-Provence: Librairie de l'Université, 1981); H. Atlan and J.-P. Dupuy, 'Mimesis and Social Morphogenesis: Violence and the Sacred from a Systems Analysis Viewpoint', in G. E. Lasker (ed.), *Applied Systems and Cybernetics*, vol. III (New York: Pergamon, 1981); J.-P. Dupuy, 'Paradoxes de l'erreur créatrice; prophéties autoréalisatrices', in *L'Erreur* (Presses Universitaires de Lyon, 1982); J.-P. Dupuy, 'La Mimésis et l'économie', in *Economies et Sociétés*, 'La logique et la science économique', ed. P. Chanier, vol. XVI, No. 3 (March 1982); J.-P. Dupuy, 'De l'économie considérée comme théorie de la foule', *Stanford French Review* (Summer 1983); P. Dumouchel, 'Mimétisme et Autonomie', in P. Dumouchel and J.-P. Dupuy (eds), *Colloque de Cerisy: l'Auto-organisation: de la physique au politique* (Paris: Seuil, 1983).
6. R. Girard, 'Camus's Stranger Retried', in R. Girard, *'To Double Business*

Bound': Essays on Literature, Mimesis and Anthropology (Baltimore: Johns Hopkins University Press; London: The Athlone Press, 1988).

7. L. Scubla, '*Ménon*, la logique sacrificielle et le problème de l'interprétation', *Poésie* 39 (December 1986).
8. Guy Lefort, in R. Girard, *Des choses cachées depuis la fondation du monde* (Paris: Grasset, 1978), pp. 150–1, English translation *Things Hidden Since the Foundation of the World* (London: The Athlone Press, 1987; Stanford: Stanford University Press), p. 128. On the theme of the importance of misrecognition, cf. pp. 149–53.
9. Ibid., p. 152.
10. Ibid., p. 150.
11. Ibid., p. 301.
12. Ibid., p. 151.
13. Ibid., p. 303.
14. Ibid., p. 159.
15. Ibid., p. 160.
16. Cf. J.-P. Dupuy, 'Le Signe et l'Envie', in P. Dumouchel and J.-P. Dupuy, *L'Enfer des choses*, op. cit., especially pp. 119–34. Since writing this text I have realized that Girard does not, as I had charged, underestimate the relative stability of the social forms invented by modernity which are substituted for the sacred in the strict sense of the term (the economy, money, etc.). They nevertheless remain for him, on the scale of his theory (the history of humanity!), destined to be devoured by the very thing on which they are based: the knowledge, partial but growing, of the mechanisms of violence.
17. H. Atlan and J.-P. Dupuy, 'Mimesis and Social Morphogenesis: Violence and the Sacred from a Systems Analysis Viewpoint', loc. cit. H. Atlan, it is true, is thinking more here of ritual than of the founding mimetic crisis itself. Cf. the discussion between H. Atlan, P. Dumouchel and R. Girard, in *Colloque de Cerisy: l'Auto-organisation*, op. cit., pp. 369–71.
18. Cf. P. Dumouchel, 'L'Ambivalence de la rareté', in P. Dumouchel and J.-P. Dupuy, *L'Enfer des choses*, op. cit., pp. 217–18, n. 1.
19. I have used the French edition: *Essais de psychanalyse*, trans. S. Jankélévitch (Payot, Paris, 1925). [Translator's note: In the original German, Freud employs the more encompassing term *Masse* to designate both McDougall's 'group' and Le Bon's 'foule' (crowd). The French edition uses the word 'foule' exclusively, whereas the standard edition of Freud in English always uses 'group' even where 'crowd' would be more appropriate. For the sake of consistency with Dupuy's text, I have systematically substituted 'crowd' for 'group' in quotations from the English translation.]
20. I am taking up again here, while developing more completely its epistemological side, the demonstration to be found in my 'De l'économie considérée comme théorie de la foule', loc. cit. Cf. also J.-P.

Dupuy, 'La Main invisible et l'Indétermination de la totalisation sociale', *Cahier du CREA*, No. 1 (1982).

21. *The Standard Edition of the Complete Psychological Works of Sigmund Freud*, ed. James Strachey, vol. XVIII (London: Hogarth Press, 1955), p. 79.
22. Ibid., p. 102.
23. Ibid., p. 92.
24. Ibid., p. 100.
25. Ibid., p. 84.
26. Serge Moscovici, *L'Age des foules* (Paris: Fayard, 1981), p. 331.
27. *Standard Edition*, op. cit., vol. XVIII, p. 96.
28. Ibid., p. 97.
29. Ibid., p. 96.
30. Ibid., p. 97.
31. Ibid.
32. Ibid., p. 96.
33. S. Moscovici, *L'Age des foules*, op. cit., pp. 363–4.
34. In a passage remarkable for its lucidity, but unfortunately isolated from the rest of his argumentation, Freud envisages exactly this diversity of forms and the possibility of their being substituted for the leader: cf. *Standard Edition*, op. cit., vol XVIII, p. 100.
35. Cf. Elias Canetti, *Crowds and Power*, trans. Carol Stewart (Harmondsworth: Penguin, 1973), p. 32.
36. Cf. the 'conjecture of Heinz von Foerster' which I recapitulate at the beginning of my *Ordres et désordres*, op. cit., p. 14.
37. Cf. P. Dumouchel's analysis of modernity as a process in which the members of society are *exteriorized*, in *L'Enfer des choses*, op. cit.
38. Cf., in 'De l'économie considérée comme théorie de la foule', loc. cit., the paragraph entitled 'la Panique et le Marché'.
39. Cf. G. Debreu and M. Scarf, 'A limit theorem on the core of an economy', *International Economic Review* (September 1963).
40. The situation in question here is therefore not the one, frequently considered in economics, where an individual rationality becomes a collective irrationality (externalities, non-optimal Nash equilibria of the 'prisoner's dilemma' type, etc.).
41. Cf., among others, the 'Séminaire: de la prophétie autoréalisatrice en économie', in *Colloque de Cerisy: l'Auto-organisation*, op. cit., with contributions by R. Guesnerie, B. Walliser and P. Mongin; M. Aglietta and A. Orléan, *La Violence de la monnaie* (Paris: Presses Universitaires de France, 1982); Y. Parfait and T. Facon, 'Economie, autoréférence et points fixes', CREA, Ecole Polytechnique, 1981; J.-P. Dupuy, 'Autoréférence et points fixes: à propos de la controverse Aubert-Simon dans *Social Science Information*', in A. Demailly and J. L. Le Moigne (eds), *Sciences de l'Intelligence, Sciences de l'Artificiel* (Presses Universitaires de Lyon, 1986), pp. 568–74.

42. Marcel Mauss, *The Gift: Forms and Functions of Exchange in Archaic Societies*, trans. Ian Cunnison (London: Cohen & West, 1970) [originally published in *Année sociologique*, 2nd series, vol. I (1923–4)].
43. Ibid., p. 1.
44. Ibid. [Translator's note: The translation of the English edition has been criticized as reflecting an overly economistic reading of Mauss's text. I have followed the more faithful alternative rendering of this passage proposed by Jonathan Parry in '*The Gift*, the Indian Gift and the "Indian Gift",' *Man*, vol. 21, No. 3 (September 1986): 455–6.]
45. Ibid.
46. Ibid., p. 41.
47. C. Lévi-Strauss, 'Introduction à l'œuvre de Marcel Mauss', loc. cit., p. XXXVIII. Firth, for his part, reproaches Mauss for not having understood what the native was trying to tell him . . .
48. Ibid.
49. Ibid., p. XXXIX.
50. Ibid., p. XL.
51. Ibid., p. XLVI.
52. Ibid., p. XLVIII.
53. V. Descombes, 'L'Equivoque du symbolique', loc. cit., pp. 660–1.
54. P. Bourdieu, *Outline of a Theory of Practice*, trans. Richard Nice (Cambridge: Cambridge University Press, 1977). I thank Mark Anspach for having led me to see that Bourdieu's criticism of Lévi-Strauss could be relevant to a discussion of Girard. Cf. M. Anspach, 'La Boucle émissaire: vers un cercle mimétique non vicieux', *Cahier du CREA*, No. 2 (1983).
55. P. Bourdieu, *Outline*, op. cit., pp. 3–4.
56. Ibid., p. 4.
57. M. Gauchet, 'Politique et société: la leçon des sauvages (II)', in *Textures* 75/12–13: 71.
58. P. Bourdieu, *Outline*, op. cit., p. 5. [Translator's note: I have restored the word 'reciprocity', which appears in the original French, in the place of the word 'reversibility' in the English edition.]
59. Ibid., p. 171.
60. Ibid., p. 6. [Translator's note: I have modified the English translation of this sentence to restore aspects of the French original important to Dupuy's argument.]
61. On the super-economism of Bourdieu, who intends to escape from economism by 'carrying out in full what economism does only partially', see the astonishing passages to be found towards the end of the *Outline*, pp. 177–83. Cf. also Alain Caillé, 'La Sociologie de l'intérêt est-elle intéressante?', *Sociologie du travail* 3 (1981).
62. R. Girard, *Le Bouc émissaire* (Paris: Grasset, 1982), pp. 24–5. (Emphasis added.) English translation, *The Scapegoat* (Baltimore: Johns Hopkins University Press, 1986; London: The Athlone Press).

63. P. Bourdieu, *Outline*, op. cit., p. 173.
64. Cf. J.-P. Dupuy, 'La Main invisible et l'indétermination de la totalisation sociale', loc. cit.
65. R. Guidieri, 'Essai sur le prêt', in *L'Abondance des pauvres* (Paris: Seuil, 1984).
66. P. Manent, 'La Leçon de Ténèbres de René Girard', *Commentaire* 19 (Fall 1982). This very polemical text is not, by the way, exempt from misconstructions of Girard's meaning due to an overly hasty perusal of the latter's writing.
67. Cf. the 'Débat Cornélius Castoriadis–René Girard', in *Colloque de Cerisy: l'Auto-organisation*, op. cit., especially pp. 288–9.
68. Cf. P. Bourdieu, *Outline*, op. cit., pp. 171–2.
69. M. Sahlins, *Stone Age Economics* (Chicago: Aldine Atherton, 1972).
70. Ibid., pp. 172–4. Cf. also a series of two articles by M. Anspach, 'Le Don paisible?' and 'Tuer ou substituer: l'échange de victimes', *Bulletin du MAUSS* 11 and 12 (1984).
71. For Louis Dumont, the non-closure of the exchange due to this distance is an example of the difference separating egalitarian and hierarchical forms. Cf. his remarks on Sahlins in *Essais sur l'individualisme* (Paris: Seuil, 1983), p. 260, n. 63 (English edition: *Essays on Individualism: Modern Ideology in Anthropological Perspective* [Chicago: University of Chicago Press, 1986]) Cf. also M. Anspach, 'La Spontanéité exigeante, la réification libératrice: Intermédiation et double bind', *Cahier du CREA*, No. 10 (1987).
72. R. Girard, *Le Bouc émissaire*, op. cit., p. 25.
73. P. Livet, *L'Autonomie du Social*, forthcoming.
74. P. Livet, *L'Autonomie du Social*, op. cit.; J.-P. Dupuy, 'Mimésis et Morphogénèse', loc. cit.; P. Dumouchel, J.-P. Dupuy, L. Scubla, M. Aglietta and A. Orléan, 'Modèles formels de la philosophie sociale et politique', *Cahier du CREA*, No. 1 (1982).
75. Cf. *Cahier du CREA*, No. 1, op. cit.
76. It must be recalled that in 'The Purloined Letter', the Chevalier Dupin pronounces these memorable words: 'Mathematical axioms are *not* axioms of general truth. What is true of relation – of form and quantity – is often grossly false in regard to morals, for example. In this latter science it is very usually *un*true that the aggregated parts are equal to the whole.' I confess that the attribution of this parable to Lacan is wholly imaginary, albeit perfectly plausible. Cf. J. Lacan, 'Le nombre treize et la forme logique de la suspicion', *Cahiers d'art*, 1945.
77. See the reference in note 57.
78. M. Gauchet, ibid., pp. 82–3.
79. Cf. Louis Dumont, *Essais sur l'individualisme*, op. cit.
80. M. Gauchet, loc. cit., p. 87.
81. Ibid., p. 84.
82. Ibid.

83. M. Gauchet, 'De l'avènement de l'individu à la découverte de la société', *Annales* (May–June 1979).
84. Louis Dumont, *From Mandeville to Marx: The Genesis and Triumph of Economic Ideology* (Chicago and London: University of Chicago Press, 1977), p. 78.
85. M. Gauchet, 'De l'avènement de l'individu à la découverte de la société', loc. cit., p. 458.
86. In this sense social contract theories, which combine modern individualism and artificialism on the one hand, and the traditional vision of society as belonging to the scheme of conscious will on the other, constitute an intermediate stage, probably unstable, in the evolution of representations of society. Cf. M. Gauchet, loc. cit., pp. 461–2.
87. Cf. the penetrating introduction by Marcel Gauchet to the political opus of Benjamin Constant in B. Constant, *De la liberté chez les modernes* (Paris: Pluriel, Le Livre de Poche, 1980).
88. Ibid., p. 28.
89. Cf., for example, the three volumes of *Law, Legislation and Liberty* (London: Routledge & Kegan Paul), especially volume 2, 'The Mirage of Social Justice' (1976).
90. For a skilful defence of Hayek, read Bernard Manin, 'Friedrich-August Hayek et la question du libéralisme', *Revue française de science politique* 1 (February 1983).

Money and Mimetic Speculation

1. H. G. Frankfurt, 'Freedom of the Will and the Concept of a Person', *Journal of Philosophy*, vol. 68, No. 1 (January 14, 1971): 5–20.
2. A. Sen, 'Rational Fools: A Critique of the Behavioral Foundations of Economic Theory', *Philosophy and Public Affairs*, vol. 6, No. 4 (Summer 1977): 317–44.
3. Jean-Pierre Dupuy, 'De l'économie considerée comme théorie de la foule', *Stanford French Review* (Summer 1983): 245–64.
4. J. M. Keynes, *The General Theory of Employment, Interest and Money* (London: Macmillan, 1936), p. 156.
5. R. Girard, *Violence and the Sacred*, trans. Patrick Gregory (Baltimore: Johns Hopkins University Press, 1977; London: The Athlone Press, 1988) p. 78.
6. Ibid., p. 79.
7. F. P. Kelly, 'How a group reaches agreement: a stochastic model', *Mathematical Social Sciences*, North Holland Publishing Company, vol. 2 (1981): pp. 1–8, J. Gazon, 'La Transmission de l'opinion, une approche structurale du pouvoir au sein des structures fortement connexes', *Cahiers de l'ISMEA*.
8. J. M. Keynes, op cit., pp. 203–4.
9. For greater mathematical precision, see the articles cited above by J.

Gazon and F. P. Kelly. In the present text, we will not refer to the problem of periodicity that gives rise to limit cycles.

10. Cf. Michel Aglietta and André Orléan, *La Violence de la monnaie* (Paris: Presses Universitaires de France, 1982), Chapters 5–7.
11. Cf. J.-P. Benassy, 'Théorie du déséquilibre et fondements micro-économiques de la macro-économie', *Revue économique*, vol. 27, No. 5 (1976).
12. R. Girard, op. cit., p. 148.

Demystification and History in Girard and Durkheim

1. Contemporary rejections of Durkheim's realism are, of course, motivated by many different social and intellectual considerations and it is impossible to provide here an adequate documentation of the many forms of anti-Durkheimian social thought. For the tendency mentioned, see Peter Winch, *The Idea of a Social Science* (London: Routledge & Kegan Paul, 1958); Derek L. Phillips, *Wittgenstein and Scientific Knowledge* (London: Macmillan, 1977). Another kind of example entirely would be that of Stanley R. Barrett, *The Rebirth of Anthropological Theory* (Toronto: University of Toronto Press, 1984), which includes a chapter entitled 'Structuralism and the Second Burial of Emile Durkheim', pp. 115–44. The chapter ends with a section extolling the virtues of field work. Durkheim is attacked on wholly different grounds (namely as an incoherent rationalist) in Terry Johnson, Christopher Dandekes and Clive Ashworth, *The Structure of Social Theory: Dilemmas and Strategies* (London: Macmillan, 1984).
2. René Girard, 'Differentiation and Reciprocity in Lévi-Strauss and Contemporary Theory', in *'To Double Business Bound': Essays on Literature, Mimesis, and Anthropology* (Baltimore: Johns Hopkins University Press, 1978; London: The Athlone Press, 1988), p. 163.
3. Emile Durkheim, *The Elementary Forms of the Religious Life*, trans. Joseph Ward Swain (New York: Free Press, 1965), pp. 14–15. All citations of Durkheim will be to English translations with modifications based on the original French.
4. In what we call the *Metaphysics*, Aristotle expounds upon the different senses of the notion of *arche*, senses that we might do well to recollect: The *arche* is an origin or a temporal endpoint, but also an ethical aim or a *telos*. It designates what is essential in a process, what guides or governs it. The *arche* is also the crucial part of something: it is a nature, an intention, or a substance. Finally, it is a phenomenon's fundamental cause as well as the basic principle in its explanation. Thus the *arche* is the determining essence, the knowledge of which guarantees the validity of knowledge, Delta, 1023a 1–25.
5. A striking example would be Peter Berger and Thomas Luckmann's classic *The Social Construction of Reality* (Harmondsworth: Penguin,

1967). This shortcoming is convincingly attributed to Pierre Bourdieu by Luc Ferry and Alain Renaut in their trenchant work *La Pensée 68: essai sur l'anti-humanisme contemporain* (Paris: Gallimard, 1985), pp. 199–235. What is at stake is the methodological requirement that David Bloor has called that of 'reflexivity', by which he means to say that the patterns of explanation employed in the sociology of knowledge must be applied to the sociological practice as well. It will become clear that I do not share Bloor's insistence also on a supposed 'neutrality' requirement. See his *Knowledge and Social Imagery* (London: Routledge & Kegan Paul, 1976), p. 6; also James Robert Brown (ed.), *Scientific Rationality: The Sociological Turn* (Dordrecht: Reidel, 1984).

6. This point is made by Robert Nisbet in *The Sociology of Emile Durkheim* (New York: Oxford University Press, 1974), p. 238; by W. S. F. Pickering, *Durkheim's Sociology of Religion: Themes and Theories* (London: Routledge & Kegan Paul, 1984), p. 381; and by Dominick LaCapra, *Emile Durkheim: Sociologist and Philosopher* (Ithaca: Cornell University Press, 1972), p. 123.
7. Durkheim makes this statement in the first paragraph of his preface to the first edition of *The Rules of Sociological Method*, trans. Sarah A. Solovay and John H. Mueller (New York: Free Press, 1938), p. xxxvii.
8. Ian Hamnett poses this question very clearly in his recent contribution to a volume on Durkheim which I discovered after writing the first draft of this paper. See 'Durkheim and the Study of Religion', in Steve Fenton, Robert Reiner and Ian Hamnett, *Durkheim and Modern Sociology* (Cambridge: Cambridge University Press, 1984), pp. 205–6.
9. *Elementary Forms*, pp. 239–40.
10. Ibid., p. 171.
11. Paul Q. Hirst, *Durkheim, Bernard and Epistemology* (London: Routledge & Kegan Paul, 1975), p. 88.
12. *The Division of Labour in Society*, trans. George Simpson (New York: Free Press, 1933), p. 302.
13. *Suicide: A Study in Sociology*, trans. John A. Spaulding and George Simpson (Glencoe, Ill.: Free Press, 1951), pp. 278–89.
14. Hirst's point is based on a narrow understanding of 'Kant's epistemology'. See his *Durkheim*, pp. 2, 4, 193, 197. The very real Kantian elements in Durkheim are clearly suggested by Steven Lukes in his massive *Emile Durkheim: His Life and Work* (New York: Harper & Row, 1972). One place to begin is the Kantian texts gathered in Lewis White Beck (ed.), *On History* (Indianapolis: Bobbs-Merrill, 1963), yet the Second Critique should also be kept in view in regard to Durkheim's most basic manner of conceiving of '*un fait moral*'.
15. Jürgen Habermas, *Theorie des kommunikativen Handelns*, vol. 2 (Frankfurt: Suhrkamp, 1981), pp. 75–170.
16. *Elementary Forms*, p. 493.
17. Cf. Eric Gans, 'Scandal to the Jews, Folly to the Pagans', *Diacritics* 9:3

(1979): 43–53; 'Le *logos* de René Girard', in *René Girard et le problème du mal*, ed. Michel Deguy and Jean-Pierre Dupuy (Paris: Grasset, 1982), pp. 179–213; 'Désir, représentation, culture', in *Violence et vérité*, ed. Paul Dumouchel (Grasset, 1985), pp. 395–404. Gans's most recent book, to which I cannot begin to do justice in this context, is a strong reworking of the Girardian hypotheses along these lines. See his *The End of Culture: Toward a Generative Anthropology* (Berkeley: University of California Press, 1985), as well as *The Origin of Language* (University of California Press, 1981).

18. *Elementary Forms*, p. 493.
19. For a valuable reconstruction of Merton on this issue, see Ian Mitroff, *The Subjective Side of Science* (Amsterdam: Elsevier, 1974), p. 12. For a more recent and sociologically realistic view, see Richard Whitley, *The Intellectual and Social Organization of the Sciences* (Oxford: Clarendon, 1984).
20. 'Individual and Collective Representations', in *Sociology and Philosophy*, trans. D. F. Pocock (New York: Free Press, 1974), p. 3. Pocock's translation of the articles in this volume strikes me as particularly unreliable. '*Conscience*' becomes 'thought' and then 'reason'; '*un mystérieux au-délà*' is rendered as the laughable 'cloud-cuckoo-land' (p. 94).
21. *Des Choses cachées depuis la fondation du monde* (Paris: Grasset, 1978), p. 109. English translation, *Things Hidden since the Foundation of the World* (London: The Athlone Press, 1987; Stanford: Stanford University Press).
22. '*To Double Business Bound*', pp. 161–4.
23. 'Natur ist das Dasein der Dinge, sofern es nach allgemeinen Gesetzen bestimmt ist.' Immanuel Kant, *Prolegomena zu einer jeden künftigen Metaphysik* (Hamburg: Felix Meiner), p. 49. In English, *Prolegomena* (Indianapolis: Bobbs-Merrill, 1950), p. 42.
24. *Le Bouc émissaire* (Paris: Grasset, 1982), English translation, *The Scapegoat* (Baltimore: Johns Hopkins University Press, 1986; London: The Athlone Press); *La Route antique des hommes pervers* (Grasset, 1985), English translation, *Job the Victim of his People* (London: The Athlone Press 1987; Stanford: Stanford University Press). See also 'Hamlet's Dull Revenge', in *Stanford Literature Review* (Fall 1984): 159–200.
25. *Le Bouc émissaire*, p. 285.
26. *La Route antique*, pp. 52–63, 216–24.
27. *Le Bouc émissaire*, p. 289.
28. See pp. 27–43.
29. *Violence et vérité*, p. 264.
30. See pp. 110–112; see also the work Orléan co-authored with Michel Aglietta, *La Violence de la monnaie* (Paris: Presses Universitaires de France, 1982).
31. *Violence and the Sacred* (Baltimore: Johns Hopkins University Press,

1977; London: The Athlone Press, 1988), p. 306 (it should be noted that this English translation of Girard's 1972 *La Violence et le sacré* was modified by the author, and is therefore of independent interest). Elsewhere Girard flatly states his view that such an 'education' will always be limited: 'Ritual thought can never turn back upon its own origin. It is perpetuated in philosophical thought, and, in our days, in our modern sciences of man, which have inherited the powers of ritual as well as its fundamental impotence' (*La Route antique*, p. 144).

32. Jean-Pierre Dupuy, 'Mimésis et morphogénèse', in *René Girard et le problème du mal*, pp. 225–78; 'De l'économie considerée comme théorie de la foule', in *Stanford French Review* 7:2 (1983): 245–64; pp. 75–100 above. On the problematic of self-organizing systems in general, see Dupuy and Paul Dumouchel, eds, *L'Auto-organisation: de la physique au politique* (Paris: Seuil, 1983), as well as Erich Jantsch, *The Self-Organizing Universe* (New York: Pergamon, 1980), and Milan Zeleny (ed.), *Autopoiesis: A Theory of Living Organization* (New York: North Holland, 1981). I am particularly grateful to Dupuy, whose work has been of particular value to my own attempt to learn about these issues. Dupuy's research group at the Ecole Polytechnique, the 'Centre de Recherche Epistémologie et Autonomie', or CREA, has created a valuable series of 'cahiers' on related theoretical problems. Of special pertinence in this context is *Cahier* No. 2 (May 1983).

33. Pierre Livet, 'Un modèle de l'imprédictible', in *Violence et vérité*, pp. 558–68.

34. Girard's most immediate target in this regard is Sartre, yet there are implications for more contemporary existentialisms as well.

35. *Suicide*, op. cit., pp. 124–30.

36. See the Introduction to *To Double Business Bound* pp. vii–xvi.

37. In what is essentially an optimistic survey of scientific explanations of mind, we find the following statement:

> Philosophers, logicians, and A1 workers are still a long distance away from a real understanding of creative induction. We must learn to represent large-scale semantic systems and systematic knowledge bases in such a way that their rational evolution – an occasionally *discontinuous* evolution – is the natural outcome of their internal dynamic. This is of course the central unsolved problem of A1, cognitive psychology, epistemology, and inductive logic alike.

Paul M. Churchland, *Matter and Consciousness: A Contemporary Introduction to the Philosophy of Mind* (Cambridge, Mass.: MIT Press, 1984), p. 113.

38. *Deceit, Desire, and the Novel: Self and Other in Literary Structure*, trans. Yvonne Freccero (Baltimore: Johns Hopkins University Press, 1965; London: The Athlone Press, 1988), *passim*.

39. Girard restated this analysis succinctly during the Cerisy debates: *Violence et vérité*, p. 140.

40. The reader is encouraged to refer to Girard's rigorous definitions in the

second chapter of *Le Bouc émissaire*, 'Les stéréotypes de la persécution', as well as the definition of mythology at the beginning of the third chapter, 'Qu'est-ce qu'un mythe?'.

41. A poignant discussion of this problem is that of Michel Serres in his 'Thanatocratie', *Critique* 298 (March 1972): 199–227.

Fetishism and Form

1. Lucien Goldmann, 'Introduction aux problèmes d'une sociologie du roman', in *Pour une sociologie du Roman* (Paris: Gallimard, 1964).
2. See René Girard, *Mensonge romantique et vérité romanesque* (Paris: Grasset, 1961); and Georg Lukács, *Theory of the Novel* (Cambridge, Mass.: MIT, 1971).
3. Lucien Goldmann, op. cit., p. 36.
4. See René Girard, *La Violence et le sacré* (Paris: Grasset, 1972), English translation, *Violence and the Sacred* (Baltimore: Johns Hopkins University Press, 1977; London: The Athlone Press, 1988). For an excellent introduction to Girard's thought, see Christine Orsini, 'Introduction à la Lecture de René Girard', in Michel Deguy and Jean-Pierre Dupuy (eds), *René Girard et le problème du mal* (Grasset, 1982).
5. Paul Dumouchel and Jean-Pierre Dupuy, *L'Enfer des choses*, (Paris: Seuil, 1979).
6. Michel Aglietta and André Orléan, *La Violence de la monnaie*, (Paris: Presses Universitaires de France, 1982).
7. Jorge Luis Borges, *El Aleph* (Madrid: Allianza Editorial, 1981), p. 182.
8. Borges, 'The Zahir', trans. A. Kerrigan, in *Labyrinths* (New York: New Directions, 1964), p. 161.
9. H. G. Wells, 'The Crystal Egg', in Leslie Fiedler (ed.), *In Dreams Awake* (New York: Dell, 1975), p. 41.
10. Borges, 'El Aleph', in *El Aleph* op. cit., p. 158.
11. Ibid., p. 173.
12. Borges, 'The Zahir', in *Labyrinths*, op. cit., p. 158.
13. Ibid., p. 157.
14. Ibid., p. 162.
15. Ibid., p. 163.
16. Ibid., p. 163.
17. Ibid., p. 164.
18. Jean-Paul Sartre, *Being and Nothingness*, trans. H. Barnes (New York: Philosophical Library, 1956), p. 177.
19. Ibid., p. 372.
20. Borges, 'The Zahir', op. cit., p. 157.
21. Ibid., p. 157.
22. Dumouchel and Dupuy, op. cit., p. 113.
23. Aglietta and Orléan, op. cit., pp. 59–60.
24. Ibid., pp. 47–8.

25. Borges, 'El Aleph', op. cit., p. 174.
26. René Girard, *Dostoïevski: du double à l'unité* (Paris: Plon, 1963), p. 77.
27. Ibid., p. 78.
28. The role of money in this text clearly reveals the error of Lukács' own remarks at the end of *The Theory of the Novel* to the effect that Dostoevsky did not write novels, but was engaged in the creation of a new epic form. The later Lukács attempts to explain this error in his 1962 *Preface* to this work. (See Lukács, op. cit., pp. 152, 20.)
29. Fyodor Dostoevsky, 'The Gambler', *Great Short Works of Dostoevsky*, trans. Constance Garnett (New York: Harper & Row, 1968), p. 404.
30. Ibid., p. 410.
31. Ibid., p. 497.
32. René Girard, *Dostoïevski: du double à l'unité*, op. cit., p. 76.
33. Dumouchel and Dupuy, op. cit., p. 95.
34. Aglietta and Orléan, op cit., p. 44.
35. Dostoevsky, op. cit., p. 511.
36. Ferenc Feher, 'Is the Novel Problematic?', trans. Anne-Marie Dibon, *Telos* 15 (Spring 1979).
37. Karl Marx, *Capital* (New York: Modern Library, 1906 reprint), vol. I, p. 128.

Voyage to the End of the Sciences of Man

1. Georges Cuer, 'Girard et Domenach', *Economie et Humanisme* (May–June 1982).
2. Domenach–Girard conversation II, *La France catholique* (25 June 1982).
3. Ibid.
4. Cf. the reference to the story of Joseph (ibid.): 'Joseph forgives . . .'
5. André Dumas, 'La mort du Christ n'est-elle pas sacrificielle?' *Études théologiques et religieuses* 4 (1981).
6. I use this expression to designate not the crisis which culminates in a sacrifice, but the crisis which arises when the sacrificial mechanism wears out: the impossibility of sacrificing innocently engenders various processes of repression, diversion and avoidance.
7. In the conversation cited above (*La France catholique*), Girard grows indignant when, alluding to human rights, I speak of a transitory sacred.
8. Marcel Gauchet, 'Fin de la religion?' *Le Débat* (January 1984).
9. Claude Lévi-Strauss, *The Naked Man*, trans. John and Doreen Waitman (London: Harper & Row, 1981).

The Christianity of René Girard and the Nature of Religion

1. *Violence and the Sacred* [= *VS*], trans. Patrick Gregory (Baltimore: Johns Hopkins University Press, 1977; London: The Athlone Press, 1988).
2. *Des Chose cachées depuis la fondation du monde* [= *CC*] (Paris: Grasset,

1978), *Things Hidden since the Foundation of the World*, trans. S. Bann and M. Metteer (London: The Athlone Press, 1987; Stanford: Stanford University Press). *Le Bouc émissaire* [= *BE*], *The Scapegoat*, trans. Yvonne Freccero (Baltimore: Johns Hopkins University Press, 1986; London: The Athlone Press).

3. In so far as no science is possible except in a stable society, and in so far as the stability of a society depends on misrecognition of the violence on which it rests, the 'recognition of misrecognition' is forbidden men as a matter of principle. It is on this assertion that the whole Girardian interpretation of the Revelation rests – an assertion which, as one sees, does not have the status of a religious or metaphysical thesis, but rather that of an epistemological theorem. It remains to be seen whether it is truly to the evangelical Revelation that we are indebted for this theorem. In principle, it is the Revelation and nothing else which allows men to know and to understand that on the *inside* of the sacrificial order it is impossible for the actors to lift the veil of *misrecognition* that is this order's very condition of possibility. And it is solely because it places them *outside* the sacrificial system that the Revelation lets them see this fundamental truth. But, in fact, Girard's position is more complex than it appears at first glance. For it sometimes happens that he attributes the power to take man out of the sacrificial order to the spontaneous evolution of ritual, and sometimes to the enlightenment brought by the Revelation alone. Sometimes he affirms that only Christ can pull humanity out of the circle of founding violence in which it is completely enclosed (*CC*, p. 242); sometimes he declares that Jesus came only to take away from men the last 'ritual crutches' of a worn-out sacrificial system ('Discussion avec René Girard', *Esprit* 429 [November 1973], p. 553; *CC*, p. 465). Sometimes he maintains that the 'authentic knowledge of violence and its works' contained in the Gospels 'cannot be of merely human origin' (*CC*, p. 242); sometimes he grants judicial rituals – which one could hardly consider the offspring of the Revelation – the ability to give us access to an intellectual knowledge of violence (*CC*, p. 20). The central thesis remains: it is not to their 'reason' that men owe their escape from the circle of misrecognition (all attempts at demystification can but displace or enlarge the misrecognition which they claim to dissipate); it is, one way or another, to religion.

We shall return to this point in the second part of our presentation. The reader is also referred to the text by Jean-Pierre Dupuy, included in the present volume (pp. 75–100), which studies the possibility and the potential effects of a recognition of misrecognition.

4. We know that the case of Orphism is particularly complex and that it has long given rise to numerous controversies. Thanks to the converging and complementary efforts of Nilsson, Guthrie, Linforth and Detienne, we can none the less consider the following three points to be established:

   a) the antiquity of the Orphic tradition and in particular of the myth of Dionysus-Zagreus;

b) the radically anti-sacrificial character of the Orphic movement;
c) the absence of an Orphic religion in the strict sense of the term that would imply specific institutions, places of worship and rites.

Cf. M. P. Nilsson, 'Early Orphism and Kindred Religious Movements', *Harvard Theological Review*, vol. XXVIII, No. 3 (July 1935); William Keith Chambers Guthrie, *Orpheus and Greek Religion*, 2nd rev. edn (London: Methuen, 1952); Ivan M. Linforth, *The Arts of Orpheus* (Berkeley: University of California Press, 1941, reprinted New York: Arno Press, 1973); Marcel Detienne, *Dionysus Slain*, trans. Mireille Muellner and Leonard Muellner (Baltimore and London: Johns Hopkins University Press, 1979); Marcel Detienne and Jean-Pierre Vernant, *La Cuisine du sacrifice en pays grec* (Paris: Gallimard, 1979).

5. Here is the myth as summarized in Detienne and Vernant (pp. 7–8):

> A god who assumes the guise of a child is slaughtered by the unanimous group of Titans, the Royalty of olden times. Covered with gypsum and wearing plaster masks, the murderers form a circle around the victim; with discreet gestures, they show the child fascinating toys: a top, a rhombus, some articulated dolls, knucklebones, a mirror. And while the child Dionysus contemplates his own image captured in the circle of polished metal, the Titans strike him, cut off his limbs, throw them in a cauldron and then roast them over the fire. Once the victim's flesh is laid out, they undertake to consume it; and they have the time to devour everything but the heart, which escaped the sharing-out in equal parts, before Zeus's thunderbolt, come to punish their crime, reduces the supping Titans to smoke and ashes, from which will rise the human race of today.

Nilsson was the first to show that this myth amounts to assimilating the Bacchic sacrament of omophagia to an odious crime, and that we have here quite naturally the explanation of the death of Orpheus:

> The central rite of Bacchic orgia – the dismembering and eating of an animal representing Dionysus himself, whose place, in myths, is often taken by a child – was transmuted into a crime in the Orphic myth, the dismembering of the child-god Dionysus by the wicked Titans. The Bacchants were thus put on a level with the Titans, the principle of evil. Thus, the bitter enmity between the adherents of Orpheus and those of Dionysus is fully understandable, and so the death of Orpheus at the hands of Maenads is explained. I should not dare to say that Orpheus died as a martyr to his religion, but this manner of death is the mystical vengeance for his blasphemy according to the *jus talionis*. He had turned the Bacchic sacrament into a crime and was torn into pieces by Maenads like another enemy of the orgia, Pentheus. (op. cit., pp. 203–4)

For a demonstration of the anti-sacrificial character of the Orphic myth of Dionysus, see Detienne, *Dionysus Slain*, ch. 4; and Detienne and Vernant, *La Cuisine du sacrifice*, ch. 1. For the opposition between Orphism and Dionysism, see Detienne, *Dionysus Slain*, ch. 3, and for the opposition between the Orphic myth of Dionysus and the Hesiodic myth of Prometheus, see Detienne and Vernant, pp. 71–84.

Girard alludes at least twice to the myth of Dionysus (*VS*, p. 347; *BE*, pp. 105–6), but he does not notice its anti-sacrificial character, and Detienne reproaches him, not without reason, with having confused Dionysism and Orphism (*Dionysus Slain*, p. 209, note 24). It is true, however, that even in the presence of a properly Orphic version of the myth, Girard could still argue that the punishment of the Titans by Zeus – that is to say, the theme of 'divine wrath' – connects this text, despite everything, to the corpus of violent and sacrificial mythology.

However this may be exactly, if we lean here on Detienne's works in order to refuse Christianity the monopoly on the 'revelation' Girard generously concedes to it, we wish to make a point of emphasizing that we absolutely do not subscribe to the global condemnation of the Girardian theory by that Hellenist scholar (Detienne and Vernant, p. 35). Indeed, our evaluation of Girard's work is exactly the opposite of his. Detienne asserts that the Girardian theory of sacrifice is false because it is warped by Judaeo-Christian assumptions; we believe, however, that it is true, and that for this reason it is difficult to reconcile with the interpretation of Christianity proposed by *Des Choses cachées depuis la fondation du monde*.

In a review of *La Cuisine du sacrifice* ('Diversité culturelle et unité de l'homme', *Critique* 437 [October 1983]) we endeavoured to show that Detienne and his collaborators contribute, in spite of themselves, supplementary proofs on behalf of the Girardian point of view. And the reader will have no problem convincing himself that the anti-sacrificial interpretation of the Orphic myth of Dionysus becomes all the more natural and all the more powerful when one begins by adopting the Girardian theory of sacrifice and of mythology.

6. On this aspect of Orpheus, see Guthrie, op. cit., pp. 40–1.
7. Guthrie has forcefully underscored the fact that the vases representing the death of Orpheus do not depict a ritual murder but a lynching:

> On these Orpheus is never depicted as torn to pieces . . . but the infuriated women are provided with a large assortment of weapons for the deed. Sometimes only one attacker is shown, sometimes more. Some are armed with spears, some with axes, some with stones; others have snatched up in haste more homely implements, sickles, pestles, even spits. This seems to imply the story of natural feminine wrath rather than of divine command, which is better suited to making him the victim in a Bacchic orgy. (op. cit., p. 33)

Therefore one sees that if the Orphic myth of Dionysus can still be branded sacrificial (it has recourse to divine violence and it denounces sacrifice, not the victimage mechanism), the account of the death of Orpheus, on the other hand, is not far from assembling all the characteristics Girard requires of a revelation: for the only violence here is human, and the victim around which the community leagues together is the very same one who threatens the social order by denouncing sacrifice. In short, like

Jesus and for the same reason, Orpheus occupies the position of the surrogate victim. It remains true that the murder of Orpheus is not committed by the unanimous collectivity, but only by the women, so that the account of his death can be read as a myth tending to justify the exclusion of women – a hypothesis all the more plausible in that the Orphic movement and its sects wished, as we know, to be exclusively masculine.

8. *CC*, pp. 223–4.
9. *CC*, p. 203.
10. 'Therefore if thou bring thy gift to the altar, and there rememberest that thy brother hath ought against thee; Leave there thy gift before the altar, and go thy way; first be reconciled to thy brother, and then come and offer thy gift.' (Matthew 5:23–4. All quotations from the Bible are taken from the Authorized [King James] version.)
11. *CC*, p. 203.
12. Matthew 8:1–4; Mark 1:40–4; Luke 5:12–16.
13. See Leviticus 13–14.
14. Matthew 26:17–19; Mark 14:12–16; Luke 22:7–13.
15. Mark 12:33.
16. See Isaiah 1:11; Jeremiah 6:20; Amos 5:22.
17. 'And the multitude sat about him, and they said unto him, Behold, thy mother and thy brethren without seek for thee. And he answered them, saying, Who is my mother, or my brethren? And he looked round about on them which sat about him, and said, Behold my mother and my brethren! For whosoever shall do the will of God, the same is my brother, and my sister, and mother.' (Mark 3:32–5)

'Think not that I am come to send peace on earth: I came not to send peace, but a sword. For I am come to set a man at variance against his father, and the daughter against her mother, and the daughter-in-law against her mother-in-law. And a man's foes shall be they of his own household. He that loveth father or mother more than me is not worthy of me.' (Matthew 10:34–7)

If any man come to me, and hate not his father, and mother, and wife, and children, and brethren, and sisters, yea, and his own life also, he cannot be my disciple.' (Luke 14:26)

18. One will notice that in the text from Matthew cited in the preceding note, all the 'variances' mentioned by Christ affect individuals of different generations. And one will find, on this subject, some very penetrating remarks by André Stéphane, the pseudonym of two psychoanalysts, in a little book of humour and of circumstance inspired by the events of May 1968 in Paris: *L'Univers contestationnaire* (Paris: Payot, 1969).
19. Cf. Jacques Gernet, *Chine et Christianisme* (Paris: Gallimard, 1982), notably pp. 217–23 and 253–5. It is true that the author seeks the

ultimate reason for the failure of Christianity to take root in China in the nature of the Chinese language, held to be incompatible with Christian metaphysics. But, as Emmanuel Todd notes,

> one senses, in reading him, that other factors deeper and more powerful than language were at work in China's refusal of Christianity . . . The ideal of filial piety is at the centre of the Chinese social and cultural systems. Now Christianity places religion above the family and affirms the primacy of God over the real, biological or adoptive, father. It affirms the primacy of the Holy Father over the natural family. And that horrifies traditional China. ('Dieu peut-il être chinois?', *Le Monde* [16 April 1982], p. 20)

20. Cf. Louis Dumont, 'La Genèse chrétienne de l'individualisme moderne', *Le Débat* 15 (September–October 1981), pp. 124–46. Reprinted in Dumont, Essais sur l'individualisme (Paris: Seuil, 1982; English edition: *Essays on Individualism: Modern Ideology in Anthropological Perspective* [Chicago: University of Chicago Press, 1986]). Note, however, that Dumont emphasizes the detachment of the individual in relation to the community and not to the family.
21. 'And another of his disciples said unto him, Lord, suffer me first to go and bury my father. But Jesus said unto him, Follow me; and let the dead bury their dead.' (Matthew 8:21–2)
22. *CC*, pp. 186–9.
23. On the Essene way of life, see the converging testimony of Philo of Alexandria, Pliny the Elder and Flavius Josephus, assembled by J. Steinman in his *Jean-Baptiste* (Paris: Seuil, 1955), pp. 19 ff.
24. One could argue, in defence of the Orphics, that in Ancient Greece, where the butcher's shop was a sort of annexe to the temple, the refusal of a meat diet was certainly not a neutral form of asceticism but the refusal of a social order founded on violence. As has been underscored many a time by Detienne, the 'so-called Orphic way of life is not reducible to an insipid vegetarianism. To abstain from eating meat in the Greek city-state is a highly subversive act' (*Dionysus Slain*, p. 72).

But we will not insist on this point, for it is in their relation to women more than to food that Orpheus and Jesus seem to us most significantly opposed. In effect, if Christ devalues the earthly family in favour of the celestial family, He does not condemn marriage and manifests no misogyny. On the contrary, female characters play an important role in the Gospels; they are presented in a favourable light and contribute to giving a positive image of woman. On the other hand, 'when the Orphic texts break their scornful silence, it is only to repeat the formula: "Nothing more bitchy than a woman"' (*Dionysus Slain*, p. 117, n. 138). And it is, it seems, that horror of femininity already encountered in the story of the death of Orpheus which drives his disciples to proscribe marriage and to reject the family.

Even were it not for other aspects of Christianity, one would find here the dividing line between the rigorously 'non-sacrificial' attitude of Jesus and the still-sacrificial character of the 'anti-sacrificial' attitude of Orpheus.

25. 'There is nothing from without a man, that entering into him can defile him: but the things which come out of him, those are they that defile the man . . . For from within, out of the heart of men, proceed evil thoughts, adulteries, fornications, murders, thefts, covetousness, wickedness, deceit, lasciviousness, an evil eye, blasphemy, pride, foolishness: All these evil things come from within, and defile the man.' (Mark 7:15, 21–3)
26. On the 'Skandalon', cf. *CC*, pp. 438–53.
27. Ibid., p. 295.
28. Ibid., p. 205.
29. Matthew 23:35; Luke 11:51.
30. Matthew 5:29. [Translator's note: where the word 'offend' appears in the King James version, I have substituted 'scandalize' in conformity with the French text.]
31. Some commentators assert that this passage is put together from a hotchpotch of different texts (cf. A. Loisy, *Études évangéliques* [Paris, 1902], p. 16 ff.), but we can get along without this hypothesis. Whether the text of each of the Gospels has one or several sources, one or several authors, one or several successive versions, the only thing that counts for us is its internal coherence, manifest or hidden: it is a question of whether or not one finds somewhere assembled and made explicit all the elements necessary to a complete revelation of the victimage mechanism.
32. Matthew 18:10–14.
33. We know that Gehenna is the valley of the sons of Hinnom, a ravine south of Jerusalem where once children were burned in honour of idols. It was Josiah who 'defiled Topheth, which is in the valley of the children of Hinnom, that no man might make his son or his daughter to pass through the fire to Molech' (II Kings 23:10).
34. Matthew 18:14.
35. Matthew 21:33–46.
36. Matthew 22:1–14.
37. Matthew 23:1–36.
38. Matthew 23:33–6.
39. Luke 11:50–1.
40. *CC*, pp. 181–6.
41. 'Symétrie et dissymétrie dans le mythe d'Oedipe', *Critique* 249 (February 1968); pp. 127–30; 'Discussion avec René Girard', *Esprit* (November 1973), p. 553.
42. *BE*, p. 153.
43. *CC*, p. 213.
44. Matthew 21:33–46; Mark 12:1–12; Luke 20:9–19; *CC*, pp. 211–12.
45. Matthew 21:40–1.
46. Matthew 25:14–30.

47. Matthew 22:1–14.
48. Matthew 22:7.
49. Matthew 22:13.
50. *BE*, p. 270.
51. It is the Hebrew word *mâschâl* which corresponds to the Greek *parabolè*. But *mâschâl* signifies comparison or analogy and seems to be devoid of any 'sacrificial' connotation.
52. *CC*, p. 162.
53. Ibid., pp. 269–72.
54. Ibid., p. 270.
55. Matthew 27:3–10.
56. *CC*, p. 270.
57. Thomas Stern, *Thésée ou la puissance du spectre* (Paris: Seghers, 1981), pp. 88–9.
58. Acts 1:18–19.
59. John 6:48–59.
60. John 1:29, 36.
61. Revelation 7:14–15.
62. Paul, I Corinthians 5:7.
63. John 1:29; cf. also John's first epistle which expresses the idea that the blood of Jesus 'cleanseth us from all sin' (1:7) and that Jesus 'is the propitiation for our sins: and not for ours only, but also for the sins of the whole world' (2:2).
64. On the Epistle to the Hebrews and on the *sui generis* character of the Christian sacrifice which oscillates between an 'effective' pole and a 'symbolic' pole, one may read with profit the article by the Indologist Olivier Herrenschmidt, 'Sacrifice: Symbolic or Effective?' in *Between Belief and Transgression*, ed. Michel Izard and Pierre Smith, trans. John Leavitt (Chicago and London: University of Chicago Press, 1982), pp. 24–42. At the end of a comparison with Brahminism and with Judaism, the author shows clearly that the Christian tradition has always been tempted to 'reduce the effective to the symbolic' (p. 39), but without ever being able to do so completely, except at the price of losing its identity as a religion and thereby being threatened with dissolution: 'For when a religion ceases to believe in the efficacy of its rites, it can turn into anything at all' (p. 40).
65. *CC*, p. 216.
66. Cf. on this point Herrenschmidt, op. cit., pp. 34–9.
67. John 13. Cf. on this point Manuel de Dieguez, *Jesus* Paris: Fayard, 1985), p. 250.
68. Not only would this promotion of the rite of the washing of the feet have to be reconciled with the long development of the theme of the 'bread of life' that precedes it; it would also have to be made to agree with the comparison of the vine and the branches that follows it (John 15:1–6). For if the foot-washing scene is dominated by pure reciprocity, the

allegory of the vine restores a dissymmetrical relationship between Christ and His disciples ('the branch cannot bear fruit of itself, except it abide in the vine; no more can ye, except ye abide in me') and rehabilitates the sacrificial scheme ('If a man abide not in me, he is cast forth as a branch, and is withered; and men gather them, and cast them into the fire, and they are burned').

69. Cf. *Tractatus Theologico-Politicus*, Chapters 4 and 5; *letter 73* from Spinoza to Oldenburg.
70. Cf. the end of Chapter 3 of *Tractatus Theologico-Politicus*.
71. On this question, one may consult Jean Lacroix, *Spinoza et le problème du salut* (Paris: Presses Universitaires de France: 1970) and Stanislas Breton, *Politique, religion et écriture chez Spinoza* (Lyon: Profac, 1973).
72. This comparison leads us from now on to doubt the originality Girard attributes to Christianity. In effect, from the outset of Book I of the *De natura rerum*, Lucretius denounces the sacrifice of Iphigenia and lauds Epicurus for having delivered men from the false religion that is ritual and sacrificial; for having been the first to dare lift his gaze against the religious monster that 'from the heights of the celestial regions, threatens men with its horrible demeanour', for having fought it and brought it down to the point, he writes, where having crushed men, 'religion is toppled in its turn and trampled underfoot while as for us, victory lifts us up to the very skies.'

We can see that this apotheosis of Epicurus still bears the traces of sacrificial logic, or rather that it conforms rigorously to its canons. For in reality all indications are that Lucretius has the figures he is employing in the poem under perfect control and that the text must be read *cum grano salis*, just like the paradoxical invocation to Venus (since the gods demand neither prayers nor sacrifices and do not trouble themselves about men) that he has maliciously placed at the threshold of his book. Otherwise, Girard himself must be chided for being a prisoner of sacrificial logic when he bases the divinity of Christ on the elimination of the sacred. (*CC*, p. 254).

73. Nor, indeed, does Epicurus propose such a return to the state of nature, for his thinking is much more complex. We are refraining from discussing here his theory of law and of social life but we will have the occasion to mention, a little later, his attitude regarding ritual.
74. 'Discussion avec René Girard', op. cit., p. 553.
75. Cf. for example 'Discussion avec René Girard', op. cit., p. 548. Remember also that for Girard, 'if primitive religious thought is mistaken in deifying violence, it is correct in its refusal to attribute to mankind's design the principle of social unity' (*VS*, p. 259). [Translator's note: I have modified the published translation of this sentence, to make it better reflect part of the French original important to Scubla's argument.]
76. P. Manent, 'René Girard, la violence et le sacré', *Contrepoint* 14 (1974),

p. 169. Girard seems to subscribe to this interpretation: 'We know that we are on our own, without a stern heavenly father to disturb our small affairs . . . The decisive word of the apocalypse hardly does more than state man's absolute responsibility in history: you want to be left to yourself in your home; well then, you are left to yourself' (*CC*, p. 219).

77. *CC*, p. 232.

78. Machiavelli also affirms that the foundation and the preservation of communities are *essentially* violent, and that men live continually on the good effects of this violence that they do not want to look in the eye. But Machiavelli, for his part, knows what he is saying: if what we call humanity is founded on violence, then this active power of violence must be preserved and men must be kept from falling under the influence of a deceptive non-violence – that of Christianity – which tends to destroy the very conditions for humanity . . . If human culture is essentially founded on violence, then Christianity can bring nothing other than the destruction of humanity in the fallacious guise of non-violence.

(P. Manent, 'La leçon de ténèbres de René Girard', *Commentaire* 19 [Autumn 1982]: 462–3.

79. Practitioners of the human sciences, always apt to make abusive simplifications, cannot be reminded too often of the usefulness of the old Aristotelian model of the plurality of causes.

As far as René Girard is concerned, we readily recognize that he has the great virtue of wanting to explain the genesis of cultural forms which structuralism is content to describe as if they were always already there. But we also believe that his morphogenetic preoccupation leads him to reject a little too hastily what he refers to contemptuously as Platonic essences, even though it is quite possible – and even necessary, as for example René Thom has shown – to reconcile morphogenesis and Platonism.

80. See the numerous works cited in the bibliography of Michel Aglietta and André Orléan's book *La Violence de la monnaie* (Paris: Presses Universitaires de France, 1982).

81. J. G. Frazer, *The Golden Bough*; A. M. Hocart, *Kingship* (London: Oxford University Press, 1927, reprinted 1969); *Kings and Councillors*, ed. R. Needham (Chicago and London: University of Chicago Press, 1970 [1936]); *Social Origins* (London, 1954); and on the king as 'future sacrificial victim' R. Girard, *VS*, pp. 269–73 and *CC*, pp. 59–66.

82. In *Kings and Councillors* Hocart showed that the Constitution is not a recent invention of democratic societies and that the principle of the separation of powers derives from the system of dual monarchy, which is itself of ritual origin. See also our brief note on the sacrificial origin of democracy in the *Cahiers du CREA*, No. 2 (Ecole Polytechnique, Paris, May 1983): 'De la démocratie comme rite ou comme pure procédure.'

83. On the decrease in the number of crimes of violence over the last two centuries, cf. Jean-Claude Chesnais, *Histoire de la violence en Occident de 1800 à nos jours* (Paris: Robert Laffont, 1981).

84. Girard himself is the first to say so. 'The surrogate victim', he writes, 'appears as the ideal educator of humanity . . . The rite gradually leads men away from the sacred; it permits them to escape their own violence, removes them from violence, and bestows on them all the institutions and beliefs that define their humanity' (*VS*, p. 306).
85. Marx maintained that capitalist society dissimulates the exploitation of man by man that feudal and slave societies displayed in broad daylight. In postulating that men need to hide the violent foundations of their society under a thicker and thicker shroud of darkness, Girard takes up the same scheme without giving it a justification that is any more convincing. On the other hand, he too flatters what Nietzsche called our 'desire to suffer' (*The Gay Science*, para. 56), for many of our contemporaries take delight in the idea that the Western world could be as violent as – or even more violent (because more 'hypocritical') than – those societies which practise human sacrifice, and it is paradoxically the figure of an accusing Christ that fascinates them in Girard's work.

But nothing is in our opinion weaker than the interpretation Girard offers of the history of mythology (*BE*, pp. 107 ff): for in truth, if men expurgate little by little from their myths the most violent scenes (collective murder, then 'crimes of the gods') it is not in order to dissimulate to a greater and greater extent the violence on which their civilization has always rested; rather it is quite clearly for the same reason that they have abandoned their bloodiest rites one after the other: habituated to a lesser violence and as it were 'tamed' or 'domesticated' by the long refinement and natural evolution of their rituals, they are no longer able to recognize their most ancient myths as their own.

86. *CC*, p. 20.
87. O. Mannoni, 'Je sais bien, mais quand même . . .', in *Clefs pour l'imaginaire ou l'autre scène* (Paris: Seuil, 1969), p. 16.
88. Ibid.
89. Cf. A.-J. Festugière, *Epicure et ses dieux* (Paris: Presses Universitaires de France, 1968), pp. 86–92.
90. Ibid., pp. 31–5.
91. A. Loisy, *La religion d'Israel*, 2nd edn (published by the author, Ceffonds, by Montier-en-Der, Haute-Marne, 1908), p. 210.
92. *CC*, p. 458.

Towards a Poetics of the Scapegoat

1. *Esprit*, Paris, February 1973.
2. J. G. Frazer, *The Golden Bough*.
3. M. Bakhtine, *Problems of Dostoevsky's Poetics* (Minneapolis: University of Minnesota Press, 1984); *Rabelais and His World* (Cambridge, Mass.: MIT Press, 1968, 1971).
4. *Le Mythe de l'Eternel Retour* (Paris: Gallimard, 1969).

5. Paris: Plon, 1963.
6. Paris, 1970.
7. Paris, 1973.
8. New York, 2 vols, 1961.
9. Alexandre and Margaret Mitcherlich, *The Inability to Mourn* (New York: Grove Press, 1975).
10. Chicago, 1962.
11. London: Penguin, 1966.
12. New York, 1966.
13. A. Storr, *Human Aggression* (London: Penguin, 1968).
14. R. Otto, *The Idea of the Holy* (New York: Oxford University Press, 1958).
15. See M. Yamaguchi, 'La Royauté et le Symbolisme dualiste chez les Jukun du Nigeria', *Journal of Asian and African Studies* 8, Tokyo, 1974.
16. See S. Ortner, 'Is Women the Nature to Men as the Nature is to Culture', in M. Rosalto (ed.), *Women, Culture and Society* (Stanford, 1974).
17. Kristeva.
18. In Japanese; Tokyo, 1983.
19. In Japanese; Tokyo, 1974.

Founding Violence and Divine Referent

1. M. Detienne et J.-P. Vernant, *Les Ruses de l'intelligence*: *la métis des Grecs* (Paris: Flammarion, 1974).
2. See for example *Zohar-Genesis*, p. 32, on the 'light that shines from the shadows', with R. Aschlag's commentary '*Soulam*'; and the same commentary on *Zohar-Genesis*, pp. 52a, 68a, and 68b, and *Zohar-Exodus*, p. 34b, where 'the secret' of the sacrifices is explicitly related to the serpent's trick which is to be turned back against him.
3. H. Atlan and J.-P. Dupuy, 'Mimesis and Social Morphogenesis: Violence and the Sacred from a Systems Analysis Viewpoint', in G. E. Lasker (ed.), *Applied Systems and Cybernetics*, vol. III (New York: Pergamon, 1981), pp. 1263–8.
4. H. Atlan, *Entre le cristal et la fumée* (Paris: Seuil, 1979).
5. Leviticus, Chapter 16.
6. *Zohar* on Exodus, Bechalah section, p. 56a: 'All the wars of the world are but rivalries and destructions; and all the wars of the Torah lead finally to peace and love.'
7. Jonah 4:1–4.
8. *Babylonian Talmud*, *Hulin* Treatise, p. 60b.
9. 'One kid of the goats for a sin offering unto the Lord', Numbers 28:15.
10. Exodus 13:9.
11. Genesis 4:15.
12. Genesis 3:20.

13. Genesis 4:1 ('Caniti', i.e. 'I have gotten' has the same root as 'Cain').
14. Genesis 4:7.
15. *Midrash Raba* on Exodus 14:15, Bechalah section, Chapter 21, par. 7.
16. *Zohar* on Exodus, Section Bo, p. 33a.
17. Job, Chapter 1.
18. See H. Atlan, 'Niveaux de signification et athéisme de l'écriture', in J. Halperin and G. Levitte (eds), *La Bible au présent* (Paris: Gallimard-Idées, 1982), pp. 55–88.
19. The scandal is somewhat attenuated by another legend (*Zohar-Exodus*, Section Bo, p. 33a) which 'recalls' that Job was a counsellor to the Pharaoh who was supposed to have advised Pharaoh to enslave the Hebrews while avoiding killing them. That is why, in return, God delivers him up to Satan but on condition that he should not be killed. (One can find several different opinions in the Talmud [*Baba Batra*, p. 15a] as to the reality of Job. While some hold that he never existed and his story is only a parable, others feel that the text presents him as a contemporary of various personalities such as Isaac, Jacob, Joseph, or David, or Ahasuerus, or, still yet, Moses . . . So many words from the Midrash [18] which must be understood, of course, by their implications more than as historical statements.)
20. *Babylonian Talmud, Moed Katane*, p. 16b. One also finds, of course, in other contexts the pursuit of imitation, notably in the notion of 'Dvekout' (attachment) to God. But it is in any case much more a question of the kabbalist and naturalist idea of the divinity as macrocosm than of the transcendent-immanent God of Faith and theology.

From Mythical Bees to Medieval Anti-Semitism

1. (Duaci: Ex Typographia Baltazaris Belleri, 1627.) There had been at least two previous printings of Thomas' work, in 1597 and in 1605. The book begins with a life of Thomas. I thank Professor Ciriaco Moron-Arroyo, of Cornell University, for his invaluable help in locating this rare book and with the translation.
2. In quo ex mirifica apum repub. universa vitae bene atque Christiane instituendae ratio traditur, atque artificiose pertractatur, opus varium atque iucundum, insertis ubique miraculis et exemplis memorabilibus sui temporis.
3. K. R. Prowse, 'The Vestal Circle', *Greece and Rome* XIV (1967), p. 183.
4. Neque enim ullo inter se concubitu miscentur, nec in libidinem resolvuntur, et tamen maximum filiorum examen emittunt. Et in hoc maximum mirum secundum litteram videri potest, et unum ex abditissimis naturae secretis. Si hoc ergo in nimibus animalibus reperitur, quid calumniaris Iudee, unam apud Christianos virginem peperisse?
5. Because the Colvenerius edition to which I had access was difficult to

read in some places, I have used Alfonso de Spina's *Fortalitium Fidei* (Lyons: Guillaume Balcarin, 1487), where Thomas' text is quoted, to fill in the gaps:

> Contigit autem ut qaedam vetula malignissima Iudeis familiaris effecta, puellam eis annorum septem, orbatam parentibus venderet occidendam. Hanc igitur in secreto super pulchra et plura lintheamia, obstructa ore eius, in omnibus fere iuncturis membrorum incisionibus vulnerarunt maximo conamine sanguinem exprimentes et in ipsis lintheaminibus diligentissime receptantes. Hanc autem post tormenta defuncta, Iudei in aquam fluidam prope oppidum proiecerunt et super eam conderiem lapidum posuerunt. Tertia vero vel quarta die, per manum erectam ad celum a piscatoribus est inventa et in oppidum deportata, horrentibus et clamantibus populis ab impiis Iudeis tantum flagitium perpetratum. Erat autem in vicino Marchio de Badem princeps qui mox, audito tanto piaculo, pervenit ad corpus, statimque ipsum corpus erectum residens, tetendit manus ad principem, quasi vindictam sanguinem, vel forte misericordiam imploraret; post ora vero dimidiam iterum se deposuit defuncti more suppinam. Adductisque ad hoc spectaculum impiis Iudeis statin eruperunt omnia vulnera corporis et in testimonium horrendae necis copiosum sanguinem effunderunt. Mox clamor vulgi ad sidera tollitur, et in vindictam sceleris totaliter animatur. Ex quibusdam indiciis capta vetula, atque convicta: maxime cum filia ejus parvula omnia prodiderit, quia a puero et ebreo extorquetur veritas. Iudei quoque capti sunt qui in puellam manus nefarias extenderant, rotatique et suspensi sunt cum vetula. Duo vero mutuo se jugularunt. Haec nobis duo fratres Reynerus et Aegidius sicut illi qui in villa fuerunt post triduum quo haec gesta sunt, veraciter retulerunt.

A number of elements in the narrative are worth noticing, even though they cannot be analysed here. For example, the deliberate ambiguity of the sign made by the girl's hand extended towards the prince. Is it asking for vengeance or for mercy? And if mercy, for whom? For herself or for the Jews? Or does it make any difference, since the scandal of the crime and the need for vengeance can be emphasized only if the gesture is taken as one of innocent pleading for mercy? And what about the parallel between the child victim and the child that appears among the victimizers? For one must wonder how the 'evil old woman' could have a daughter of such a tender age (*filia parvula*). Is this subtle association of the hated victims of the lynching mob with innocence still an echo of the old sacrificial process that turns the victim into a god?

6. Antoine de Lalaing, *Primer viaje de Felipe de Austria a España* (1501), in A. García Mercadal, *Viajes de extranjeros por España* (Madrid: Aguilar, 1952), vol. I, p. 453. The translation is mine.
7. *Patrologia Latina*, vol. 50, cols 205–8.
8. See Hilda M. Ransome, *The Sacred Bee in Ancient Times and Folklore* (Boston and New York, 1937), p. 118.
9. In addition to Virgil I have used a collection of short writings on agriculture by ancient authors, originally published in Greek, translated by Rev. T. Owen with the title *Geoponica* (London, 1805). See especially pp. 200–2.

10. *Pat. Lat.*, loc. cit., col. 208. Pliny, for example, in his *Natural History*, says that 'when entirely lost they [i.e. bees] can be restored by being covered with fresh ox-paunches together with mud, or according to Virgil with the dead bodies of bullocks . . . since nature can change some things from one kind into another' (XI, 23). Other sources talk about burying the body of the bull.
11. *Pat. Lat.*, op. cit., vol. 50, col. 207. Ambrosius is quoted by Alardus Gazeus in his detailed commentary on Cassianus' work in the *Patrologia Latina* edition.
12. Apparently Virgil's mythical story is to a large extent his own. It might be interesting, although completely outside the scope of this essay, to meditate on Virgil's reasons for linking the myth of Orpheus to that of Aristeus: 'This is not a hackneyed subject, like the labours of Hercules or the adventure of young Hylas, or of Pelops, which can speak directly to its readers. Eurydice's moving death had not yet entered the realms of the commonplace. Apart from a very brief account by the mythographer Apollodorus, none of the Greek or latin writers before Virgil gives us anything on this subject. No one else, as far as we know, had had the idea of linking this myth to that of Aristeus.' André Oltramare, *Étude sur l'épisode d'Aristée dans les Georgiques* (Geneva, 1892) p. 14.
13. I use H. R. Fairclough's translation in the Loeb Classical Library.
14. See Robert W. Cruttwell, *Virgil's Mind at Work* (New York, 1969), pp. 120–1.
15. See my 'Sacrificial levels in Virgil's Aeneid', *Arethusa* 14 (1981): 217–39.

Index